Play Behavior

Play
Behavior

Joseph Levy
University of Waterloo

John Wiley & Sons
New York · Santa Barbara · Chichester · Brisbane · Toronto

Library of Congress Cataloging in Publication Data:

Levy, Joseph, 1942–
   Play behavior.

   Bibliography: p.
   Includes index.
   1. Play.   I. Title.

BF717.L46   150   77-12504
ISBN 0-471-01712-4

Printed in the United States of America

10 9 8 7 6 5 4 3 2

To my children Jason, Robyn, and Tamara
whose creative spirit has taught me the true
meaning of play.

Foreword

Authors like to think that the topic of their work is important; some like to feel that it is very important; and a few will claim that their subject matter is, indeed, among the most important of all, if not the most important. But the nature of the universe (i.e., too many authors and too few important topics) requires most such claims to turn out as authors' illusions. Joseph Levy is fortunate. His claim for the importance of play is no self-delusion but an ever more widely recognized fact of our postindustrial society. It is not that we have suddenly grown tired of work; we have been tired of work for a long time. It is not that we have suddenly shaken off the yoke of the Protestant Ethic; we were suspect of that philosophy for a long while. It is not that all of a sudden we assumed the desire to return to a more childlike existence, in which play once more has a dominant place; we had that desire ever since we left childhood. All of these factors, and many more, enter into an explanation of why play is presently receiving such increased attention. But the primary and all-encompassing reason is that we finally may be approaching the point where we can reap the fruits of the industrial and technological developments of the past hundred or more years: not in terms of more products (we already have more than we need); not in terms of greater luxuries (more expensive soaps and gold-plated water faucets), but in terms of freedom from toil, freedom from the tyranny of work perceived and understood only as paid employment.

This condition is as yet only true for a small proportion of the world's population. It will mean that the production of goods necessary for survival no longer requires that the vast majority of the population be employed for interminable hours of their days. It is this condition that has the potential to produce a new person. Such persons will have the freedom to raise their heads toward the sky, to contemplate the stars, listen to the murmur of the brook, dance in free abandon for the joy of the world, and become one with the wonders of nature. Are we about to produce such a person?

Joseph Levy has written a most informative work. It is all about play, a behavior category that most animals have no problem recognizing as distinct from others, but that social scientists still do not agree on how to define. Why is play so important? Because it is the road to becoming oneself. As Levy phrases it, it allows one "the paradox of pursuing what is at once essential and inconsequential." In play, any activity, no matter how trifling, can become the most important event of life, at that moment, with a total involvement that knows no limits. Your activity becomes your universe. It is essential, because *you* make it so. It is inconsequential, because it has no purpose beyond itself. "Minutes later it is forgotten or irrelevant."

Irrelevant, yes . . . as an event in itself, but not in the makeup of the person, or of society. Picture the person who never plays or the nation that never plays. It is a frightening thought. But it also explains why a book of this nature, while objective in its approach and unbiased in its presentation of the many viewpoints, theories, and research findings on play, makes and must make value statements that reflect the author's convictions. For example, Levy suggests that "the goal of any society should be to promote and reinforce both intrinsic experiences and intrinsic personalities." Although this position indicates a lessening of controls, the author also recognizes the dangers involved in a society that is "moving toward the moral dictum that the individual has the right to any form of play."

These, and many others, are issues that are examined in this book. It is written as a textbook; it includes a comprehensive survey of the area of play, and provides exercises that help bring the material to life through actual experiences. It is research oriented and offers guidance to people who would want to pursue such endeavors on their own.

Let me conclude by asking once more the question: Are we about to produce a person in the years to come, who can and will play? Or are we about to produce an individual who, through a misunderstanding of the nature of play, is bound for self-destruction and the destruction of our global environment? Levy has written a book that helps us understand what play is, and what it can be. We, as a society and as individuals, will have to make up our minds and will have to work for what we will want play to be in the years to come.

John Neulinger

Preface

The purpose of this book is to explain a phenomenon of human behavior previously considered too trivial and nonutilitarian to be worthy of serious study. Play behavior, the creative human expression examined in this book, encompasses what I consider to be major social, psychological, and cultural dimensions for survival in our postindustrial age of leisure.

Traditionally the people who have studied play behavior have taken a philosophical and phenomenological approach, almost as if to imbue play with some religious and mystical qualities that are not amenable to rigorous, systematic, and precise examination. Some armchair philosophers in the fields of recreation and leisure have even stated that to study and monitor play behavior, is to vitiate and diminish its essence. Thus it appears that some "old guard" pseudophilosophers would like to clothe play behavior with rich veils of mysticism and reductionism that leave no room for the reasoning paradigms of science. Although there is nothing wrong with beginning the study of play behavior using intuitive and metaphysical explanations, it should be possible to translate these explanations into a constituent model of elements, variables, or components. Then the scientist of play behavior would be able to test and predict the relationships among these intuitive and speculative variables.

It is not the aim of this book to generate or introduce new explanations of play behavior to replace some of the more paramount classical and contemporary philosophical and reductionistic theories. Quite the contrary, this book is intended to complement those reductionist models that have enjoyed such an excessive amount of reliance from the professions (e.g., recreation, planning, architecture, physical education, psychiatry, education, and nursing,) and disciplines (e.g., psychology, sociology, political science, philosophy, and anthropology). As I have often explained to some of my psychoanalytically oriented colleagues, while it is perfectly possible and ontogenetically correct to impute death wishes or latent homosexuality to motor cycle racers, these reductionist explanations based on sublimation cannot be empirically tested. For example, the reductionist explanations do not permit us to obtain systematic answers to questions such as: What is play behavior? Why is it enjoyable? And, what are the determinants and consequences of play behavior?

However, while it is one of the major goals of this book to move beyond the metaphysical and intrapsychic models of play behavior, it is still crucial that the neophyte researcher review and put into proper perspective the classical, contemporary, and modern explanations of play behavior. A thorough discussion of its intuitive, speculative, philosophic, and more scientific explanations will provide the student with the background necessary to examine, understand, plan, and monitor it.

Although this book is intended to be scholarly in the sense that it breaks new academic ground, it has also been directed toward providing a paradigm for integrating the scattered pieces of information on play behavior. This paradigm has been articulated in such a way that professionals concerned with play will be able to understand and improve the delivery of play service systems in an age when play is of fundamental concern to planners, educators, architects, social workers, and psychiatrists alike.

This book is divided into twelve chapters. The first chapter delineates the three criteria of play behavior that permit the reader to distinguish between play and nonplay. The second chapter reviews the major methods of knowing and the importance of recognizing that the research process may be initiated at either the inductive or deductive level. The third chapter addresses itself to the multitude of social, psychological, economic, and environmental reasons for studying play behavior. The fourth chapter breaks new theoretical ground by proposing a conceptual paradigm for the study of play behavior. This paradigm will undoubtedly help to provide a focus and direction for the diverse and scattered enquiries into play behavior. This chapter should be of particular interest to social and behavioral scientists interested in inter- and trans-disciplinary research. Chapters 5 through 10 review the major classical and contemporary theories of play behavior. However, unlike previous books that have reviewed these theories, I have made a special effort to identify the heuristic and practical potential in each of these theories as well as their most obvious limitations. Too often we are very critical of theories without ever taking the time and effort to identify the potential within the theory. Chapter 11 is a recapitulation of some of the more salient functional and realistic issues associated with human play behavior. This chapter provided me with the opportunity to relive those euphoric moments in the book when I was able to express my own notions, viewpoints, explanations, and contentions. In particular this chapter is in response to Dr. Max Kaplan who requested that I expose the reader to some of my own personal viewpoints and scenarios. I am most grateful to him for encouraging me to step out from behind the massive literature and empiricism. In the last chapter (Chapter 12) I return to a major research project on children's play that should be of great interest to those engaged in experimental research. This chapter clearly points out that it is possible and feasible to isolate certain parameters in play and to study them in a highly controlled environment.

In summary, the book provides anyone interested in the study of play with a very extensive exposure to the study of play behavior and provides more mature researchers in the field with a conceptual framework within which to articulate their own research problems.

In addition to the most obvious academic reasons presented thus far, I have written this book for very personal reasons. Writing this book has given me the opportunity to synthesize into one communicable package my views, notions, experiences and research on a topic that has been close to me for many years. However, in addition to giving me the opportunity for synthesis and personal expression, it has also enabled me to share my knowledge and background with individuals dedicated and committed to critically examining and planning for the optimal and equitable play needs of all our citizens living in a pluralistic society.

Joseph Levy

Acknowledgments

This book has become a reality because of some outstanding research and writing by some of my colleagues. People whose work on play has made a substantive contribution to the theories, notions, and ideas in this book are Brian Sutton-Smith (Teachers College, Columbia University), John Neulinger (New York University), Igor Kusyszyn (York University), Mihalyi Csikszentmihalyi (University of Chicago), Doyle Bishop (University of Ottawa), Terry Orlick (University of Ottawa), Mike Ellis (Dalhousie University), Gerald Kenyon (University of Waterloo), Kyo Izumi (University of Waterloo), and Allan Sapora (University of Illinois).

At Waterloo I am indebted to my Theories of Play students whose keen and perceptive interest in the course motivated me to work through my ideas from both a theoretical and pragmatic framework.

My deepest gratitude goes to three individuals who read the entire original manuscript: Dr. Max Kaplan (University of South Florida) whose editorial review for Wiley was exhaustive and extremely constructive; Dr. John Neulinger who provided the Foreword; and my wife Myra who always managed to find the time to give her honest opinion to the material at its early conceptual stages and who proceeded to unremittingly proofread the many subsequent drafts.

J. L.

Contents

PlayBehavior

1
Toward a Definition of Play Behavior

Living in a state of play means living more humanly. In play we *confirm our existence and affirm our worth* (Kusyszyn, 1977). In a consideration of the definition of play, the basic assumption is "that man is not born free; he is to become free." In other words, play simply cannot be "freedom from." Indeed, Aristotle's definition of happiness shifts the emphasis from "freedom from" to "freedom for." Man[1] must win his freedom; he must experience his freedom by living every moment to the fullest. To be free, and therefore to know play (know oneself), means to realize simultaneously the supreme importance and utter insignificance of our existence. To play means to accept the paradox of pursuing what is at once essential and inconsequential. Only in play can we totally commit ourselves to a goal that minutes later is forgotten or irrelevant.

Play, then, is necessary to affirm our lives. It is through experiencing play that we answer the puzzle of our existence. Play is where our lives live. When we slip into play, we slip into a self-experience where we can afford to "let go" and respond to ourselves, to others, and to the environment in an unpredictable, personal way. When we slip out of play, we slip into regimentation, lose our sense of personal freedom, and fail to see the incongruities of everything we hold to be important.

The person at play, then, is not driven by external forces but is characteristically motivated from within. Realization that the confirmation of our lives is, to some extent, within our jurisdiction makes us feel more responsible to be aware of our personal existence (White, 1959).

Living in play means confirming our existence and celebrating life. We celebrate life when we explore new boundaries that give additional impetus to our growing consciousness. This means using our senses — eyes, ears, nose, taste buds, skin, even our lungs and heart — in order to experience the world as it

[1] Throughout this book, the term "man" is used in the generic sense and does not imply any sexual connotation.

really is and not as we would like it to be or as someone has portrayed it to be.

Play brings out the greatness, dignity, and sacredness of our existence, which in turn gives impetus and meaning to our lives. On this topic, Kusyszyn (1977) a humanistic psychologist summarized the feedback mechanism operating in play.

> How do we confirm our existence and affirm our worth? By having an effect on our world (White, 1959). (The effect can even be an imagined one.) We can affect both objects and people by producing changes in them, transforming them, fixing them, or destroying them. We can affect people by getting them to respond to what we do or say.
>
> By affecting our world we in turn are affected by the feedback we get. The feedback can produce a variety of emotions in us. It's through experiencing these emotions that we confirm our existence and affirm our worth.
>
> (Kusyszyn, 1977, p. 3)

Play offers us the opportunity to transcend the ordinary organic and ego levels of functioning and to experience the world of wonder, peace, love, and anguish at a very intuitive level; but these experiences must come from within, not from external pressures of influences as is often the case. What, then, is the model of man and the world that will foster this "in-spiriting" aspect of human behavior?

MODELS OF HUMAN BEHAVIOR

Extrinsic Model

Western industrial society has developed, flourished, and maintained its major social institutions through the use of positive and negative external incentives. These incentives have been provided by doctors, parents, schools, churches, governments, and industries in the form of cures, corporal punishment, personal love, money, status, prestige, and security. Through a process of primary and secondary reinforcement contingencies, our society has thus molded and produced the type of individual and system that we have today.

In general, one may classify our *society as motivated and monitored by external reward and punishment systems*. When the extrinsic positive or negative system is removed, the behavior toward the goal is terminated. Given the fact that our extrinsic systems have produced the highest productivity in the history of our country, why should we be concerned with other motivational systems? Although the success of using extrinsic incentives has been clearly proven, there are strong indications that complete reliance upon extrinsic incentives can have deleterious effects on the mental health and motivation of the individual. Thus, although it is possible to condition children to provide the correct arithmetical response by using red stars, corporal punishment, or chewing gum, this form of motivation does not consider the intrinsic potential of the activity or the unique makeup of the organism.

We have reached a point in our society where individuals are beginning to rebel against activities whose major motivating force is an extrinsic reward at the end of the process — grade, trophy, paycheck, and the like. The labor unions in the postindustrial era have clearly given up hope on the intrinsic potential of the work place and are bargaining exclusively for extrinsic benefits — health and dental plans, higher salaries, more holidays, earlier retirement, cleaner and safer working conditions, and so forth. The extrinsic orientation of most of the labor work force has produced an alienated and bored working population who are extrinsically reinforced for behavior that they dislike and that fails to meet their human needs.

Juxtaposed to extrinsically motivated work for the majority of the population is an abundant amount of free time, which has the potential of satisfying man's need for wholeness and self-fulfillment. Unlike work behavior, however, free-time behavior does not generally evoke the extrinsic reward contingencies associated with work. Quite the contrary! In some free-time behavior individuals actually subject themselves to pain, humiliation, and even the risk of death. Alas, if this kind of polarization between work and free time exists, why is it that individuals report achieving such heightened states of excitement, wonder, happiness, joy, and a host of other human emotions (Csikszentmihalyi, 1975b)? These free-time ego functioning activities are clearly not motivated by the traditional primary and secondary extrinsic models; instead, they appear to derive their motivating force from within and to give form and shape to our unique humaneness.

Intrinsic Model

In view of our industrial society's obsession with regimentation, predictability, and homogeneity through disintegration of the individual, it is little wonder that the personalized inner side has usually been omitted in any serious and rigorous models of man. However, a few writers, most notably Murphy (1958), Rogers (1961), Maslow (1962, 1964, 1971), Levy (1971b), Csikszentmihalyi (1975b), and Kusyszyn (1977) have addressed themselves to the inner and integrated states experienced by the individual.

It is thus the goal of the intrinsic model of man to incorporate the subjective and humanly *integrating* experiences of behavior into the traditional extrinsic *disintegrative* model. As a result, life must be interpreted in terms of both individual disintegration (extrinsically monitored responses) and individual integration (intrinsically monitored responses).

What then are the characteristics of the intrinsic model of man that will aid in the examination of human behavior, which does not appear to be motivated by externally monitored rewards? Only by understanding these characteristics in their present form can we explain play—the most unique, diverse, and creative expressions of the human organism.

While wading through these "intuitively" and "empirically" arrived at characteristics of play behavior, the following salient assumptions are a *sine qua non* for any comprehensive discussion of these characteristics.

1. *Characteristics Not Mutually Exclusive*

Several characteristics of play behavior may, at any point in time, explain the motivation and satisfaction derived from the behavior. For example, an individual may ski because of the opportunity it provides to have control over one's body, skis, and the like, as well as to gamble and take risks without real-world repercussions.

The fact that play offers the individual the opportunity to satisfy several of these needs concurrently makes play behavior an excellent arena for trying out combinations and permutations of individual traits that would not be tolerated and reinforced in the real world. In other words, it is quite possible, while playing, to take grave risks in order to test ourselves and heighten our awareness about ourselves while, at the same time, being completely apart from the routine activities of everyday working life. For example, the surgeon, whose profession no longer provides the opportunity to flirt with danger or explore innovative surgical procedures, may find an outlet for self-stimulation, self-testing, and suspension of reality in skiing trips, rock-climbing expeditions, or photography.

2. *The Valence (Strength) of Each Characteristic May Change as the Structure of Play Behavior Changes*

The risk, challenge, and feeling of control will differ in a rock climb, for example, that takes place on a clear and sunny day when visibility is excellent as opposed to a wet and cloudy day when visibility is poor and footing is unpredictable. The same variability in the play characteristics may be expected when the structure of any activity is altered.

3. *Lack of Empirical Validity*

The majority of the characteristics and typologies of play behavior thus far proposed have been either useful insights (Caillois, 1958; Kusyszyn, 1974, 1975, 1977) or recently formulated models (Ellis, 1973; Neulinger, 1974; Csikszentmihalyi, 1975b) in their neophyte state of empiricism. In the aftermath of Berlyne's (1968) own struggle with the characteristics of play behavior, he comments on the perplexing and arduous task of attempting to compile the most salient characteristics of play. He writes:

It is evident from these attempts — and others could have been added — that a characterization of playful behavior is not easy. In such lists of criteria, certain themes continually reappear, and one writer after another tries desperately to pin them down. There is, however, obvious disagreement on what ought to be regarded as the salient defining characteristics of play. Some of the criteria, even when there is fair agreement on their importance, are put so imprecisely that they raise more problems than they solve, It is not clear how the various criteria are related. Furthermore, one suspects that some of them would not apply to all behavior that one would want to count as "play" and that some of them might apply to behavior to which one would not want to attach this label.

(Berlyne, 1968, p. 814)

4. Subjective Definition of Play

For the sake of clarity, it ought to be briefly mentioned why the author has elected to use the term "play" rather than "leisure" or "recreation." Ostensibly, there have been two major conceptualizations of leisure: the residual free time objective definition of sociologists, which dates back to Veblen's *The Theory of the Leisure Class* (1899); and the subjective, existential definition, which dates back to Aristotle, who defined leisure as the performance of activity "for its own sake or as its own end" (de Grazia, 1962, p. 13). De Grazia, who did not believe that everyone was capable of being in a state of leisure, points out that

the word leisure has always referred to something personal, a state of mind or a quality of feeling. It seemed that in changing from the term leisure to the term free time we had gone from a qualitative to a quantitative concept. We now had something that could be measured with ease.

(De Grazia, 1962, p. 59)

In view of the confusion that is still evident in the literature and in the minds of most professionals regarding the distinction between the objective and subjective definition of leisure, the term "play" has always enjoyed the unique status of being conceived and perceived as a very subjective and idiosyncratic human form of expression. Thus, by using the subjective conceptualization of play, it becomes possible to examine the creative and growth-producing characteristics of both residual (nonwork) and nonresidual (work) activities. In research terms, we have made *play behavior* the *dependent variable* and *free-time* versus *non-free-time* activities the *independent variables*.

We shall now identify and discuss the characteristics of this vital and complex class of human behavior. Although the evidence on play dating back to both Peking and Neanderthal[2] man suggests that there are a host of characteristics of this creative phenomena, the author has identified three criteria that are both heuristic and well documented in the emergence of man down through the ages (Neumann, 1971).

INTRINSIC MOTIVATION

Theoretical Definition
Intrinsic motivation is the drive to become involved in an activity originating from within the person or the activity; the reward is generated by the transaction itself.

One of the most germane and often discussed characteristics of play behavior by social scientists (Berlyne, 1960, 1968; Levy, 1971a, Neulinger, 1974; Greene and Lepper, 1974; Csikszentmihalyi, 1975a; Kusyszyn, 1977) is intrinsic motivation.

The author, in an article entitled "Intrinsic-Extrinsic Framework of Therapeutic Recreation," draws upon the field of social psychology to propose an inextricable relationship between intrinsic motivation, mental health, and recreation service systems. A brief recapitulation of some of the major concepts in that article are presented below.

1. Intrinsic factors produce self-realization, self-actualization and self-esteem . . . .

2. Satisfaction of the self-esteem needs leads to feelings of self-confidence, worth, strength, capability and adequacy . . . .

3. Extrinsic factors are associated with . . . dissatisfaction and which constitute a negative, avoidance dimension . . . .

4. Extrinsic factors are considered to prevent dissatisfaction but to have little effect in creating positive attitudes . . . .

5. Similarly the reduction of intrinsic factors may result in diminished satisfaction but not in the creation of dissatisfaction . . . .

6. Recreation's key role in promoting mental health, therefore, is seen as lying in its potential for promoting and planning experiences which will contribute to the satisfaction of intrinsic needs.

[2] Greendorfer (1975) points out that Neanderthal man's tools were designed with a perfection and aesthetic appreciation beyond that dictated by functionalism. She goes on to report that archeological evidence reveals a picture of Neanderthal man involved in ritual and cultural "play activity" equivalent to that cited by Huizinga (1955) in the ancient Chinese cultures.

> Similarly, mental illness and failure to find satisfying recreational activities that meet the intrinsic needs of the organism may be seen as closely related . . . .
>
> 7. What is being postulated is that mental health and mental illness are two independent dimensions of adjustment with the degree of illness or health reflecting the individual's disposition toward primary satisfaction of extrinsic or intrinsic needs . . . .
>
> (Levy, 1971a, p. 31)

Without a doubt, Dr. Daniel Berlyne, of the University of Toronto, is perhaps the most outstanding researcher in the field of motivation. In his concluding chapter on "Laughter, Humor and Play," he discusses "intrinsically motivated behavior":

> It is repeatedly asserted that playful activities are carried on "for their own sake" or for the sake of "pleasure." They are contrasted with "serious" activities, which deal with readily identifiable bodily needs or external threats or otherwise achieve specifiable practical ends . . . .
>
> When we say that play or some other activity is engaged in "for its own sake," what we really mean is that it is engaged in for the sake of these inner consequences. It follows that it will be engaged in only when the organism is in the kind of motivational condition that makes these inner consequences rewarding. Behavior of this kind is what we call "intrinsically motivated" behavior.
>
> Berlyne, 1968, pp. 840-841)

Dr. John Neulinger[3], author of *The Psychology of Leisure* (1974), the first comprehensive text on the subject, has proposed a leisure paradigm in which "intrinsic motivation," along with "goal" and "perceived freedom," forms the essential characteristics of leisure. Neulinger describes intrinsic and extrinsic motivation in the following terms:

> We are concerned with the question, is the satisfaction gained through the activity seen as coming from engaging in the activity itself (*intrinsic motivation*), or from the result of some pay-off from the activity (*extrinsic motivation*)? Is the activity itself the reward, or does the activity only lead to the reward? A picture

[3] Dr. John Neulinger, associate professor in psychology at City College of the City University of New York, has organized and chaired the first and second symposium on *Leisure* at the 1973 and 1974 American Psychological Association meetings. He is former associate editor of *The Journal of Leisure Research* and has been most active in empirical research on the phenomenon of *leisure*.

> comes to mind of a country fair at which children were searching
> through a haystack in which small gifts had been randomly dis-
> tributed. If a child found a gift, he could keep it, but had to leave.
> Many a child did just that. They searched found their reward, and
> left happily smiling. But there were some others, although few,
> who searched, found the gift, quickly hid it again in the straw,
> and continued searching. For them, searching was the reward!
>
> (Neulinger, 1974, p. 17)

Green and Lepper (1974), in an article entitled "Intrinsic Motivation: How to Turn Play into Work," have reported that when children are extrinsically re-warded for an enjoyable task (play), pleasure in the activity decreases and so does involvement in it. Furthermore, they point out that there is the "danger that extrinsic rewards may undermine intrinsic motivation . . . " and "turn play into work" (p. 50). Of even graver consequence is the finding that extrinsic rewards "can backfire" and seriously retard the interest and commitment to the activity, be it reading, running, skating, or piano lessons.

The findings reported by Greene and Lepper (1974) and the intrinsic-extrin-sic paradigm of recreation proposed by the author (Levy, 1971) suggest, how-ever, that for a variety of psychosocial reasons, extrinsic and intrinsic motivation may supplement and complement each other. As a result of the motivational disposition of the mentally retarded individual, Levy (1971a) suggests the appli-cation of both extrinsic and intrinsic rewards in the education, recreation, and rehabilitation of this group of individuals.

If one must introduce extrinsic reward systems in order to achieve certain positive human goals, Greene and Lepper (1974) set out the following guide-lines:

> If they are necessary, extrinsic rewards should be just powerful
> enough to bring the desired behavior under control. To prevent the
> undermining of intrinsic motivation, extrinsic rewards should be
> phased out as soon as possible. In addition, training in self-control
> can be used in place of extrinsic rewards. This training will help to
> maintain intrinsic motivation rather than undermine it.
>
> (Greene and Lepper, 1974, p. 54)

In addition to the need to recognize that intrinsic rewards will have direct growth-enhancing effects on the individual there is also an ecological rationale for using intrinsic rewards. Our biosphere is undergoing a tremendous strain because of man's failure to recognize the finite nature of our natural resources. If as a society we perpetuate a heavy reliance upon extrinsic rewards, there will continue to be a severe drain on the natural and synthetic resources of our envi-ronment. The same case could be posited for the reliance upon human-oriented extrinsic artifacts — status, promotions, prestige, salaries, and individual comparisons. All these extrinsic social rewards are based upon individual comparisons, which can only lead to an ultimate zero-sum product; that is, the benefits allocated are a limited resource, which means that, by definition, some end up being "winners" and some end up being "losers." We must, therefore, strive to minimize reliance upon extrinsic rewards and maximize reliance upon intrinsic rewards for human(e), social, and ecological, reasons.

Although the discussion in this chapter is mainly concerned with the play episode itself rather than its determinants or consequences, it must be pointed out that, in addition to discussing the intrinsic characteristics of play behavior, it is also possible to discuss the intrinsic characteristics of people. An intrinsically motivated individual is one who is predisposed to intrinsically enjoying events and situations to a greater degree than the individual who must always be extrinsically rewarded before becoming involved. There is no question that some activities, by their very nature, are more intrinsically rewarding than others and hence provide more intrinsic pleasure to everyone. However, some people, as a consequence of their socialization and unique innate makeup, are able to generate the experience of pleasure from the most mundane and boring activities, whereas others need extrinsic rewards even to participate in activities that are overloaded with intrinsic satisfiers. It is most obvious that the relationship between intrinsic experiences and intrinsic personalities becomes a circular one and that the goal of any society should be to promote and reinforce both of them.

What is an intrinsic experience? What are the elements of this phenomenon that constitutes such a salient characteristic of play behavior? Based upon a thorough review of the literature and research on intrinsic motivation and play behavior, the following operational elements have been compiled. It is anticipated that each of these operational elements will facilitate further empirical research and validation.

Converging of Self-Consciousness and Behavior

Individuals who have been intrinsically involved in such activities as chess, bridge, painting, skiing, jogging, gambling, writing, meditating, and a number of other similar endeavors have reported a convergence of their self-awareness with their behavior and environment (Csikszentmihalyi, 1974). During this convergence, individuals and their behavior become one, that is, they stop being aware of their own actions and feelings and become interphased with the activity. Olympic figure skaters at the 1976 Winter Olympics in Innsbruck, Austria, reported that once their routines were initiated, they lost complete self-consciousness — that is, they no longer cared about questions that would reflect an awareness of self, such as Who am I? What am I wearing? What am I doing here? How well am I going to skate? However, as soon as the skaters had a major fault in their skating routines, they seemed to be jolted out of this convergence of the self and behavior and immediately became aware of their identity that is, they began to think "I have just faulted; I look very silly; I am blushing; I am letting down my country by not winning a gold medal." Thus, as soon as players become aware of their selves (self-consciousness) and then behavior from the outside, the intrinsic characteristic of play behavior is eliminated. Csikszentmihalyi (1974), whose research on "flow"[4] involved interviews with people engaged in flow-producing activities, captures most clearly the converging of self and behavior.

> An outstanding chess-player:
> The game is a struggle, and the concentration is like breathing—you never think of it. The roof could fall in and if it missed you, you would be unaware of it.
> An expert Rock-climber:
> *You are so involved in what you are doing, you aren't thinking of yourself as separate from the immediate activity* . . . . . you don't see yourself as separate from what you are doing . . . .
> A dancer describing how it feels when a performance is going well:
> Your concentration is very complete. Your mind isn't wandering, you are not thinking of something else; you are totally involved in what you are doing. Your body feels good. You are not aware of any stiffness. Your body is awake all over . . . Your energy is flowing very smoothly. You feel relaxed, comfortable and energetic.
>
> (Csikszentmihalyi, 1974, p. 63)

Kusyszyn (1977) discusses the converging of self-consciousness with the activity in terms of the "altered state of consciousness' experienced during a gambling episode.

> It is the placing of the wager which provides for the placing of the self in the hands of risk and uncertainty. While in this position the player experiences a heightened awareness of his existence . . . . The arousal coupled with the already confirmed belief that the situation is a safe one, free from the possibility of real failures and social punishments, leave the gambler in a very comfortable state—in a *released* or *selfless* state.
>
> (Kusyszyn, 1977, p. 7)

[4] Play is the flow experience par excellence" (Csikszentmihalyi, 1974, p. 59).

Optimal Information Flow

Individuals who are intrinsically involved maintain their complete involvement by processing every relevant piece of important information about the activity being performed. Stimulus seeking human organisms try to maximize their enjoyment by finding an optimal relationship between their skills and the requirements of the activity. In order not to become bored (i.e., their skills are superior to the requirements of the activity) or overly anxious (i.e., their skills are inferior to the requirements of the activity), players monitor all their information-feedback mechanisms to ensure that all relevant stimuli have been processed and their impact analyzed. In order to carry out this complex and necessary information-processing exercise, players must delimit their relevant boundaries of information. All other incidental, irrelevant, and confounding stimuli are consciously or unconsciously eliminated from the information processing. The actual mental exercise of delimiting and processing relevant stimuli has been referred to as "arousal" by Hebb (1955), Duffy (1962), and Ellis (1973); "epistemic" by Berlyne (1960); "sensoristasis" by Schultz (1965); "narrowing of consciousness" by Maslow (1971); and "centering of attention" by Csikszentmihalyi (1974).

For years, coaches, mentors, mothers, and teachers have intuitively advised their pupils to eliminate irrelevant cues and stimuli and focus all attention only on those cues that are directly related to the activity. Golf's great immortals, Jack Nicklaus and Sam Snead, have clearly demonstrated their disciplined and conditioned ability to shut out all stimuli (televisions cameras, crowds, opponents, million dollar salary, sore back, etc.) that are not directly relevant to hitting the golf ball.

Csikszentmihalyi's (1974) interviewees volunteered the following phrases, which provide strong content validity for the need to maintain optimal information flow, if intrinsic motivation is to prevail.

> One respondent, a university professor in science who climbs rock, phrased it as follows:
>
> When I start on a climb, it is as if my memory input has been cut off. All I can remember is the last thirty seconds, and all I can think ahead is the next five minutes.
> This is what the chess experts say:
>
> When the game is exciting, I don't seem to hear nothing—the world seems to be cut off from me and all there's to think about is my game.
>
> (Csikszentmihalyi, 1974, p. 65)

Optimal flow of information must not be conceived as being an attempt on the part of the individual to have total control and predictability over the outcome. To the contrary, play theorists such as Huizinga (1955), Caillois (1961), and Berlyne (1960) have identified tension and uncertainty as one of the prime motives of play behavior. Hence, the term "optimal flow of information" must be examined in light of man's search for situations and activities where optimal uncertainty, challenge, and risk prevail. It is the constant attempt on the part of the player to keep the activity from losing its uncertainty that generates the intrinsic involvement. Ironically, it is often only through the use of extrinsic intervening variables that one maintains an optimal flow of uncertainty (information). The concept of "handicap" in footracing, horse racing, and golf must be looked upon as a way of injecting an added extrinsic dimension to the activity for purposes of stimulating both the superior and inferior opponents. In essence, the intervening handicap optimizes the skills of the player with the requirements of the activity.

From a concern with the information properties of the activity and the individual, we proceed to the second salient characteristic of play behavior — suspension of reality.

SUSPENSION OF REALITY

Theoretical Definition
Suspension of reality is the loss of the "real self" and the temporary acceptance of an "illusory self" or "imaginary self." Through this form of make-believe, individuals achieve the freedom from the real world (e. g., rules, roles, expectations, etc.) to experience their inner egoless personality.

The retreat from the physical, social, and moral specifications of the real world affords the individual the opportunity to test abilities and other human(e) powers and in this way become more intensely aware of self and environment. This heightened awareness of one's internal processes — love, hate, compassion, humility, power, risk, danger, and other expressions of the disinhibited self — has become a critical need in a society where one has little opportunity to confirm one's *existence* and *worth* (Kusyszyn, 1977). This need has been reported to be so great that some individuals have abandoned their lucrative medical, legal, and business practices to pursue the quest and search for meaning and identity.

This search, absorption, and loss of self-consciousness (i.e., who am I in the real world?), is most obviously manifested in gambling, mystic activities, yoga, and various religious rituals. The suspension of reality evident in many forms of gambling is poignantly described by Kusyszyn (1977), who is speaking as a researcher and a gambler.

> Gambling also provides a release . . . from reality through activity.
> The gambler very quickly, usually as soon as he begins to contem-
> plate making his first wager, transports his self into a play world, a
> fantasy world in which he stays suspended until he is jarred back
> into reality by the finish of the last race or the disappearance of
> his money. While on this mental midway, he can and usually does
> act, feel and think with abandon, without superego control, and
> without any psychological defenses. We say his Free Child (Berne),
> id (Freud) or instinctoid impulses (Maslow) emerge and indulge
> themselves in cognitive-emotional pleasures. Thus the gambler sus-
> pends himself at a comfortable level of arousal (Hans Selye calls it
> stress drunkenness), bravely tests his decision-making and predic-
> tive powers and in this way gain a glimpse of his pure, unrealized,
> pushing-for-expression, becoming self. Gambling allows him to be
> an actor, but not merely an actor but the hero of his own little
> drama.
>
> (Kusyszyn, 1977, pp. 6–7)

Suspension of reality is not exclusively limited to highly stimulating environments such as casinos, race tracks, or meditation sessions. We often fail to see
this self-forgetfulness and loss of ego in such popular play environments as the
local "Y", the ski resort, the dance floor, and the backyard badminton court.
For example, picture the local "Y" at noon, where business executives can
throw themselves completely into a game of volleyball, basketball, water polo,
or handball, with every ounce of energy and determination in order to try to
defeat their opponents. However, all the time that they are "playing their guts
out," they know that, win or lose, the game outcome will not have a serious or
enduring effect upon their "real" world. But if they behaved in such an "all or
nothing" absorbing manner on the stock market with their clients' investments
and lost, the outcome could mean tragic setbacks in the "real" world of these
executives. Such is certainly not the case in play behavior, when one has the
liberty to suspend reality.

The late Paul Haun (1965), a highly regarded psychiatrist and leader in the
field of leisure and mental health, gave this description of the value of the "suspension of reality" characteristic of play behavior in the young child.

> The business of childhood is play. Those of you who have watched
> the moppets in your neighborhood pedalling their tricycles, throw-
> ing their balls, skipping their ropes, and running their courses know
> with what intensity, with what singleness of purpose, with what ab-
> sorption such pursuits are followed. Should you watch long enough
> —at the kind of game that is not adapted from the adult world, but
> is truly the creation of childhood, like hide-and-seek or tag—you

will observe a marvellous custom. When the tension mounts too high and the pressure becomes quite unendurable, one of the children is bound to call out: "King X" Instantly—and until he is ready to resume the game—all rules are off. He cannot be chased or pushed or caught or found. He is, in a genuinely primitive sense, taboo (temporary suspension of reality). A marvellous and truly necessary custom! When business [the real world], which at this time of life happens to be play, becomes intolerable the seven-year-old executive takes a brief vacation from its anxieties and concerns. His fellows, aware of his need [to suspend reality] and recognizing that each of them will soon be in an identical state, support encourage, and respect his action.

(Haun, 1965, p. 20)

With regard to the need of adults to engage in play behavior as a result of its inherent ability to transcend the world of reality, Haun (1965) stated:

As adults, our business is no longer play. We work at doing our jobs, living within our conscience, raising our families, getting along with other people, trying to succeed. At times the tension mounts too high, the pressures become quite unendurable—just as they did in childhood. Where are we to look for the same kind of temporary immunity, for the same brief but inviolable sanctuary we found perfectly adapted to our needs in those old games of hide-and seek? Where but in play itself, which we now expand and dignify by the word recreation? I like to think of the recreation specialist as the perfect "king's X-er" for today's jittery world . . . .

(Haun, 1965, p. 20)

Today in our society we face a crisis around this characteristic of play behavior. Whereas in the majority of cases children seem to have extraordinary abilities to distinguish between the message "this is play" and "this is the real world," adults who are monitored by extrinsic contingencies often will not heed the message and will slip into "reality" during a play episode. Berlyne (1968) points out the distinction between "play" and the "real" world in play episodes that involve physical aggression.

In play, an animal or child or an adult human being may attack another. Aggressive responses are likely to be inhibited in the presence of this other individual most of the time, but, if a situation is defined as "playful," aggressive responses can be performed with impunity and are therefore disinhibited. On the other hand, in "real" aggressive behavior, each of the antagonists tries to hurt the

> other as much as possible and may even kill him. In playful fighting some of the components of fighting are suppressed, and most of them are under partial inhibition, reducing their vigor. Signals are given to indicate that the aggressive responses do not have the meaning that they normally have, so that the retaliative reactions of the opponent are likewise subject to inhibition . . . .
>
> (Berlyne, 1968, p. 841)

Needless to say, the insidious violence that has become so commonplace in competitive hockey at all age levels is evidence that this form of human behavior cannot be called play. And it is for this reason that Huizinga (1955) maintained that when sport loses its suspension of reality play characteristic, it loses its ability to fulfill a critical cultural and humanistic function in the socialization of man.

In addition to a state of self-forgetfulness where one loses touch with the physical reality, play also encompasses a feeling of *personal* control, commitment, and effectiveness. The third characteristic of play behavior is internal locus of control.

INTERNAL LOCUS OF CONTROL

Theoretical Definition
Internal locus of control refers to the degree to which individuals perceive that they are in control of their actions and outcomes.

The locus of control construct was originally derived from Rotter's social learning theory (Rotter, 1954, 1966). "Internals" are considered to be individuals who believe that they have at least some modicum of responsibility and control over their own destiny. Those having an "external" disposition believe that personal effort may be of little use and often feel that their outcomes are under the control of such extrinsic factors as "fate, luck, chance, powerful others or the unpredictable" (Brok, 1974).

Neulinger (1974) subsumes internal locus of control under his primary dimension of leisure — "perceived freedom"

> By this we simply mean a state in which the person feels that what he is doing, he is doing by choice and because he wants to do it . . . .
>
> One might argue that the person high on the external control factor sees himself as having less freedom and thus will be less likely to experience a given situation as leisure. He may also be less prepared for a situation that imposes relatively little control.
>
> (Neulinger, 1974, pp. 15–16)

Recently, Brok (1974) reported some interesting research results on "the way internals and externals relate to the concepts work, leisure, and various free time activities" (p. 122). Brok's exploratory work provides empirical evidence that locus of control does play a role in determining attitudes toward leisure. Brok's discussion of his findings are strongly related to the other two characteristics of play behavior discussed previously. Brok (1974) summarized his findings in the following terms:

> Those who feel at least some modicum of responsibility for their own destiny tend to view free time in a more favorable and positive light than those who believe their lives are often determined by fate, powerful others or the unpredictable. The fact that internals valued achievement oriented free time activities more highly than externals seems consonant with the former group's general orientation . . . .
>
> Externals seem to prefer free time activities that involve considerable social support. . . . It appears that externals not only valued being cooperative with others, but equally care about free time pursuits which provide considerable external benevolent control.
>
> The fact that internals saw both *leisure* and *work* as more satisfying than the external group, suggests that those who are socialized to believe they are in control over their own destinies are generally content with the totality of their lives. . . .
>
> (Brok, 1974, p. 124)

In the closing section of his research report, Brok (1974) pointed out the association between internal locus of control, intrinsic motivation, and the need to monitor the "ecological factors" so that individuals will have the opportunity to develop healthy and creative personalities. It is most obvious from Brok's research that not all individuals have developed the internal resources to play.

> Any activity considered meaningful, involves the perception of free choice, often demands effort, and is felt to be intrinsically rewarding. Interestingly, recent work seems to show that these factors are characteristic of those who believe in internal control. . . .
>
> I am not advocating that the way to meaningful leisure may solely lie in changing people's locus of control from external to internal. Ecological factors must also be considered . . . "for some people, especially for members of certain minority groups, the belief that there is little connection between effort and payoff is often realistic. For such people, an effective program for changing control orientations must produce change in the individual and his

immediate social surroundings." It may well be that in order to promote meaningful leisure, we must also create the appropriate social milieu for its appreciation.

(Brok, 1974, p. 125)

Returning to Kusyszyn's astute behavioral and phenomenological discussion of gambling, it will again be possible to see how vividly this activity is play *par excellence*. Kusyszyn describes the internal locus of control characteristic of gambling in the following terms:

A very important and special feature of the enterprise is the fact that the gambler has under complete personal control the degree of his commitment to the activity. The degree of commitment can be altered at almost any point. For example, the gambler can commit himself to a large degree at the beginning by placing a large initial wager; should he lose that wager, his next wager may be smaller or it may be larger; the wager may even be twice as large if he is the type who believes in the gambler's fallacy "double-up and catch-up" and chases his losses. The self-regulation of involvement may be looked at psychologically as providing self-stimulation, self-testing, arousal-oscillation, feelings of individuation, power, effectiveness, and so on.

(Kusyszyn, 1974, p. 3)

Although the above characteristics of play behavior may be easily translated into practice, as a society we are still perpetuating free-time activities that are the antithesis of play. In minor-league hockey, football, and baseball, for example, our young budding citizens are socialized to subject their minds, souls, and bodies to external and extrinsic forces — be they Vince Lombardi-type ideologies (win at all costs!) or externally imposed rules, standards of excellence, officials, schedules, facilities, and rewards! Leonard (1968), in his most influential futuristic discussion on humanism and education, clearly points out that the play behavior of the future will be structured and motivated to accommodate the internal locus of control and intrinsic motivation dimensions of man. Leonard writes:

... the playfield. We enter it through a break in the border of flowering shrubs — a large, grassy expanse of flat and rolling ground. People from earlier times might be surprised that it is unmarked by lines or artificial boundaries of any kind. The games of limitation — which include most of the sports of civilization — faded so rapidly after the late 1980's that the last lined area disappeared from the playfield a couple of years ago. Touch football was among the last to go. In its many permutations, football was fluid and interwoven enough to remain interesting and relevant in the new age, and some children even now play a version of it that requires no fixed boundaries and no "officials." But the aggression it sometimes encourages leaves a bad taste in the mouths of most children.

Baseball, by contrast, lost its relevance long ago. Played now in four major domes across the nation before small invitational audiences . . . . Baseball, indeed characterizes much that has passed away. Its rigid rules, its fixed angles and distances, shape players to repetitive, stereotyped behaviors. Its complete reliance on officials to enforce rules and decide close plays removes the players from all moral and personal decisions, and encourages them, in fact, to get away with whatever they can. Its preoccupation with statistics reveals its view of human worth: players are valued for how many percentage points, hits, home runs, runs batted in and the like they can accumulate. Everything is acquisitive, comparative, competitive, limiting.

Children who have played the games of expansion are hard pressed to comprehend baseball's great past appeal. As for these present games, many are improvised by the children themselves, then revised day by day. Refinement generally runs toward simplicity, elegance and an absolute minimum of rules. With no officials to intervene, the players themselves are repeatedly up against moral decisions.

On the flatland, several pairs of children are sailing plastic aerodynamic disks back and forth . . . . Rules may vary, but are generally quite simple . . . . There is no appeal, no intervening referee, no out-of-bounds sanctuary. Thus the receiver is making frequent statements about his own ultimate capabilities. He is practicing moral judgement. The greatest joy comes from a perfectly executed throw and a spectacular catch. In this case no score whatever changes hands. The reward is intrinsic. There are no external standards no statistical comparisons — only the absolute of individual ability, desire and honesty.

(Leonard, 1968, pp. 168–170)

It would seem that Leonard's scenario is with us today. His future is the present to many individuals who want to "do their thing." And when we examine closely and translate undistilled, we can see that the younger generation is demanding more *internal locus of control* and *intrinsic motivation* in their play behavior options. They do not want to be "monitored," "managed," "conditioned," or "programmed" in their play behavior. Those terms are the antithesis of play behavior. The contempt and disfavor of some mature adults for sports

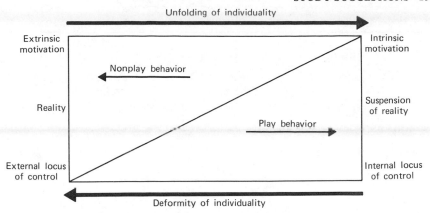

Figure 1 Play Behavior: The Unfolding of Individuality

has undoubtedly has its genesis in the extinction of the play characteristics in their physical education classes in early childhood and adolescence. Although running around a stuffy gym or a monotonous track to the sound of a shrill whistle and a bellowing "drill sergeant" *may* have been a worthwhile form of cardiovascular fitness, it certainly was *not* play.

In summary, the characteristics of play behavior describe a dynamic process that facilitates the unfolding of the most creative and profound traits of the individual. Figure 1 is a schematic representation of the *unfolding of individuality through play behavior.*

STUDY SUGGESTIONS

1. Using the outline provided below, select one activity that has traditionally been defined as play and describe the degree to which that activity fulfills the characteristics of play behavior. An interview and observational approach is recommended.

Name of Activity _____

Description of Player _____

Characteristics of Play Behavior _____

Intrinsic Motivation	Suspension of Reality	Internal Locus of Control
Body, golf club, and golf ball become part of total feeling. Lose feeling of being separate from equipment and environment.	When playing, the role of father, manager, wife, etc. are temporarily forgotten.	How to play particular shots are individual decisions. In control of club and ball.

Extrinsic Motivation	Adherence of Reality	External Locus of Control
Social interaction with friends. Golf trophy for winners. Recognition by members.	Concerned about how well the game proceeds. Would like to win club championship.	Attributing poor shot to selection of wrong club or weather conditions.

2. Using the scoring provided for each of the characteristics of play behavior, compile a *Play Score* for the activity selected above.

(i) Motivation

3	2	1	0	−1	−2	−3	Play score
Extremely intrinsic	Moderately intrinsic	Slightly intrinsic	Undecided	Slightly extrinsic	Moderately extrinsic	Extremely extrinsic	

(ii) Reality

3	2	1	0	−1	−2	−3	Play score
Extreme suspension of reality	Moderate suspension of reality	Slight suspension of reality	Undecided	Slight adherence to reality	Moderate adherence to reality	Extreme adherence to reality	

(iii) Locus of Control

3	2	1	0	−1	−2	−3	Play score
Extreme internal locus of control	Moderate internal locus of control	Slight internal locus of control	Undecided	Slight external locus of control	Moderate external locus of control	Extreme external locus of control	

Total Play score

Total Activity Play Score
(Range: +9 to −9)

2

The Scientific Approach to the Study of Play Behavior

Human behavior has long attracted the attention and concern of serious thinkers. The writings on play from Aristotle's *Ethics,* to the Swiss psychologist Piaget, and into our contemporary research and heuristic approach (Herron and Sutton-Smith, 1971; Ellis, 1973; Neulinger, 1974; Csikszentmihalyi, 1975b) have been voluminous to say the least. However, despite this concerted effort to study a specific substantive subject, most conclusions have been equivocal, pseudoscientific, and armchair explanations for this important domain of man's behavior.

SCIENTIFIC RESEARCH EVIDENCE ON PLAY BEHAVIOR

Beach (1945), one of the earliest to study the essential characteristics of play in the animal kingdom and to make play generalizations to the "higher animals," severely criticized the lack of scientific knowledge in the study of play.

> Present day understanding of animal play is regrettably limited and current views on the subject are considerably confused. On the other hand, there are the hundreds of observations made by naturalists, by animal breeders and by nearly everyone who has kept a household pet to indicate that animals of many species do exhibit various types of behavior which, if they were observed in humans, would undoubtedly be called play. On the other hand stands our undeniable ignorance as to the essential nature of play, its causes and its results. The richness of the observational evidence is in sharp contrast to the poverty of scientific knowledge. . . . The majority of interpretations purporting to define or explain play are speculative in nature, deductively derived and completely untested.
> (Beach, 1945, pp. 523, 527)

The criticism levied by Beach in 1945 has been repeated by contemporary scientists from a variety of disciplines. Inbar and Stoll (1968), in their investigation on the role of play ("autotelic") behavior in the socialization process, point out the discrepancy between the theories proposed and the paucity of empirical research to support these claims. They write:

> Given the thrust of the theories concerning autotelic behavior in socialization along with the renown attached to certain theories (e.g. Mead, Piaget, Erikson, etc.), we should expect a large body of empirical test. The case is otherwise. There are a few investigations of play and games, let alone in regard to socialization.
> (Inbar and Stoll, 1968, pp. 9-10)

Marion Clawson (1962), an outstanding writer and advocate of the optimal planning and utilization of natural resources, reinforces Beach's stand on the lack of empirical support for many of the claims in the fields of play and recreation. In Perloff's *The Quality of the Urban Environment*, Clawson laments on the absence of quantifiable experiments.

> The fact that man plays, as do many other animals, has been widely noted; it is asserted that play and relaxation are necessary for emotional and perhaps for physical and mental health. Recreation is supported by some as a necessary form of self-expression in a complex modern industrial age, when the individual is all too often submerged in an overwhelming and anonymous society. Recreation is also defined as a means of reducing juvenile delinquency and other socially deviant behavior. The frequency of assertion of these viewpoints, often by men of long and varied experience, and the obvious sincerity and conviction with which these views are held, should give even the most cynical critic pause.
> There have indeed been many who doubted these claims for recreation in general and for use of outdoor natural resources for this purpose in particular. Whether or not the doubters have been as numerous as the advocates, one cannot say; they have been less vocal, at least in print. One can indeed safely say that the usual claims of human need for recreation rest on intuitive experience, not upon carefully devised and conducted experimentation; and quantification of such asserted need, which would be necessary if one were to judge the rationality of different amounts of expenditure for different kinds of recreation, has been totally lacking —if indeed not impossible.
> (Clawson, 1962, pp. 144)

With specific reference to children's play, Herron and Sutton-Smith (1971), in their collection of readings on play entitled *Child's Play,* succinctly and candidly summarized the need for a scientific approach to this field.

> The study of children's play has attracted the attention of individual researchers and professionals from many fields, including anthropology, biology, child development, education, psychology, psychiatry, recreation, and sociology, but it has never been an organized focus of attention in science.
>
> (Herron and Sutton-Smith, 1971, p. vii)

Perhaps the most outspoken and articulate critic of the reductionist and armchair approach to explaining play behavior has been Dr. Michael J. Ellis (1973, 1975). In a paper presented to the American Medical Association's Conference on Mental Health Aspects of Sports, Exercise, and Recreation, Ellis (1975) reiterated the theme that prevailed in his book, entitled *Why People Play* (1973).

> When we talk of play, many of us wish to imbue it with a special status. It is generally presumed to lie outside the world of rewards and punishments. It is not work and has been allowed to acquire some magical significance. To study it, to manage it, is presumed to diminish it in some way. It is as if people wished to put play in a reserve, where science is not allowed to sully it with reason. It is the purpose of this presentation to move beyond the mystical and provide the beginnings of a vocabulary and an ordering mechanism that allows us to think about the play of people, and where appropriate, to plan and manipulate it.
>
> (Ellis, 1975, p. 1)

METHODS OF KNOWING OR UNDERSTANDING PLAY BEHAVIOR

The research into play behavior, to date, has been meager and devoid of the traditional scientific approaches used in the physical sciences, such as biology, chemistry, physics, astronomy, and the like. However, although it must be recognized that there are great substantive gains to be made from using the scientific method to study play behavior, a caveat must be introduced regarding the scientific method. The major purpose of the scientific method is to *eliminate human subjectivity in the procedure of ordering events, facts, relationships, and other observable phenomena.* The scientific method, vis-à-vis computers and other approaches, cannot and will not replace creative and innovative human thinking and speculation. It is only by following the expression of an observation, idea, hunch, notion, and curiosity about phenomena that one can impose the scientific method on one's thinking. But first the thinking!

How do play behavior researchers initiate their thinking; Kerlinger has proposed four methods "of knowing . . . or fixing belief": the method of intuition, the method of authority, the a priori method, and the scientific method (Kerlinger, 1973, p. 5).

Method of Intuition, Mysticism, Existentialism, and Aestheticism

Perhaps the oldest and most prevalent way of knowing or experiencing oneself dates back to the time of the second temple in the second century B.C. The Jewish mysticism, Merkabalism (Scholem), involved a form of meditation in which a man would sit with his head between his knees, whisper hymns and songs, and repeat the name of a magical seal.

Kerlinger (1973) presents a more contemporary definition of intuition as it applies to knowing the truth.

> Here men hold firmly to the truth, the truth that they know to be true because they hold firmly to it, because they have always known it to be true. Frequent repetition of such "truths" seems to enhance their validity.
>
> Recent psychological evidence has shown us that men will often cling to their beliefs in the face of clearly conflicting facts. And they will also infer "new" knowledge from propositions that may be false.
>
> (Kerlinger, 1973, p. 5)

The revitalization of play as an appropriate aesthetic, epistemological, and spiritual expression by various religious sects (e.g., Zen Buddhism, Shintoism, Taoism, Hare Krishna, Scientology, Black Muslimism, and Meher Baba) and "hippie" groups has generated a disciplined[1] form of self-actualization and peak experience based on intuitive and spiritual knowledge about oneself and the universe. According to Pieper (1952), culture depends for its very existence on play, and play in turn is not possible unless it has durable and inextricable ties with spiritual and divine contemplation. Although Pieper is regarded by

---

[1] Zen and Yoga are examples of Eastern religions that can elicit this intuitive altered state of subjective consciousness by employing disciplined mental and physical techniques, including the repetition of a word or sound, the exclusion of meaningful thoughts, a quiet environment, a comfortable position, and a trained (play) leader. One of the meditative practices of Zen Buddhism, Zazen, employs a yogalike technique of coupling respirations with counting to ten—i.e., one on inhaling, two on exhaling, and so on, to ten. The deep concentration and blotting out of irrelevant stimuli necessary for reaching the soul's deeper regions has, for many years, been described by artists, chess players, and mountain climbers as the major characteristics of those activities.

many sociologists as a classic philosopher in the study of play and leisure, his words are identical to the Christian work, *The Third Spiritual Alphabet,* written in the tenth century by Fray Francisco de Osuna. Osuna, like Pieper, was talking about a subjective altered state of consciousness. He wrote that "contemplation requires us to blind ourselves to all that is not God" (Osuna, 1931, p. viii). His discussion on intuitive play behavior would fit appropriately into a twenty-first-century text on relaxation techniques. Osuna recommended that this meditation should be performed for one hour in the morning and evening and should be taught by a qualified teacher. He wrote that such an activity would help in all endeavors, making us more efficient in our tasks and making the tasks more enjoyable. All people, the secular as well as the religious, should be taught this meditative activity, for it is a refuge to which one can retreat when faced with stressful situations.

However, while the subjective writings supporting the existence and need for intuitive knowledge and play date back to the Christian and Jewish mystics, the empirical data supporting the apparent widespread use of this mode of knowing only date back to the early 1960s (Gellhorn, 1967, Barber, 1961, 1975; Luthe, 1969, 1975). Suffice to say that, to date, despite the philosophical attention that has been paid to intuitive and mystical play service systems (Murphy, 1972), there has been absolutely no empirical research on this topic.

From a complete reliance and dependence on the inner aspects of the being for knowledge, some derive all their knowledge from authoritative sources.

Method of Authority

Knowledge based on authority is often referred to as "institutionalized" knowledge. Kerlinger (1973) describes this mode as

> the method established belief. If the Bible says it, it is so. If an idea has the weight of tradition and public sanction behind it, it is so. ... This method is superior to the method of tenacity because human progress although slow, can be achieved using the method. Actually, life could not go on without the method of authority. We must take a large body of facts and information on the basis of authority. Thus, it should not be concluded that the method of authority is unsound; it is only unsound under certain circumstances.
>
> (Kerlinger, 1973, p. 5)

Jurisprudence (courts, police, corrections, etc.), religion, and the military are three principle examples of societal systems that derive their knowledge from this method. The majority of the knowledge based on authority is incorporated into our personality and cognitive schemas through primary (family) and secondary (school, church, government, etc.) socialization processes and is transmitted from one generation to the next. This transmission and monitoring of authoritarian knowledge is achieved through the use of norms, mores, customs, history, and education.

When there is a breakdown in the transmission of authoritarian knowledge, viewpoints, ideology, and dogma, we refer to it as a "cultural gap." History has indicated that this form of knowledge may persist despite the fact that its contemporary relevancy may not be appropriate.

Difficulties with this method of knowledge arise when one individual or group in society is forced overtly or covertly to comply with the wishes, perceptions, and ideologies of another individual or group who claims to have authority or expertise on a particular topic. The question of what is productive leisure or play versus nonproductive leisure or play has been debated from an authoritarian model. The dominant social order in society is demanding that society spell out what should be considered lowbrow and highbrow play behavior and foster the development of highbrow activities while eliminating the opportunities for lowbrow activities. Reacting to the traditional and historical authoritarian leisure ethic and practices is the counterculture. The counterculture advocates a leisure ethic and play behavior that is derived from man's natural and internal perceptions, needs, and rhythmic relations to his fellow man and to the universe.

Notwithstanding the fact that the intuitive and authoritarian methods of knowing derive their input of information from different sources, that is internalist (intuition) as opposed to externalist (authoritarian) sources, both these procedures are based on subjective rather than objective awareness. The next two methods of knowing discussed by Kerlinger (1973) are based on the objective approach.

A Priori Method (Rational Method)

The third mode of knowing or perceiving is the a priori (rational) method. Kerlinger (1973) states that this method

> rests its case for superiority on the assumption that the propositions accepted by the "a priorist" are self-evident. Note that a priori propositions "agree with reason" and not necessarily with experience. The idea seems to be that men, by free communication and intercourse, can reach the truth because their natural inclinations tend toward truth. The difficulty with this rationalistic position lies in the expression "agree with reason." Whose reason? Suppose two good men, using rational processes, reach different conclusions, as they often do. Which one is right? Is it a matter of taste. . . . If something is self-evident to many men—for instance, that learning hard subjects trains the mind and builds moral char-

acter, that American education is inferior to Russian and European education, that women are poor drivers—does this mean it is so? According to the a priori method, it does — it just "stands to reason."

(Kerlinger, 1973, pp. 5-6)

The a priori rationalistic method of knowing assumes that all knowledge comes from the reasoning processes. This method considers the senses to be fallible and points out that all people do not hear, feel, or see equally well. Plato, St. Thomas Aquinas, Descartes, Spinoza, Kant, and Hegel are among the philosophers who derived their knowledge through this method. The Platonic concept, that only reason could determine the true and perfect form of things and that the objects in the world that our senses perceive are imperfect and distorted, still influences scientists and general academic thinking to a considerable extent today.

The a priori method of reasoning, may be exemplified by the following "rationale syllogistic" model.

Major Premise: Tall boys make outstanding basketball players.

Minor Premise: John is a tall boy.

Conclusion: John will make an outstanding basketball player.

Scientific Method of Knowing

Since the late 1950s, shortly after the Soviet Union launched Sputnik, the world began to attribute the success of the Russian space program to the scientific method. So much has been said about the powers of the scientific method that many professionals and lay citizens seem to think it involves some secret formula intelligible only to scientists in white coats. It involves no such secret mental gymnastics. The scientific method is used to some extent by almost everyone today. Its power in the hands of a good scientist stems from the rigor of its application. Let us briefly examine this method.

The essence of the scientific method is its reliance upon "things that can be publicly observed and tested" (Kerlinger, 1973, p. 5). The procedure for producing scientific results must be publicly produced so that other investigators can understand the research procedures of their fellow scientists.

Kerlinger (1973), a leading education researcher and expert on research methods, discusses the elements of the *scientific method* that sets it apart from the other three methods of knowing.

To satisfy our doubts ... therefore, it is necessary that a method should be found by which our beliefs may be determined by nothing human, but by some external permanency—by something upon

> which our thinking has no effect. . . . The method must be such
> that the ultimate conclusion of every man shall be the same. Such
> is the method of science. Its fundamental hypothesis . . . is this:
> There are real things, whose characters are entirely independent of
> our opinions of them. . . . The scientific approach has one char-
> acteristic that no other method of attaining knowledge has: self-
> correction. There are built-in checks all along the way to scientific
> knowledge. These checks are so conceived and used that they con-
> trol and verify the scientist's activities and conclusions to the end
> of attaining dependable knowledge outside himself.
>
> (Kerlinger, 1973, p. 6)

The scientific procedure, much to the surprise of the nonscientist, may be
initiated by information obtained from any of the four methods of knowing discussed here. However, once the initial spark of insight has been generated, the
scientific procedure from then on is very precise, rigorous, repeatable, and quantifiable. By definition, the scientific method assumes that information is only
more or less correct, in view of the various kinds of errors introduced by man
and his scientific tools. It is for this reason that the scientific process has developed procedures for calculating the error factor in each piece of information.
And in order to minimize the error factor and maximize the information factor,
the scientific process is a verification process ad infinitum.

Bolan (1971) introduces the fact that the scientific process may be imple-
mented through two major methods — *inductive* and *deductive*—and combinations of these.

Inductive Process: The inductive process implies reasoning that proceeds
from the specific to the general (from specific observations to a general
statement).

Deductive Process: The deductive process implies reasoning that proceeds
from the general to the specific.

Bolan outlined the relationship between the scientific approach and the in-
ductive-deductive processes:

> The scientific approach is based on developing knowledge in which
> causal relationships are presumed to be experimentally verifiable,
> and both deductive and inductive methods of reasoning are used to
> develop propositions and assertions of the world. The underlying
> basis of the power of scientific knowledge is its eventual use of
> empirical observations based on pre-designed experiments for verif-
> ications of its hypotheses. Unlike other modes of understanding
> with deductive reasoning, these experiments can be planned in ad-
> vance and can be controlled and replicated through a set of meas-

> uring operations. Scientific knowledge based primarily on the relations between things rather than the essence of things.
>
> (Bolan, 1971, p. 376)

For many years there has been a paucity of scientific research by practitioners in such diversified fields as education, social work, recreation, and medicine because of the false assumption that the scientific process can only be initiated with a deductive theory or hypothesis. It is most tragic that practitioners who have deep intuitive knowledge of some of the major problems in the field are not versed in research methodology and statistics and hence miss the opportunity to formulate an inductively oriented research question. Far too much of the research on play behavior has been deductively conceived and tested without any inductive validation.

Goldstein (1963) points out that it is essential to consider beginning the reasoning process at either the inductive and deductive levels and to consider reversing the process several times:

> Some persons question whether theories can be developed without some explicit or unconscious observations preceding them, but because this is difficult to confirm or refute, there is general agreement one may start at either point. Scientists have spent much time arguing about which point one should start from, but because as many reasons can be advanced for one as for the other, choice between the two given is a matter of personal preference. One may start with certain observations [*inductive*] and attempt to find relationships between these observations; develop an explanation of the presence of these relationships; test this explanation to see if further observations and relationships between these can be predicted; modify the explanation on the basis of findings during these later observations; make further predictions by the modified explanation and tests by further observations and so on.
>
> One may start with a certain theory [*deductive*] about what relationships will be found if certain observations are made; these observations may then be made to determine if the relationships between them fit the theory previously developed; the scientific theory may be modified to fit the relationships between the observations; predictions may be developed further about other observations and relationships between them; further observations may be made and predictions checked, etc.
>
> (Goldstein, 1963, p. 8)

Figure 2, a schematic representation of the scientific method of knowing, summarizes the inductive and deductive processes.

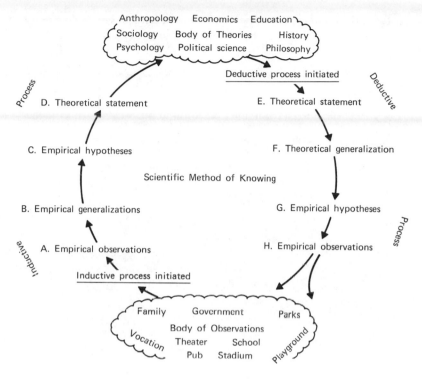

Figure 2 A Schematic Representation of the Scientific Method of Knowing.

The Inductive-Deductive Process on the Playground

Inductive Reasoning. Suppose, for example, that a playground leader observes that children from lower socioeconomic backgrounds prefer to climb higher on the play apparatus than do children from middle and upper socioeconomic backgrounds. If the playground leader were interested in pursuing this observation and proceeded to keep some form of records on play behavior, the leader would perhaps also observe that children from lower socioeconomic backgrounds do not like to play competitive games whose outcome is determined by skill, whereas children from upper and middle socioeconomic backgrounds show a greater disposition toward games and play whose outcome is determined by skill. Based on a number of reliably made observations, the playground leader can move from isolated empirical observations to broader empirical generalizations of the relationships between socioeconomic class and play behavior. Following the formulation of the empirical generalizations, the researcher formulates testable empirical hypotheses. After selecting the appropriate measurement technique and testing the empirical hypotheses, the researcher is ready to consider the formulation of a theoretical (explanation) statement on the relationship between the variables under investigation. Presented here is the development of the inductive reasoning process for the hypothetical case given above.

A Hypothetical Example of the Inductive Scientific Approach to the Study of Play

Body of observations:
Summer playground
Community
Family

Empirical observations:
Observation of children playing in various situations and on various types of apparatus. The characteristics of the community, school, and family are delineated for purposes of describing the children.

Empirical generalizations:
1. Children from low socioeconomic backgrounds attend community and school skill activities less frequently than children from high socioeconomic backgrounds.
2. Children from low socioeconomic backgrounds attend community and school activities that have no adult leadership more frequently than children from high socioeconomic backgrounds.

Empirical hypotheses:
1. Children from low socioeconomic backgrounds will sign up to play on the baseball team less often than to play in the penny-pitching contest, whereas children from high socioeconomic backgrounds will sign up to play on the baseball team more often than to play in the penny-pitching contest.
2. Children from low socioeconomic backgrounds will attend the "adventure playground" (less leadership) more frequently than the "creative playground" (more leadership), whereas children from high socioeconomic background will attend the "creative playground" more frequently than the "adventure playground."

Theoretical statement:
Children's preference for play behavior and situations in which the outcome is predictable, controllable, and a consequence of optimizing skill levels with activity demands is directly related to socioeconomic level, whereas childrens' preference for play behavior and situations in which outcome is unpredictable, uncontrollable, and of no consequence to how well the skill levels and activity de-

mands are optimized is inversely related to socioeconomic level.

Deductive Reasoning. Having reasoned inductively from the specific empirical observations to the theoretical statement, the good researcher must next reverse the field and engage in the deductive reasoning process — from the general to the specific.

Suppose, for example, that, following the inductive development of the theoretical statement discussed above, the researcher reviews a number of theories from psychology and sociology that point out the relation of "the need for aggression" to socioeconomic background. Thus the theories from the literature on aggression may state that the lower the socioeconomic level of the individual, the greater the "need for aggression." Based upon the inductive evidence and the evidence on aggression from the literature, the researcher is now ready to formulate a number of theoretical hypotheses about the relationship between socioeconomic class, "need for aggression," and play behavior. All these theoretical hypotheses would be about relationships not yet observed. For the sake of discussion, let us suppose that the researcher has articulated the following theoretical hypothesis: as the socioeconomic level decreases, the frequency of aggressive play behavior will increase. This hypothesis would be empirically tested, and if the researcher finds that, beyond pure levels of chance, children from low socioeconomic levels do indeed exhibit more aggressive play behavior, the researcher's deductive theory would be supported.

Should a discrepancy be found between the theoretical statement and the findings from the empirical hypotheses vis-à-vis the empirical observations, the theoretical statement may have to be changed or modified, or the empirical observations used to test the empirical hypotheses may have to be altered. Any good researcher must be ready to modify or even abandon the most cherished general theories when new empirical facts contradict them. The researcher must always remember that the general theories and the hypotheses are dependent upon observable facts.

In summary, scientific knowledge may be developed inductively from A to D or deductively from E to H. The process of theory building would continue using these two methods of knowing. In this regard, Hebb (1958) has stated the mandate incumbent upon the scientific investigator:

> Theory is not an affirmation but a method of analysis and can't produce any belief. Knowledge progresses by stages, so the theory one holds today must be provisional, as much a formulation of one's ignorance as anything else, to be used as long as it is useful and then discarded. Its function is to organize for better evidence. It is really only a working assumption which the user may actively disbelieve.
>
> (Hebb, 1958, p. 211)

Recently the author (Levy, 1972a, 1972b, 1973, 1974, 1976) has reported the results of his research on children's competitive play. Of great value to the discussion on the deductive reasoning process is the fact that the author's research was totally conceived from the social psychology body of theories on "achievement motivation." A brief example of the deductive scientific approach used by the author in his research is presented below.

An Actual Example of the Deductive Scientific Approach to the Study of Children's Competitive Play[2]

Body of theory:	Social psychology (Atkinson's theory of achievement motivation).
Theoretical statement:	Individuals in society differ as to their motivation to approach or avoid achievement-defined situations.
Theoretical generalization:	The more individuals are disposed toward success and achievement in society, the more likely they are to seek out situations where the criteria used for evaluating success and failure is objective and under the control of the individual.
Theoretical hypotheses:	1. Avoidance-oriented children will tend to select play environments for which the possibility of success is as far away from .50 (i.e., there exists a fifty percent chance of success and fifty percent chance of failure) as possible, thus selecting play behavior options in which their level of skill and competence is extremely inadequate (i.e., high probability of failure) or extremely adequate (i.e., high probability of success) for the play situation. 2. Approach-oriented children will tend to select play environments for which the probability of success is as close to .50 as possible, thus selecting play behavior options in which their level of skill and competence is adequate and challenging for the play situation.
Empirical hypotheses:	1. Avoidance-oriented children will tend to select opponents of inferior or superior ability in a competitive play situation. 2. Approach-oriented children will tend to select opponents of equal ability in a competitive play situation.

[2] Levy (1972a, 1972b, 1973, 1974, 1975, 1976).

Empirical observations: 1. *Ability opponent.* An individual whom the player is familiar with as to his or her relative skill or competence level in a specific play situation.
2. *Ability opponent level.* A superior opponent is an individual whom the player recognizes and has experienced as being superior in ability to himself or herself. An inferior opponent is . . . inferior in ability. An equal opponent is . . . equal in ability.

Although the inductive and deductive scientific method of knowing appears to be a very rigid step-by-step process, such is not the case in real life. The actual scientific process generally involves some skipping back and forth between the inductive and deductive approaches. It may be most advantageous, once an empirical observation at the inductive level has been made, to go straight to the body of theories and scan the literature prior to formulating empirical generalizations and hypotheses. Similarly, when the researcher initiates the deductive process, it may be advantageous to scan the body of observations prior to formulating theoretical generalizations and empirical hypotheses. Often, the best research resembles the production of a first-rate movie: the final product is produced from millions of individual frames, which were most certainly not shot in the same sequence as they appear to the moviegoer.

Limitations of the Scientific Method

The limitations of science have been debated for almost as long as science has been used as a way of gaining knowledge. Science cannot make value judgments; it cannot say that playing bridge or listening to a musical concert is more worthwhile than watching the bowling match of the week on television. Science cannot make moral judgments; it cannot say that reading *Playboy* or *Playgirl* is immoral behavior and attending a spiritual revival meeting with Billy Graham is moral. Some "experts" would disagree and would argue strongly that a moral— immoral continuum for play behavior is possible. It may indeed be possible — but not by using the scientific method exclusively. Moral, ethical, and philosophical decisions take place outside the scientific domain. The complex and continuing dialogue on the relationship between science and moral obligations is discussed by Sieghart (1973):

> Scientists come to be blamed for the use which society makes of their work; in their turn, scientists become troubled about the extent of their moral responsibility, both for social problems themselves, and for devising solutions for them.
> In that situation, the interplay of science and technology on the one hand, and social ethics on the other, is much discussed today. These two are not easy to discuss in a common language: science

uses concepts which are in themselves morally neutral, while ethics does not yield readily to analysis by the scientific method. Moral problems cannot be answered by devising an appropriate set of experiments. There may be general agreement about some moral issues, but there will always be large areas of dispute which cannot be resolved by objective tests.

(Sieghart, 1973, p. 7)

Science can, however, analyze elements in a play experience, be it painting, camping, running, or resting, that are regarded as contributing to the understanding of the term "play." Science can, within limitations, predict what people will consider as an enjoyable play experience or an unsatisfying play experience, and it can provide the policymaker with unbiased information that can be used in making critical value or moral judgments. But the act of making the judgment itself is not science.

STUDY SUGGESTIONS

1. Using the inductive scientific method of knowing, select an accessible and measurable body of observation and develop an empirical observation, followed by an empirical generalization, empirical hypothesis, and theoretical statement, related to play behavior.

2. Select a theoretical statement from a body of theory and develop an empirical hypothesis on play behavior using the deductive process.

3. Using the following inductively derived empirical generalizations, formulate an empirical hypothesis for each.
   (a) Activities that are reinforced by spectator attendance are valued greatly in society.
   (b) Academically successful children select competitive play activities more often than academically unsuccessful children.
   (c) Children's use of leisure time is a concomitant of parental use of leisure time.
   (d) Societies with highly structured and complex social institutions foster highly competitive play.
   (e) Job satisfaction and play satisfaction are related positively.

4. For each of the statements below, indicate which of the four methods of knowing would best describe the statement.
   (a) Australians have always been outstanding runners. Robyn was born and raised in Melbourne until the age of ten, at which time her parents moved to Iceland. It is most certain that she will do well in the marathon race, in view of her Australian background.

(b) The U.S. Marine Corps has been training the finest infantry soldiers for over 100 years by using the traditional training methods. In view of their success, they will continue to use the ten-mile march in full battle gear every morning at 5:00 A.M.

(c) I can always feel when I am going to meet someone who will dislike me.

(d) One out of four people in North America has experienced some form of mental illness.

3
Why Study Play Behavior?

As social scientists interested in monitoring the present in order to predict the future, we have to be sensitive and recognize that there are a plethora of trends and indices that indicate the urgency of studying play behavior.

WORK AND PLAY

Theoretical Statement:
Play, not work, has become the major source of personal dignity and identity in society.

Technological progress has changed the total concept of work. Whereas at the turn of the century, work was viewed with respect and as the major source of personal identity and meaning, such is not the case in the twentieth century. Our commitment to technology, science, and efficiency has diminished the humanizing potential of the work place. MacLean, in Staley and Miller's *Leisure and the Quality of Life* (1972), discussed the lack of dignity and intrinsic satisfaction in the work place:

> A century ago our nation was engaged primarily in farming and handicraft manufacturing. A man sowed his seed and reaped his crop; he was his own boss. Another person took a fine piece of leather and from it created a beautiful pair of boots which someone purchased and praised the workman for his art. One had a "calling" to the ministry, to the teaching profession, to medicine. He knew his vocational goal and the process for attaining it apprenticeship or education. One of our greatest satisfactions should come from our work; work used to be the means for fulfillment, recognition, and service. Times have changed. For many of us, work is less demanding and no longer intrinsically rewarding.
> Staley and Miller, 1972, pp. 96-97)

While Maclean laments in a most nostalgic tone a return to the "good old days," Perlis,[3] in Kaplan and Bosserman's *Technology, Human Values, and Leisure* (1971), paints a dismal picture of the work place for the majority of the work force in our postindustrial society:

> Automation is rapidly revolutionizing our industrial society. Plant after plant produces more and more goods with less and less labor. ... Much of our current unemployment is due to this scientific revolution. ...
>
> Assembly-line or push-button work in modern times is no great joy in itself. There is no opportunity for achievement. There is no chance for excellence. There is only the time clock every day and the paycheck every week. In the long run, I see no real religious, educational, cultural, physiological, or psychological satisfactions on the modern assembly-line, push-button job. ...
>
> Kaplan and Bosserman, 1971, pp. 98-99)

Notwithstanding the inherent problems of the work place, some would argue philosophically (Parker, 1971; Haworth, 1975) and pragmatically (Kaplan and Bosserman, 1971) that the maximum human potential can only be reached when work and play behavior are complementary relationships. Whether the work-play sequential life-style will indeed promote and fulfill the human(e) needs of the worker is a moot point at this stage of society. However, what is not a moot point is the fact that as a result of our intensive commitment and application of labor-saving technologies, we will most certainly reach a condition where only two percent of the population will produce the necessary goods to keep North America operational (Kahn and Weiner, 1967). Even if these figures are somewhat inflated and subject to regression as a result of changes in the work place and other fiscal and economic policies, the future is still predictable: the average Canadian and American worker will have more free time in the future than ever before. Add to this the growing body of retired citizens who have put in their work time and are anxiously wondering how they are to spend their earned free time.

Dr. Vic Marshall, a medical researcher at McMaster University in Hamilton, Ontario, Canada, in a recent paper ("Warning on Aging: Two Generations May Be Retired by 2000," 1976), stated that by the year 2000, Canada's population of those over age eighty-five is expected to double and the population of those over sixty-five to increase by half. Marshall has also pointed out that by the year

---

[3] Leo Perlis is national director of the AFL-CIO Department of Community Services, a founder and former secretary of CARE, and a former organizer for the Textile Workers Union of America and other unions.

2000, the typical North American family will have two generations in retirement. This means that the average couple in their forties will not only be getting their children through the final years of school but also trying to look after parents and grandparents who will be without the security, identity, and satisfaction of jobs and income. The answer to this complex geriatric crisis is certainly not to be found by building more institutions to house the senior citizens. Dr. Marshall, like many professionals in the field of aging, feels strongly that "We don't need more bricks and mortar. . . . We need more information on what's available in the community" (p. 31).

There is no question that millions of people will have to make the transition from a life-style centered on work to a life-style centered on free time, and it is clearly recognized that this free time will have to be used creatively if the individual and society are to survive in the "age of leisure." As a result attention must be focused on the fact that it is almost impossible to alter the deeply conditioned attitudes, skills, and perceptions of someone who has reached the age of forty without an appropriate repertoire of play behavior. Most recently at a symposium on aging sponsored by the Ontario Blue Cross, three emminent authorities[4] — Drs. Lee Salk, Jerome Singer, and Hans Selye — presented longitudinal research evidence that supported the theory that how well you adapt to retirement is governed by the opportunities you had as a child to be independent, creative, and resourceful ("Retirement Said Mirror of Infancy," 1976). Clearly these opportunities are actualized and manifested most clearly in children's play behavior. One may speculate with a great degree of certainty that the adult's ability to use free time for the cultivation of the mind, spirit, and personality, and not solely for entertainment, is greatly determined by the child's play experiences during the formative years.

In addition to millions of "nonworking" citizens faced with enforced free-time, there appears to be good cause for concern with the use of free time by the "working" citizen. Thus, as work becomes less of a *satisfier* and more of a *dissatisfier,* play activities of the family, community, church, synagogue, sorority, and other groups will have to emerge as the prime life interest.

ECONOMY AND PLAY

Theoretical Statement:
While the rise in per capita free time has brought with it a per capita rise
in income and a per capita rise in the purchase of leisure-time commodi-

---

[4] Dr. Lee Salk, director of the Division of Pediatric Psychology at the New York Hospital, Cornell Medical Center. Dr. Jerome Singer, dean of the Graduate School at the State University of New York at Stony Brook. Dr. Hans Selye, director of the Institute of Experimental Medicine and Surgery at the University of Montreal.

ties, it has not brought with it a concomitant state of personal tranquility and satisfaction.

In addition to a rise in per capita free time, the average person in our society is also experiencing a per capita rise in income and real purchasing power. Thus, with the aforementioned psychosocial and economic incentives and contingencies to work diminishing, the emphasis is turning to free-time pursuits. This new "earned leisure" has given birth to a booming billion dollar "leisure industry," which produces such items as powerboats, bicycles for two, family camping trailers, a "his" and "her" snowmobile, and a host of other leisure equipment. The list is endless. The only apparent condition is the ability to say "Charge it."

In 1972, the *New York Times* Sunday, December 31, 1972 reported that the leisure-time market now accounts for a total expenditure of $100 billion more than the cost of national defense. Compiled below are some of the overwhelming statistics reported by the *Times* in this age of *leisure consumership*.

Boating: Americans purchased 700,000 boats in 1972. 400,000 of them were powerboats. Rowboats and canoes accounted for 200,000 of the total. The pleasure boat industry reported a twenty-five percent increase over 1971 boat sales. Some 45.5 million Americans have taken to the water ways in one form or another. So crowded are American and Canadian waters by 9 million boats that resulting pollution has forced passage of federal legislation to require holding tanks for waste for later onshore disposal.

Tennis: Twenty percent more Americans played tennis in 1972 than in 1971. Tennis is a $420 million a year business, with all-weather court enclosures accounting for an increasing percentage of the gross figure. For $250,000, it is possible to have an all-weather tennis court installed within a few weeks. So whether you live in Anchorage, Alaska, or Sunnydale, California, you can play tennis 365 days a year. All-weather courts are being built at the rate of one per day.

Skiing: Perhaps one of the fastest leisure-time activities to "catch on" over the last decade has been skiing. Once considered an elitist activity, alpine and cross-country skiing are now billion dollar industries, with followers from all walks of life, Although there were 50,000 legs broken in America in 1972, plastic boots, fiberglass skis, and mechanical antifriction devices have already made a dent in the injury rate.

Bicycles There are bicycles for one, two three, and four and bicycles: for young, old, and in-between. There were 10.5 million bicycles sold in 1972 in the United States.Which about equals the sale of automobiles. The owner's of America's 75 million two-wheelers form a powerful lobby and have been successful in getting bike traffic lanes and trails, safe parking facilities, and safety regulations in many areas. California has a state-wide network of bike trails, and Oregon is spending one cent of every highway dollar on cycling needs.

Motorcycles: There are 3.8 million registered motorcycles, which represent an investment of at least $250 each.

Travel trailers: In 1961 there were 62,600 travel trailers produced in the United States. In 1971, there were 549,000 camping vehicles — camping trailers, truck campers, pickup covers, and motor homes. These sales represent $1.7 billion. For the less ascetic and more affluent, there are motor homes with complete living facilities, priced from $5000 to $50,000.

Games: At the more passive and cerebral end of the leisure-time spectrum, chess and backgammon are experiencing a comeback. Chess sets, ranging in price from $25 to $10,000, can hardly be manufactured quickly enough to meet the demand since the widely publicized Bobby Fisher–Boris Spassky world championship match. Backgammon, as old as King Tut but pretty much relegated to high-society resorts since an era of popularity in the 1920s, is booming because Americans are staying indoors at night instead of wandering out into the crime-infested streets. Backgammon sets range in price from $10 to about $975.

Snowmobiles: This latest motorized winter leisure-time activity is noisy, dangerous, polluting, and of concern to private property owners whose privacy is trespassed. In 1971 there were 164 snowmobile fatalities in the United States. There are 1.25 million registered snowmobiles in America.

In summary, for the American people in 1972, as compared to 1971, there has been twenty-five percent increase in pleasure boating; a twenty percent increase in tennis; a fifteen percent increase in bicycling; a ten percent increase in skiing; and a four percent increase in golf.

The economic profile in Canada is similar to that of the United States. A study of the Economic Council of Canada forecasts an increase of forty-seven percent in total per capita personal expenditures between 1970 and 1980. It also forecasts sharper increases in spending on leisure time and related goods and services—as high as sixty percent for such things as automobiles, motorcycles, entertainment, and travel and up to seventy-four percent on leisure durables such as televisions, radios, and sporting equipment. The Consumer Finance Research Division of Statistics Canada points out that, in 1953, only fifty-two percent of households had cars. In 1971, for example, seventy-seven percent of Canadian households owned automobiles. In 1953, only four percent of households were without radios, and nearly seventy-five percent had only one. Twenty years ago, ten percent of households had television sets. Last year, that figure grew to ninety-six percent, with nearly twenty-five percent owning two or more sets and twenty-four percent owning color televisions.

In Canada, in 1972, about ten percent of households reported owning an outboard motor, twelve percent had boats, and eighteen percent owned one or more snowmobiles!

Expenditures on travel also show substantial increases. Canadian tourists traveling to the United States rose fifty-seven percent between 1965 and 1970 and an amazing one-hundred-forty-one percent to countries abroad. Total travel expenditures by Canadians for foreign travel rose one-hundred-thirty-three percent between 1961 and 1971.

Within Canada, the number of establishments offering tourist accommodations rose twenty-two percent in the three-year period, 1966–1969. The tourist industry in Canada is the country's third largest industry. It also represents 6.8 percent of Ontario's gross provincial product.

In its 1972–1976 forecasts, the Economic Council of Canada predicted that these trends in leisure expenditures would grow at phenomenal rates. The data reported above unequivocally supports the relationship between a growth in free time and income and the purchase of free time commodities. However, a number of social scientists have viewed this "consumership" life-style with great concern (Linder, 1970; Auden, 1972). They raise critical questions regarding the qualitative benefits of a consumership life-style. Linder (1970) points out that, contrary to the popular belief that as income goes up and purchasing power goes up, one has a fuller life-style, the evidence indicates that consumption and maintenance of "goods" is inversely related to an optimal quality of life. It will thus become ever more critical as the standards of living improve to ensure that individuals are educated as to the wide choice of play options.

PLAY AND THE POSTINDUSTRIAL IDENTITY SOCIETY

Theoretical Statement:
When a society has been assured of fulfilling its basic survival needs, it begins to search for means to confirm its existence and affirm its worth.

In a world full of newspapers whose headlines daily report that more than sixty percent of the world's population goes to bed hungry, in a world that is rapidly depleting its vital natural resources, and in a world where, at any moment, war in the Middle East could set off a nuclear war between the super-powers, the options of play and self-actualization are ones that we are distinctly priviledged to have. It is, however, necessary to point out that play behavior has assumed a major role in our postindustrial society only because society has reached a stage of development that is beyond the survival stage. Our society has grown to demand a quality of life beyond mere subsistance. Hence, we have the revolt of dissatisfied patients, welfare clients, the unemployed, university students, women, penal inmates, the disabled, homosexuals, and a host of other groups who are *demanding confirmation* of their *existence* and *affirmation* of their *worth* through a better quality of service, care, and life. Glasser (1972), in his book the *Identity Society,* comments on the surge toward this "verification of themselves as human beings" in the "civilized identity society":

> Led by the young, the half-billion people of the Western World have begun a rapid, turmoil-filled evolution toward a new role-dominated society, the *civilized identity society*. Less anxious about fulfilling goals to obtain security within the power hierarchy, people today concern themselves more and more with an independent role—*their identity*. Arising from our need for involvement, identity or role is either totally independent of goal or, if goal and role are related, role is more important. Of course people still strive for goals; increasingly, however, they are goals, vocational or avocational, that people believe will reinforce their independent human role, their identity. The goals may or may not lead to economic security, but they do give people verification of themselves as human beings.
>
> In the traditional survival society our goal was security; an identity or independent role was rarely possible. If we gained a secure goal, and in the civilized survival society most people did not, then as time progressed we usually achieved a "dependent role," a role tied directly to our occupation. For example, if we made a living repairing shoes, then cobbler would become our dependent role. In this or any other secure occupation if we did well, we usually were able to gain a little status which motivated us to continue to work hard. If we became very secure, we usually took some regular time off to pursue some particular pleasure or interest. Through this enjoyable pursuit many of us achieved, for brief periods, an *independent role.* It was through our dependent roles, however, that most of us gained access to the people and activities which provided involvement and pleasure. If we were lucky enough to enjoy a secure dependent role we had only to look around to be constantly reminded of how much better our lives were than the lives of many more around us who in their struggle just to keep alive had no role at all.

> In the countries that have moved into the new civilized identity society, there is now suddenly enough security so that an independent role is possible for almost everyone. Rather than work for goals and then attempt to gain a dependent role as in the cobbler example, young people today strive for an independent role first and then look for goals which can establish this role.
>
> (Glasser, 1972, pp. 38–40)

Nowhere has the search for identity, independence, and affirmation been more evident than in the countercultures of our society. Murphy (1972), in a most provocative article entitled "The Counter Culture of Leisure," discussed the expressive and pluralistic shifts that are having profound effects on our postindustrial life-styles and value systems. Murphy's views are summarized here.

1. From a society oriented toward external Darwinian self-survival to a society oriented toward internal humanistic experiences

2. From a society oriented almost exclusively to life-serving work to a society oriented toward work-serving life.

3. From a society where play and work do not occur simultaneously to a society where work and play occur in a natural, complementary, and rhythmical relationship.

4. From the traditional concept of play as a "block of time" to a nonsequential, nonterminal concept of play.

5. From a society where play is a concomitant of materialism to a society where play is a concomitant of psychosocial needs.

6. From play motivated by hierarchical "payoffs" and extrinsic standards to play motivated by nonhierarchical intrinsic needs.

7. From play characterized by rational functionalism (middle class norms) to a new order of play characterized by rituals, chivalry, celebrations, community sharing, diurnal time, and the integration of the sensate and intellectual spaces of man.

8. From a few boring, stark play options to a bewildering array of stimulating choices.

Levy (1971b), in an article entitled "Recreation at the Crossroads," points out the distinction between man's *expressive* and *instrumental needs*. It is most evident from this article and the work by Murphy (1972) that the play needs of individuals in the identity society are totally different than the play needs of individuals in the preindustrial subsistence-living society.

> The recreation movement at the turn of the century came into being in order to meet the utilitarian needs of man following his long

tedious day at the factory or shop. Today, however, we are faced with changing human needs introduced by our rapidly developing technical and affluent society. Because of the need to become in-genuitive, sensitive, inventive, and adaptive to the changing societal needs, recreators must assume a critical role in meeting man's *expressive* recreative needs, as opposed to the *instrumental* and *utilitarian* recreative needs proposed by the classical theories of leisure at the turn of the century.

. . .

Operating here are two extremely different needs of man. One set of needs may be thought of as stemming from man's biological and physiological nature; these drives are related to the need to avoid pain. The classical instrumental theories of leisure were for-mulated based upon this drive-reduction model of man.

This set of instrumental needs can be seen as comparable to Maslow's (1955)[5] deficiency motives or what White (1959) calls tension reduction drives. However, since these needs serve only to reduce pain, tension, fatigue, or boredom, they do not directly lead to growth nor do they provide for growth. The expressive needs, which are like Maslow's growth motives and White's com-petence or effectance motives, are those which have to do with the uniquely human push toward self-realization, or very simply, to be psychologically more today than one was yesterday.

Since psychological growth can only be achieved through suc-cessful completion of meaningful tasks, only the factors having to do with the expressive aspects of one's life can influence these in-herent growth needs. These expressive factors are not able to re-lieve the pain caused by the lactic acid in our muscles nor satisfy our biological needs, just as the instrumental factors cannot satisfy the growth needs.

To sum up, because of the independent and distinct characteris-tics of these two needs, we find two distinct groups of factors contributing to the fulfillment of these needs.

The instrumental drive reduction factors are associated with the individual's relationship to the context or environment in which he works and plays. Concern with clean air, shorter working days, longer weekends, air-conditioning, and physical security would be examples of instrumental factors. The basic criteria for inclusion as an instrumental factor are that the factors should have short-term effects, contribute more to dissatisfaction, and be cyclical in nature — that is, need frequent replenishment.

[5] Both Maslow (1955) and White (1959) appear in Bibliography in this book.

The expressive, intrinsic factors or satisfiers include achievement, recognition for achievement, a degree of risk taking, responsibility, and possibility for growth. These factors provide satisfaction for the human need of psychological growth or competence and act as reinforcement for the "built in" generator that we usually call motivation.

(Levy, 1971b, pp. 51-52)

Levy (1971b, 1976) feels very strongly that play service systems — be they minor-league hockey, camps, skiing chalets, or drama guilds — must become sensitive to the creative and expressive needs of a society no longer in need of instrumental experiences.

PLAY AND OPTIMAL FUNCTIONING

Theoretical Statement:
The ability to play is directly related to the individual's optimal physiological and emotional functioning.

For example, as a nation, Canadians are obese, addicted, and emotionally unstable. In one year (1970–1971), Canadians smoked 60 billion cigarettes, swallowed 394 million tranquilizers, and took 470 million doses of sedatives. The Canadian people drank the equivalent of 30 million gallons of liquor. Insurance companies report that as much as ninety percent of all highway fatalities are linked to alcohol consumption. Not only are Canadians an unhappy people but they also suffer from potbellies and shortness of breath. In 1971, 2600 Canadians committed suicide, 2000 died of cirrhosis of the liver, 49,000 died of coronary disease, and 44,000 were treated in hospital for peptic ulcers.

The latest Canadian Mental Health Association (CMHA) statistics show that one in six Canadian adults will require psychiatric help sometime in life. This figure has climbed from one in ten adults just three years ago. A 1970 report on the mental health of Canadian schoolchildren showed some alarming statistics. According to that study, roughly one million school-age children across Canada required some form of psychiatric care but were not getting it. Recently, Dr. Anderson, clinical director of the outpatient and community services at Lakeshore Psychiatric Hospital, Toronto, said that about fifteen million Canadians could benefit from some kind of mental health care. Dr. Anderson said he was basing his claim on a New York study, which found that about one quarter of the population is severely disturbed, about half is mildly to moderately disturbed, and about one quarter are well.

A recent seminar in Toronto on mood-altering drugs ("Bored Canadians Quaffing More Tranquilizers, M.D. Says," 1976) reported that

> people go to doctors because they are suffering from boredom, from dissatisfaction with work and their lives. They don't know how to live and enjoy themselves . . . anxiety is increasing among Canadians. . . . We have more leisure time to think about it. We're more free about our emotions.
> (Bored Canadians Quaffing more Tranquilizers, M.D. Says, 1976, p. 32).

Ruth Cooperstock, a research scientist with the Ontario Addiction Research Foundation, predicted at the above seminar that worldwide sales of tranquilizers, now rising at a rate of eleven percent per year, will be double the 1970 sales total by 1980.

In a most recent Reuters survey of nine countries — Britain, Soviet Union, Australia, Japan, Sweden, West Germany, and the United States — drinking was found to be on the increase ("Whatever the Reasons, Booze Use Is on the Rise," 1976). Dr. Bill Spence, a specialist in alcoholism with the New South Wales Health Commission, attributed the surge in drinking to increased affluence allied with the mounting pressures of modern society.

The above statistics should tell us that the age of leisure and pushbutton technocracy is not providing creative and stabilizing outlets for our emotional needs. Intuitively and statistically, it is being pointed out that there is a growing incapacity to find self-realization, self-actualization, and other expressive needs through present use of free time. Twentieth-century living may be easier physically and economically, but statistical records attest that it is far more stressful psychologically.

It has recently been estimated by the American National Commission on Marijuana and Drug Abuse that six percent of American high-school-age youth have used heroin at least once. The survey also found that eight percent of the high-school-age group — or close to two million youths — have tried hallucinogenic drugs such as LSD, mescaline, or peyote. These kinds of statistics point out a psychosocial by-product of our postindustrial age with which we have not yet adequately dealt — disorientation, futility, lack of identity, and alienation.

For many decades the social science literature on the problems of technology, industrialization, and urbanization have made gloomy prognoses as to man's identity problem. It has, to some degree, become an institutionalized self-fulfilling prophesy. The author disagrees with this existential attitude and feels that although alienation may be a contemporary social malaise, it can be brought under control like any other learned social disease whose genesis is in society and not man.

Identity provides a sense of closure that allows the neophyte citizen to turn confidently toward the future without the need for external crutches such as drugs, alcohol, or other mind-altering chemicals. External stress, novelty, anxiety, risk taking, and other inherent elements of future shock have a growth-producing effect on the individual with a strong basic identity and strong secondary identifications.

Today's age of leisure and the explosion of the problem of identity among our youth must be hypothesized as being related. Keniston's book, *The Uncommitted: Alienated Youth in American Society* (1965), is indicative of the increasingly difficult problem many young people are facing in finding their spot in the sun. Keniston (1965) describes a small sample of withdrawn, hostile, but articulate Harvard undergraduates. For this alienated group, society, the world, and themselves are objects of intense hatred. They are distrustful, pessimistic, and resentful; see no particular way in which society can be reformed; and have only the bleakest expectations of a world that they regard as hostile, unjust, hypocritical, and abusive. They have no motivation to correct what they view to be incorrigible defects in society. Commitment to anything is a vice only less worse than the crime of attempting to adjust to the social norms.

Réne Dubos (1968), the widely read microbiologist, describes man's search for meaning in "an age of anxiety and alienation":

> The most poignant problem of modern life is probably man's feeling that life has lost significance. The ancient religious and social creeds are being eroded by scientific knowledge and by the absurdity of world events. As a result, the expression "God is dead" is widely used in both theological and secular circles. Since the concept of God symbolized the totality of creation, man now remains without anchor. Those who affirm the death of God imply thereby the death of traditional man whose life derived significance from his relation to the rest of cosmos. The search for significance, the formulation of new meanings for the words God and Man, may be the most worthwhile pursuit in the age of anxiety and alienation.
>
> (Dubos, 1968, pp. 14–15)

What then is the role of play behavior in the postindustrial age of economic and technological affluence? The major role of play down through the ages, beginning with the Sumerian civilization about 6000 years ago, has been to reestablish the unity of man with himself; his fellow man; and his environment. Etymologically it is this unity that has enabled man to become aware of his own sense of being. In other words, play behavior must facilitate the rehumanization of man as a consequence of the dehumanization that has been perpetrated in the name of the scientific progress.

In order to more fully appreciate the role of play behavior in restoring the humaneness of the organism, an account of the fundamental needs of *l'homme moyen sensuel* is presented.

MAN: THE HUMAN ANIMAL

Man has evolved into the most complex, social, emotional, and cognitive animal because of his innate capacity to adapt to ever-changing conditions. This ability to adapt to novel and inimical stimuli has permitted man to survive and unfold into his present state of existence. Other animals who have been unable to adapt to an ever-changing environment have become extinct or have evolved into less complex organisms with less elaborate behavioral repertoires.

The complexity of human behavior that has evolved as a result of man's adaptation to the rapidly changing circumstances in his environment has, in the past, given him a selective advantage in preparing for the future.

One of the most explicit discussions of man's ability to adapt to his environment has been presented by Desmond Morris (1964, 1969). Morris (1969) describes man as an "opportunist" who abhors inactivity and is willing to do anything possible to deal with boring or super-arousing environments. Morris writes:

> The opportunists are not so fortunate. They are the species — such as dogs and wolves, racoons and coatis, and monkeys and apes — that have evolved no single, specialized survival device. They are jacks-of-all-trades, always on the look-out for any small advantage the environment has to offer. In the wild, they never stop exploring and investigating. Anything and everything is examined in case it may add yet another string to the bow of survival. They cannot afford to relax for very long and evolution has made sure that they do not.
>
> They have evolved nervous systems that abhor inactivity, that keep them constantly on the go. Of all species, it is MAN himself who is the supreme opportunist. Like the others, he is intensely exploratory. Like them, he has a biologically built-in demand for a high stimulus input from his environment.
>
> (Morris, 1969, p. 184)

Unfortunately, as a result of misdirected science, technology, economics, and social organizations, man may be losing some of his opportunist traits. Geneticists, microbiologists, and other scientists are telling us that man's contemporary interaction with his environment is perverting, distorting, and stultifying the potentially adaptive responses he has already developed. Hence the twenty-first-century *Homo sapiens* will be characterized by an inability to react to novel stimuli, a lack of curiosity, and a lack of social concern. In fact, it has already occurred. For instance, on March 14, 1964, New York citizens watched or walked by, for more than 30 minutes, as a mentally deranged assailant killed Kitty Genovese. Not a single individual was aroused to intervene, even to the degree of shouting at the assailant or calling the police. Dubos laments and regrets the distorting and pathological effects of our society on man; whose biological and emotional composition may be showing the effects of the artificial and de-humanizing social and physical environment.

> There are several reasons for the widespread skepticism concerning the advantages and even the possibility of unlimited technological growth. One is the awareness . . . that beyond a certain point prosperity and abundance of goods become meaningless. It is increasingly apparent, furthermore that certain present trends are self-limiting because they lead to absurdities which, if continued, generate countertrends. The growing interest in crafts, home cooking, folk dances, and the various forms of "be-ins" certainly represents a trend against the standardization of industrial goods and commercial entertainment. . . .
>
> We wonder, indeed, whether man can long survive the artificial environment he is creating. . . . We must define with greater precision the determinants of man's responses to environmental forces — his innate limitations as well as his aspirations. . . .
>
> We lament the dehumanization of man. Anthropology has taught us that man acquired his humanness while evolving in intimate relation with other living things and we know that all phases of his development are still conditioned by the social stimuli that he receives in the course of his life. . . .
>
> (Dubos, 1968, pp. 26–28)

Dubos advocates the harnessing of science and technology for the optimal development of man, given the limitations of man's bio-psycho-social makeup.

> Scientific technology cannot and should not be uprooted, not only has it become indispensable for man's survival but it has enriched his perceptions, enlarged his vision, and deepened his concept of reality. To a very large extent the continued unfolding of civilization will depend on the imaginative creativity of scientific technologists. But it would be dangerous to assume that mankind can safely adjust to all forms of technological development. In the final analysis, the frontiers of social and technological innovations will be determined not by the extent to which man can manipulate the external world but by the limitations of his own biological and emotional nature.
>
> (Dubos, 1968, pp. 28-29)

Given man's need for individual and collective expression vis-à-vis his environment and given the impact of our scientific technology on man, what role does play have in assuring the optimal development of the true essence of man? Listed below are some direct goals of play behavior in contributing toward the humanism of the future.

1. *Environmental Information Processing*

Man's opportunity to process a variety of environmental stimuli should be considered an essential constituent of any play behavior program. The need to smell, touch, feel, hear, and see are basic human needs dating back to our earliest ancestors. Children and adults deprived of the opportunity to see the sun, hear the birds, feel the soil, or smell a tulip bush cannot be expected to develop an appreciation and respect for the cosmological development of the universe or the interdependence between man and nature.

2. *Human(e) Self-Consciousness*

In view of our society's attempt to objectify and quantify information about man, it has become apparent that man is losing his own human(e) self-consciousness. Who am I? What is unique about me as an individual? These self-reflecting questions are becoming more difficult to answer as scientific quantification and the generation of collective characteristics about man increase. Thus, *pari passu,* behavioral scientists must develop and encourage opportunities for the affirmation of human(e) self-consciousness. The growth in popularity of such play behavior manifestations as cooking, dancing, painting, poetry, outdcor recreation and camping, yoga and a variety of crafts, are, by their very nature, evidence of this need for human(e) self-consciousness not satisfied in the other major social systems (family, education, religion, vocational, etc.).

3. *Heterogeneity, Not Homogeneity*

At the turn of the century, the goal of America was to produce a unified country through a process of reducing cultural, political, and social heterogeneity to one of homogeneity. This "melting pot" concept has failed for the reasons outlined above. It is clear in our present state of affairs that while some institutions in society must operate according to an invariant set of values, norms, and aspirations, such cannot be the case for all of man's institutions. There must be opportunities in society for man to satisfy his individuality and diversity in a socially tolerant and positive way. The major rather than the residual goal of play service systems should be the planning and implementation of opportunities for the expression of individuality and unique potentialities. Such environments as the library, museum, lake, playground, ice rink, and backyard must be used for the diverse and heterogeneous unfolding of man's inner creative processes.

This concept is of major concern to this book, since it is becoming most obvious that the major contribution of play behavior in the age of leisure and technology is to guarantee and foster the diversity and pluralism in our society.

In our headlong rush to improve our life-styles, there has been the danger of mistaking the progress of science — computers (impersonalism in human affairs), planning (depersonalization of social decisions), and efficiency (maximization of objective goals) — with the progress for the quality of life.

The times demand that we carefully examine the industrial, political, and economic systems whose *raison d'être* may be incongruent with the ultimate needs of man and the biosphere. As professionals interested in promoting a quality of life through play behavior, we must stand up and speak out against the goals of powerful institutions that have desecrated our environment, failed to control organic and mental disease, failed to eliminate human persecution based upon race and political beliefs, and failed to strive for world peace.

4. *Choice of Play Behavior Based on Human Values*

While partially subsumed under the preceding discussion, it is critical that special emphasis be given to the question of "choice of play behavior."

Laymen as well as scholars can think of many forms of play behavior that are popular and enjoyable today and that, while meeting the needs of some individuals, are also detrimental to other individuals. Let us look at the growth in popularity of motorized play behavior opportunities. The motorcycle, racing car, airplane, snowmobile, and a host of other motorized forms of transportation have opened up a new field of free-time options. However, this technological innovation in play behavior brings with it some blatant, as well as not so blatant, consequences. Environmental pollution, resource depletion, noise, and the need for additional space are but a few of the dangerous and undesirable accompaniments of the growth and popularity of motorized play behavior. A similar case may be made for a number of other recently introduced forms of free-time expression.

During recent years, there has been a tendency to shy away from discussing the individual and societal benefits of choosing one form of play behavior instead of another. Today's professionals must exercise their human responsibility and advocate the implementation of one set of play behavior options over another. Hence, the statement that "We must provide a snowmobile trail through the delicate conservation site because we can do it operationally and because the public is demanding it" is tantamount to professional, intellectual, and ethical abdication. The same principle would be operating if a playground were rejected because a group of citizens did not believe that children should be spending their free time playing.

STUDY SUGGESTIONS

The student can profit from exposure to some of the literature on the essence of man. This exposure should offer the student the opportunity to place the study of play behavior in a theological, biological, anthropological and general humanistic field of discourse. The following references are recommended:

Calhoun, J. B. Population density and social pathology. *Scientific American,* 1962, *206,* 139-148.

Clark, G., and Piggott, S. *Prehistoric societies.* New York: Knopf, 1965.

Dubos, R. *Man adapting.* New Haven: Yale University Press, 1965.

Ewald, W. R. Jr. (Ed.) *Environment for man.* Bloomington: Indiana University Press, 1967.

Fiske, D. W., and Maddi, S. R. *Functions of varied experience.* Homewood, Ill.: Dorsey Press, 1961.

Hall, E. T. *The silent language.* New York: Doubleday, 1959.

Hall, E. T. *The hidden dimension.* New York: Time-Life Books, 1965.

Izumi, K. Environment and behavior. *Canadian Council on Social Development,* Spring 1975, *6,* (1) 1-3.

Kahn, H. and Wiener, A. *The year 2000. A framework for speculation on the next thirty-five years.* New York: Macmillan, 1968.

Kogan, B. A. *Health: Man in a changing environment.* New York: Harcourt, Brace and World, 1970.

Moos, R. H., and Insel, P. M. *Issues in social ecology.* Palo Alto, Calif.: National Press Books, 1974.

Neubauer, P. (Ed.) *Children in collectives, Child-rearing aims and practices in the kibbutz.* Springfield, Ill.
Charles C. Thomas, 1965.

Solomon, P. (Ed.) *Sensory deprivation.* Cambridge: Harvard University Press, 1961.

4
A Conceptual Paradigm for the Study of Play Behavior

The objective[1] of this chapter is to present a conceptual paradigm within which the concept of play can be rigorously, cohesively, and holistically studied from an *interdisciplinary* and even *transdisciplinary* approach. The paradigm should act as a *synthetic* and *holistic* model within which hypotheses can be articulated, tested, and brought to fruition. As with all theoretical concepts and models, they are not intended to be all-inclusive or true or false: they are only more or less relevant. Recently, Csikszentmihalyi (1974) discussed the need to interpret models of human behavior in "as if" and not in "nothing but" phenomenological terms.

---

[1] This objective raises issues that cut deeply across many questions about the present structures and processes for formulating, conducting, evaluating, and integrating research endeavors that focus upon human play behavior. One of the most germane issues has to do with problem identification and definition of play behavior. To date, the majority of research efforts on play behavior tend to begin by defining the *hypotheses* in *disciplinary* terms. This, in turn, predisposes and delimits the range of possible conceptualizations and methodologies for addressing the problem.

What traditionally emerges is one of two fundamental approaches for conducting research: a *disciplinary* approach in which hypotheses are conceived and operationalized solely vis-à-vis a particular discipline or profession (e.g., recreation, planning, social work, etc.) or a *multidisciplinary* approach in which hypotheses are conceived and operationalized in terms of two or more disciplines independently, with no interactions or collaborations between the separate disciplines either at the level of conceptualization or methodology. The explanations (theories) emanating from the independent disciplinary investigations are generally brought together, in aggregation, such that their implications for each other can be studied.

The conceptual model proposed in this chapter is intended to encourage and facilitate the identification, conceptualization, and operationalization of play behavior research in *interdisciplinary* and even *transdisciplinary* perspectives.

POSTULATES SUPPORTING THE PARADIGM

All paradigms of human behavior have as their foundation a number of supporting postulates without which the paradigm would only be an analytic exercise devoid of substance. These postulates should be looked upon, not as being all-inclusive statements, but rather as indicators of the fields of enquiry that may generate greater support for the paradigm.

Multiple Determinants of Behavior

All contemporary theories of human behavior explicitly or implicitly accept the principle of multiple determinants of behavior. Recognition of this multiple thrust has brought to the forefront the multivariate models of research design to replace the outmoded classical bivariate model.

It should be pointed out that both the bivariate and multivariate advocates support the principle of multiple determinants of behavior. It is the approach that distinguishes the two research camps. The bivariate classical group prefers to isolate the independent and dependent variables, either by incorporating the variables into the design (control) or by randomization procedures. On the other hand, the more contemporary multivariate model involves simultaneous statistical analysis of all independent variables.

Person-Environment Interaction Model of Man

In 1853, Auguste Comte asked how man could be at one and the same time a product of society and shaper of it. Since that question was raised by Comte, social scientists such as Newcomb (1951), Kluckholn (1954), Allport (1955) and Hollander and Hunt (1971) have clearly demonstrated the need to take into account both the uniqueness of the individual and the physical and sociocultural environment in any model explaining human behavior. It has been clearly demonstrated that all human behavior is a product of situational factors and a dynamic interpersonal model of man that treats individuals as constantly interacting with their milieu $[B = f(P \times E)]$, where B = behavior, f = function, P = person, and E = environment. (Lewin, 1951; Hollander and Hunt, 1971).

Clearly expressive of the person-environment interaction model was Bishop and Witt's (1970) classic study on leisure behavior, which advocated an "interaction" analysis, rather than the more customary "organismic" analysis, of leisure behavior. Using a "Leisure Behavior Inventory," which asked the subjects to imagine a hypothetical experience and then select the desired response for each experience, Bishop and Witt provided strong support for a person-environment interaction model of leisure behavior. These researchers concluded their study by advocating an interaction approach to the conceptualization of human leisure behavior.

> With regard to the issue of whether the major source of variation in behavior derives from the situation or from simple individual difference ... neither persons nor situations, in terms of their simple effects, have a great deal of influence on reported leisure behavior. The various interactions accounted for substantially more of the variance than did the main effects of persons, situations, or modes of responses. ... Present data suggest that both variances for the leisure behavior samples might include large triple-interaction components. If so, this might suggest the need to integrate both points of view in the development of theories that allow for individualized response patterns to different situations.
>
> (Bishop and Witt, 1970, pp. 358-359)

The innovative research by Bishop and Witt adds a third dimension to the study of leisure behavior that has heretofore been ignored in any rigorous enquiry, and that is the "modes of responses." These modes of responses may be empirically operationalized in terms of the options available to the individual for self-actualization. It thus becomes encumbent for the researcher to consider three major determinants of play behavior:

1. Unique human characteristics that have evolved as a result of socialization (person).

2. The immediate antecedent environment that has preceded the play behavior response (situation).

3. The options perceived by individuals as available to them for self-expression (structure).

PLAY PARADIGM

The schematic representation of the play paradigm in Figure 3 represents a framework for investigating three interrelationships that reflect that play behavior is both a cause and a consequence of man's socialization and evolution.

Determinants of Play Behavior

The play paradigm in Figure 3 represents play behavior as being determined by the interaction of the person by environment. Anthropologists, sociologists, and psychologists have lately uncovered evidence for this interaction thesis (Huizinga, 1955; Caillois, 1961; Roberts and Sutton-Smith, 1962; Eiferman, 1968; Loy, 1968; Norbeck, 1969). Huizinga (1955), whose impact on the study of play is witnessed in every major piece of scholarly writing on this topic, concluded that play behavior, more than any other form of human behavior, contributed to

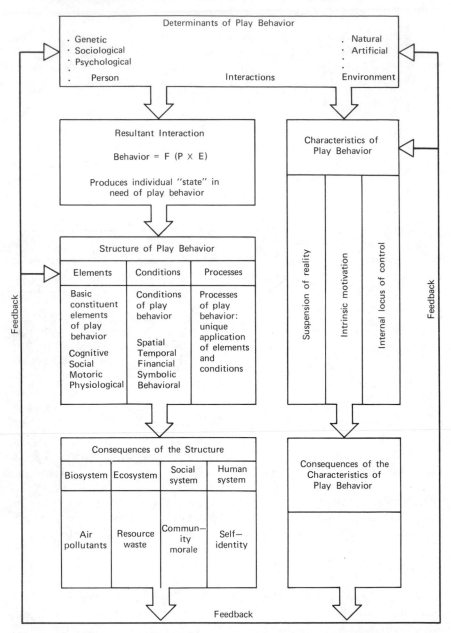

Figure 3   A Conceptual Paradigm for the Study of Play Behavior

the emergence, growth, and flourishing of civilization. Hence, Huizinga saw politics, the arts, the sciences, and even war and peace as having its genesis in human play behavior.

More recently, Roberts and Sutton-Smith (1962) have done secondary anthropological data analysis of 56 primitive societies relating prevalent play structures to sociocultural configurations. These researchers report that play in which *chance* predominates is found where the individual is socialized by a sociocultural system in which religious and educational beliefs emphasize the benevolence or coerciveness of supernatural powers. Here the sociocultural milieu stresses triumph over one's destiny rather than over an opponent. Fate and luck determine the outcome, and even when personal rivalry exists, success simply means projecting the outcome of play onto external forces — that is, the winner was luckier than the loser. The structure and characteristics of play behavior will be a concomitant of these sociocultural beliefs in external forces (gods, politicians, industry, education, etc.), over which the individual players believe they have no control.

Play in which *skill,* dedication, sacrifice, training, practice, and internal locus of control are salient is prevalent in societies where the sociocultural milieu is rooted in the belief that one has control over oneself and is capable of mastering one's environment.

The *achievement*-oriented societies have socialized their budding citizens into expressing their identity through play whose structure and characteristics is imbued with the philosophy that individuals should be given the opportunity to rely on their own abilities in order to demonstrate to themselves and to others that they are worthy or capable. In its purest sense, this means play (achievement) for play's (achievement's) sake. Part of this sociocultural treatise, which seems to be set aside by our institutionalized forms of play, is the concept of *equity.* One only has a true measure of achievement when the principles of equality, fairness, and respect are operative. In its quest for power and success, our society seems to have found it advantageous to set aside the principle of *equality in effort.* Thus, it has become acceptable to trip, blind, maim, or defame your opponent in the struggle to be a victor or winner in play; in which the purpose is the evaluation of one's true skill and competencies. The last category of play, identified by Roberts and Sutton-Smith (1962) as being structurally and characteristically isomorphic to sociocultural experiences in the larger society, is *strategy.* Play in which the outcome is determined by cognitive strategic decisions, with differential payoffs and incentives, was more popular in structurally complex societies.

Eiferman's (1968) research, based upon observations of play among Arab and Israeli children, points out a sociocultural stereotyping of children's play by sex; this finding has also been substantiated by sociologists for other areas of life-vocation, education, family roles, and the like. Boys' play in both cultures was characterized by far greater interdependence of roles, high division of labor, zero-sum competition, physical contact, and overt aggression. Girls' play displayed low division of labor, less group activity, and the absence of severe overt aggression caused by zero-sum play structures.

In a discussion in *Personality and Play,* the anthropologist, Edward Norbeck (1969), presents his observations of "some forms of play in Japan to see what kind of inferences about Japanese culture and Japanese personality might be drawn from them" (p. 47). Norbeck identifies the sociocultural practice among the Japanese of avoiding physical contact with others while in public as a determinant of play behavior. Norbeck comments:

> An examination of the whole roster of popular Japanese sports gives a key to understanding, and relates to a Japanese custom or value that goes far beyond the world of sports. This is the avoidance of physical contact with others while in public. Baseball preserves physical distances, and in a very real sense social distances. So also does skiing and I believe, all other popular sports of Japan, whether traditional or modern additions.
>
> (Norbeck, 1969, p. 47)

Historically the Japanese people have also prided themselves in being a society founded on the sociocultural ideals of *asceticism, control, rules, order, group dedication, moderation,* and *emotional* and *physical restraint.* Norbeck has shown how the sociocultural ideals of one society can shape the play behavior of all its members. Such evidence gives credence to the sociocultural determinants that are used to socialize and prepare the individual for play behavior.

Although it has been popular to examine the sociocultural determinants of play behavior, such has not been the case with the genetic or innate abilities or traits of the individual. Intuitively, it would appear logical to assume that in some forms of play behavior the genetic blueprint would contribute more to the transaction of the play process than would the sociocultural conditions. Indeed, the question of body type proposed by Sheldon and Stevens (1942) may be a most critical genetic component to consider in such physical play as boxing, wrestling, swimming, rock climbing, and soccer. This is not to assume tacitly that other *abilities* and sociocultural influences are not important. It is only intended to demonstrate the possibility that for some forms of play behavior, the final outcome may be more greatly *determined* by innate and genetic individual differences than by sociocultural differences. It may indeed be speculated that for some forms of play behavior, innate and genetic traits are a *necessary,* though not *sufficient* condition for achieving excellence and personal satisfaction. In order to have both a *necessary* and *sufficient* condition for explaining the play behavior of Bobby Orr, Nadi Comaneci, Dorothy Hamill, and Bruce Jenner, for example, one must take into account all the possible determinants of human behavior.

A number of major attempts at explaining the genetic and sociocultural determinants of play behavior have been made, albeit as they apply to competitive sports and athletic performance (Fleishman, 1964; Singer, 1972; Alderman, 1974).

Summarizing and synthesizing the literature on the determinants of athletic performance, Alderman (1974) compiled the following four major groups of variables:

(1) The natural ability, capacity, and physical endowment an individual receives via genetic inheritance. . . .
> Cardiorespiratory endurance,
> Muscular strength
> Flexibility, etc.

(2) The acquisition of the specific skills required for excellence in a particular task or sport. . . .
> Co-ordination,
> Reaction time,
> Kinesthesis,
> Agility, etc.

(3) The specific type and level of physical fitness mandatory for the task or sport. . . .
> Physique,
> Height,
> Weight,
> Motor capacity,
> Vision, etc.

(4) The general psychological makeup of the person in terms of his personality, motivational, and emotional strengths. . . .

> Achievement,
> Aggression,
> Affiliation,
> Power,   Needs
> Independence,
> Self-actualization,
> Tension seeking,

> Desire to excel,
> Desire to win,
Personality   Determination or persistence,
Factors   Poise or self-confidence,
> Emotional stability,
> Extraversion,
> Responsibility,

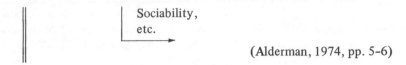

Sociability,
etc.

(Alderman, 1974, pp. 5-6)

In terms of play paradigm presented in Figure 3, Alderman's first three dimensions would clearly be subsumed by the genetic category, and his fourth dimension would more appropriately be subsumed under the sociocultural category. Alderman reiterates the *person–environment interaction* postulate discussed previously in order to assure the reader that these dimensions are dependent upon each other.

> All motor performances, regardless of a person's ability level, is a function of the meshing of these four dimensions. These factors, and the performance resulting from an interaction of them, are also very definitely influenced by the general environment in which the person lives and the specific conditions under which the situation is occurring.
>
> (Alderman, 1974, p. 6)

The *environment* as a determinant of play behavior, in Figure 3, refers specifically to the artificial and natural human environments. Having a swimming pool in one's backyard will obviously result in more time being devoted to swimming activities than other competing behavioral options. Australia, for example, has produced more international class tennis players, swimmers, and marathon runners, per capita, than any other country in the world. This result must be explained to a great degree in terms of the climatic conditions of Australia, which are conducive for year-round training in optimal temperatures and facilities. However, while these kinds of environments have acute effects on whether one can ski or swim in a certain natural or artificial setting, the critical issue in understanding and predicting play behavior following exposure to certain environments goes deeper than the availability of snow or water.

Environments that precede play behavior (e.g., work, street, school, etc.) and those in which play behavior takes place (park, theater, playground, restaurant, etc.) must be conceptualized as independent determinants affecting behavior. Environmental or physical determinism of human behavior has been comprehensively reviewed by Proshansky, Ittelson, and Rivlin (1970). There is a growing recognition of the critical impact of such environmental variables as color, form, texture, spatial dimensions, and environmental quality on the individual's bio-socio-psychological functioning (Milgram, 1970; Moos, 1973).

Clearly the incorporation of environmental variables into any explanation of play behavior will yield more valid information about play behavior in psychiatric wards, children's nurseries, children's playgrounds, libraries, theaters, wilderness areas, public housing projects, and a host of other settings in which environmental determinism has been ignored. However, there is as yet no comprehensive behavioral typology of artificial and natural environments that could be used to estimate the impact of these environments on play behavior.

The work of Roger Baker and his associates in ecological psychology is the only important and unique attempt to define various "behavior settings," with great potential for the study of play behavior. Two classical studies on children's play have adopted the behavior-setting approach of Barker (Gump and Sutton-Smith, 1955; Gump, Schoggen and Redl, 1963).

In regard to the person–environment interaction mentioned previously, it must be borne in mind that *interactions between differences in individuals and variations among environments are the determinants of variations in play behavior.*

Structure of Play Behavior

The structural elements, conditions, and processes of play behavior are concerned with the heart of play, for the establishment of a clear and universal taxonomy of play behavior would contribute greatly toward the communication and expansion of research in this field. The lack of an invariant structural taxonomy of play behavior is lamented by Avedon and Sutton-Smith in *The Study of Games* (1971):

> Personnel in the field of recreation have avoided answering the question and have subsequently avoided the adoption of a universal taxonomy for games, since to do so would demand a theory. Thus, many are content with the taxonomies that have appeared in the literature for the past fifty years, i.e., indoor games, outdoor games; games of low organization., games of high organization. . . .
>
> All of these classifications refer to an element of a game and thus different games are grouped together because they have one element in common. This leads one to ask: Are there certain structural elements that are common to all games, regardless of the differences in games or the purposes for which the games are used? Are there elements that are invariant under certain transformations? If the answer is in the affirmative, then these invariant elements would not only lend themselves to scrutiny, but would enable personnel to standardize game utilization for therapeutic purposes, as well as modify professional programme planning practices.
>
> (Avedon and Sutton-Smith, 1971, pp. 419–420)

The structure of play has been subdivided into constituent categories. It is thus hypothesized that any manifestation of play behavior may be analyzed vis-à-vis its elements, conditions, and processes.

Elements of Play Behavior

The elements deal with the specific skills, abilities, and capacities required for carrying out the specific form of play behavior. An activity such as cross-country skiing may be analyzed from a kinesiological and anatomical perspective such that one could isolate the major elements required to learn and engage in the activity. This analytical breakdown according to elements becomes critical when working with individuals who require specific therapeutic and corrective intervention and assessment.

The recognition that a number of activities may share a pool of invariant elements is important from a teaching standpoint of view if one is concerned with substitution, generalizability, and transference of learning. It may be that several card games have as their foundation the ability to carry out a number of major cognitive processes such as sequential ordering or rote memory. The ability to prescribe play havior that is congruent with the cognitive, motoric, social, and affective abilities of the individual is inextricably dependent on the leader's ability to analyze each activity according to its most prominent elements (Gallahue, Werner, and Luedke, 1975).

Conditions of Play Behavior

The conditions deal with factors surrounding the activity. In some cases, the conditions are both *necessary* and *sufficient* for carrying out the activity, for example, water for swimming. However, in some situations the conditions may alter, while the activity stays the same, for example, canoeing in a lake, river, pond, or swimming pool. Although everyone has experienced the same activity under different conditions, there exists a paucity of research on the behavioral impact of differential conditions on play (i.e., engaging in a game of chess with one's friend may be play, while engaging in a chess tournament with a national championship at stake may cause the game to lose some of its play characteristics). Hence, the symbolic,[2] temporal, spatial, and other conditions that are transcendable from activity to activity may indeed have a substantial affect on the characteristics and consequences of play behavior.

Processes of Play Behavior

The processes deal with the way the individual player decides to consciously manipulate the *elements* and *conditions* for specific effects and outcomes. The

---

[2] A symbolic condition that is predominant in Western society and hence is manifested in play behavior is competition. The major symbols that are used to reflect this condition are achievement, excellence, success, and a continual striving for identifiable goals. It is little wonder that play is also imbued with the predominant symbols of our Western civilization.

rock climber who chooses to negotiate her most difficult climb on a wet, foggy day; the tennis player who chooses to take the most difficult net shots with the lowest probability of success; and the poet who writes all his poetry while standing up in the subway—these are all examples of human play behavior in which the elements and conditions have been monitored to produce a certain state or situation. Notwithstanding unconscious wishes, the individuals are attempting to blend the *elements* and *conditions* into a formula that will provide them with their own unique optimal flow of play.[3]

It is through the analysis of these processes, "transactions" (Berne, 1964), and "encounters" (Groffman, 1961) programmed by the player that the researcher identifies the unique idiosyncratic traits of the organism. The player who is always seeking superior opponents and employing very risky strategies is phenotypically different from the player who seeks opponents of equal ability and who takes safe and moderately challenging strategies.

Consequences of Play Behavior

Throughout recorded time, there have been philosophers, pedagogues, psychologists, and many other authorities who have stated that man has survived and flourished because of his ability to play. These people have all pointed out that whenever one traces the origin of a skill or a practice that has played a crucial role in the biological, sociological, psychological, and philosophical evolution of man, one usually discovers the origin to be play. Huizinga (1955) and other play historians have documented that most utilitarian devices have evolved from some nonutilitarian unit or playful behavior. For example, the wheel, the sail, and the shovel were probably invented in the course of play, and although the Aztecs did not have the wheel, their playthings had rollers for movement. Anthropologists tell us that man as an artist is infinitely more ancient than man as a worker. Huizinga's thesis that all civilization was derived from play is reflected in the following quotation:

---

[3] Through the analysis of the way individuals uniquely *structures* their *elements* and *conditions* in play, it should be possible someday to develop *play personality profiles* representing unique combinations of motives, emotions, values, attitudes, and needs. The basic principle underlying this belief stems from psychological research, which has found that the more *unstructured* and *undefined* a stimulus or cue, the more the subject can and will project his or her true inner self onto external situations. The structure of a stimulus or cue is the *degree of choice* and *freedom* available to the subject. A highly structured stimulus or cue (role of mother, worker, student, professional athlete) leaves very little personal choice and freedom. A stimulus or cue of low structure (reading, playing cards, painting, weaving, jogging, etc.) has a wide range of *alternative choices* and *degrees of freedom*. Thus the less structured in terms of production quotas, roles, rules, expectations, and so forth, the more the player can demonstrate his or her own identity.

> The spirit of playful competition is, as a social impulse, older than culture itself and pervades all life like a veritable ferment. Ritual grew up in sacred play; poetry was born and nourished on play, music and dancing were pure play. Wisdom and philosophy found expression in words and forms derived from religious contests. The rules of warfare, the conventions of noble living were built up on play patterns. We have to conclude, therefore, that civilization is, in its earliest phases, played.
>
> (Huizinga, 1955, p. 173)

One of the earliest and perhaps most academically fruitful classification systems for the satisfaction derived from play was formulated by the French anthropologist Roger Caillois, whose work has been cited in every major piece of research on play behavior. Caillois' (1961) typology of play is based on the satisfaction of four primordial human needs.

1. *Agnon:* The need for *competition* is so strong in man that he will search for equality to a point where the imposition of a handicap becomes necessary. The opportunity to test one's speed, endurance, memory, ingenuity, and the like is clearly sometimes possible only in play.

2. *Alea:* The need to control *chance,* through games such as dice, roulette, and lotteries, where winning is the result of fate rather than individual skill.

3. *Mimicry:* The need to transcend one's own limitations through *make-believe, imitation,* and *regression.* Mimicry is evident when a child makes believe he or she is Superman, Spiderman, a Musketeer, a cowboy or the Cookie Monster. Adults who vicariously enjoy the characters of a play, movie, or masquerade party are satisfying this need for mimicry.

4. *Illinx:* The fourth need satisfied by play according to Caillois is *danger, vertigo,* and *risk taking.* Play activities such as sky diving, mountaineering, skiing, whitewater canoeing, primitive camping, and survival training will furnish "a kind of voluptuous panic upon an otherwise lucid mind" (Caillois, 1961, p. 23). Caillois also used this need to describe extreme losses of consciousness to a point of intoxication and delirium. This need for intoxication would explain the popularity of the thousands of contraptions at fairs and amusement parks that literally turn shrieking and screaming people pale, dizzy, and extremely nauseous.

In an attempt "to construct a model characterizing physical activity as a socio-psychological phenomenon," Kenyon (1968) postulated the following six subdomains, which indeed may be looked upon as being consequences of physical activity:

1. Social experience

2. Health and fitness

3. Pursuit of vertigo

4. Aesthetic experience

5. Catharsis

6. Ascetic experience

Laymen 1968, in her address at the Second International Congress of Sports Psychology, identified the following six values (consequences) of play behavior:

1. Engaging in sports promotes physical fitness; physical fitness is associated with good emotional health and a lack of fitness with poor emotional health.

2. The acquisition of the motor skills involved in sports contributes toward meeting the *basic needs of safety and esteem* in young children of both sexes and in boys and young men from the early grades through college years.

3. Supervised play presents potentialities for promoting emotional health and preventing delinquency.

4. Clinical evidence from play therapy, group therapy, and the use of physical exercise as a psychiatric adjunct in the treatment of emotionally-ill patients indicates that *when play, recreation and athletic activities* are planned with individual needs in mind, they may be very valuable means of improving emotional health.

5. Play and sports *supply outlets for the expression of emotions,* and *outward expression of emotion in approved activities is conducive to the development and maintenance of emotional health.*

6. Competitive sports, if properly used, may enhance emotional health and the acquisition of desirable personality traits.

(Layman, 1968, pp. 250–256)

In the *Power of Play,* Frank and Theresa Caplan (1974) identify the following specific functions of play as they apply to children's play:

Playtime aids growth. . . .
Play is a voluntary activity. . . .
Play offers a child freedom of action. . . .
Play provides an imaginary world a child can master. . . .
Play has elements of adventure in it. . . .

> Play provides a base for language building . . . .
> Play has unique power for building interpersonal relations . . . .
> Play offers opportunities for mastery of the physical self . . . .
> Play furthers interest and concentration. . . .
> Play is the way children investigate the material world. . . .
> Play is a way of learning adult roles. . . .
> Play refines a child's judgments. . . .
>
> (Caplan and Caplan, 1974, pp. xii–xvii)

Throughout their work, Caplan and Caplan (1974) demonstrated the critical social, emotional, physical, and cognitive consequences of play in the life of the child.

Play as a precursor to *creativity, abstract thinking, spontaneity, imagination,* and *make-believe* has received a great deal of attention from child psychologists in the last two decades. Perhaps the most substantive and continuous research in this area of play has been carried out by Dr. Brian Sutton-Smith. His research has been based on the viewpoint that:

> when a child plays with particular objects, varying his responses with them playfully, he increases the range of his associations for those particular objects. In addition, he discovers many more uses for those objects than he would otherwise. Some of these usages may be unique to himself and many will be "imaginative," "fantastic," "absurd," and perhaps "serendipitous." Presumably, almost anything in the child's repertoire of responses or cognitions can thus be combined with anything else for a novel result, though we would naturally expect recent and intensive experiences to play a salient role. While it is probable that most of this associative and combinatorial activity is of no utility except as a self-expressive, self-rewarding exercise, it is also probable that this activity increases the child's repertoire of responses and cognitions and that if asked "creativity" questions involving similar objects and associations, he is more likely to be able to make a unique (that is creative) response. That is to say that play increases the child's repertoire of responses, an increase which has potential value (though no inevitable utility) for subsequent adaptive responses.
>
> (Sutton-Smith, 1967, p. 366)

Sutton-Smith has interpreted his results as an example of the way in which responses developed and reinforced in play may be put to adaptive use when the need arises. More generally speaking, as individuals develop wider and more complex behavioral repertoires, they are better equipped to respond differentially (creatively) to an ever-changing and complex environment. And in view of the fact that the most stable characteristic of our "future shock" (Toffler, 1971) society is *change* and *novelty,* play's greatest consequences may lie in its ability to teach man to react *creatively* in a world where creativity is at a premium.

More recently, Freyberg (1975) and Pulaski (1975) have corroborated much of the earlier work by Sutton-Smith. They report that play in the form of day-dreaming, imagination, and make-believe fosters cognitive and creative skills as well as social and emotional interpersonal and intrapersonal skills.

Bruner (1975), in an excellent summary on the experimental research dealing with infrahuman and human play, cited several major cognitive and emotional consequences of play behavior.

1. Children will solve problems with greater ease if allowed to take a playful attitude toward the problem.

   We were quite struck by the tenacity with which the children in the play group stuck to the task. Even when their initial approach was misguided, they ended by solving the problem because they were able to resist frustration and the temptation to give up. They were playing.

2. The opportunity to play in early childhood may mean the ability to lead a creative and mentally healthy attitude in later years.

   Erik Erikson recently reported that in a 30 year follow-up of people who had been studied as children, those subjects who had the most interesting and fulfilling lives were ones who had managed to keep a sense of playfulness at the centre of things. ... Corine Hutt ... has shown that the opportunity for play affects a child's later creativity. ... The more inventive and exploratory the children had been in their previous play with the supertoy, the higher their originality scores were four years later. In general, the nonexploring boys viewed themselves as unadventurous and inactive, and their parents and teachers felt they lacked curiosity. The nonexploratory and unplayful girls turned out to be rather unforthcoming in social interactions, as well as more tense than their more playful comrades.
   (Bruner, 1975, pp. 82–83)

However, while research on the consequences of children's play has progressed in both quantity and quality, such has not been the case with the research on adult's play. The research on recreation and leisure has been weak in methodology and substance. The majority of the claims for the benefits of recreation and leisure have been supported by professional zeal, dogma, and philosophy. It is a serious indictment that millions of dollars are used to support leisure service systems whose benefits have not been scientifically assessed.

Most recently, the author (Levy, 1977), employing a time-budget technique that included an assessment of the psychosocial consequences of leisure behavior, reported that the only need that was consistently satisfied by leisure activities was *relaxation*. This finding on the major consequence of adult play behavior has been philosophically supported by Pieper (1950), Dumazedier (1967) and Martin (1975). But what about the other major functions of leisure so strongly espoused by the leaders and advocates of the age of leisure? The future will demand a more objective and valid documentation of the functional consequences of leisure behavior, particularly as we move into a systematic planning-oriented society in which all social service systems will be evaluated a priori according to human and cost-benefit criteria.

While the literature on the consequences of play behavior, has traditionally concerned itself with the *positive* and *functional* aspects, a strong case is beginning to be made for the study of the *negative* and *dysfunctional* consequences of play. This emphasis has been precipitated by a strong concern in our country about the deleterious effects of viewing violence on television, at the ballpark, in the arena, and in the stadium. Recent research has indicated that viewing violent and culpable acts of physical aggression in hockey, wrestling, football, basketball, boxing, roller derby, lacrosse, and soccer can stimulate and reinforce aggressive and asocial behavior (Husman, 1965; Jarvie, 1970; Kingsmore, 1970; Taylor, 1971; Rabinovitch, 1972; Hatfield, 1973; Noble, 1973; Alderman, 1974; Harrison, 1974; Cratty, 1975).

Recognizing that play behavior in and of itself may have both functional and dysfunctional consequences, Cratty (1975) and Orlick (1974, 1975a, 1975b, 1975c) have taken the initiative to propose intervention into children's play that would attempt to minimize the human dysfunctional consequences and optimize the human functional consequences. Cratty (1975) points out that, for the most part, play leaders have assumed that play was beneficial and that there was something inherent within play that would guarantee that the child benefited optimally from the experience. Cratty, however, citing the negative consequences of play at all age levels and in all facets of play, does not feel that the functional potential of play should be left to chance. He presents this viewpoint in the justification for writing this book, *Learning About Human Behavior: Through Active Games* (1975):

> The thrust of the present text is to attempt to teach the child rather important lessons about human behavior and about himself through the constructive use of games. Rather than leave to chance some of the important social and psychological outcomes of participation in sports. . . . The child himself cannot be expected to somehow tie together the often elusive models, situations, and lessons arising in and surrounding sports participation; rather he must

be led in rather direct ways to think about a number of potentially important aspects of human behavior.

(Cratty, 1975, pp. 3–4)

Cratty, recognizing that play may have both positive and negative behavioral outcomes, identifies specific psychosocial "lessons" (consequences) that may be promoted through various active games. Notwithstanding the difficulty of validating that a game of circle tag can be used to teach such lessons as "cooperative and competitive behavior" (Cratty 1975, p. 139), Cratty's identification of specific potential consequences deserves commendation and further empirical research;

Orlick (1974, 1975a, 1975b, 1975c) has recently reported research findings that reveal that many children voluntarily drop out of competitive sports because of the emotional strain caused by the win-at-all-costs philosophy of coaches, parents, and society. Orlick's findings are a strong and serious condemnation of the zero-sum (i.e., for every winner there must be at least one loser) competitive play activities that are most popular in our society for purposes of socialization. Orlick and other sport psychologists (Ogilvie and Tutko, 1971) have pointed out that in some situations, competitive zero-sum activities may be harmful to the mental health and long-term personality development of the individual. In place of the contraindicated zero-sum play activities, Orlick (1975b) has suggested the utilization of non-zero-sum play, which would promote such humanistic goals as acceptance, cooperation, and recognition of individual differences. Thus, perhaps our society should be promoting such non-zero-sum play as poetry, art, music, pleasure skating, skiing, swimming, and a host of other forms of play, in which the consequences do not lead to loss of self-esteem, self-identity, and respect for one's opponents.

Although the research by Orlick and other social scientists is in its infancy and further work is required on assessing the psychosocial consequences of play, one cannot ignore the fact that when young children are maimed in hockey and football games, when a game of baseball leads to the permanent degeneration of self-identity, or when a game of soccer leads to a riot and the death of two officials, it is then high time to balance the functional and dysfunctional consequences of certain forms of play behavior.

In light of this book's concern with the psychosocial dimensions of play behavior, it must be remembered that play is related to the natural and artificial environment. Play is related and confounded by both human and nonhuman forms of energy (Izumi, 1972). While in the past we have enjoyed the luxury of not having to concern ourselves with the environmental consequences of our play patterns, today our high play resource consumption life-styles have reached their point of diminishing returns. Play behavior, like other necessary forms of human behavior, must be transacted so that we maintain an optimal living environment around us. This assumption about play behavior stems from the increasingly visible and dire warnings that life on this planet cannot be sustained for much longer if we continue to waste our natural resources, contaminate our air, and deform our natural living environments with expressways, apartment houses, and other dehumanizing environmental alterations. The consequences on our resources and environment of such popular play preferences as watching television, motorboating, snowmobiling, motorcycling, and many other energy-consuming ecologically disturbing activities will have to be reckoned with. Philosophies, programs, and policies related to play behavior will have to be congruent with a *conserver society life-style* rather than with our traditional *consumer society life-style*.

CONCLUSION

The conceptual paradigm for the study of play behavior provides a perspective for the analysis and theorizing of a form of human behavior heretofore left to speculation, philosophy, professional zeal, bias, and dogma. The limited theorizing that has been generated on this human domain has been compartmentalized and lacking in completeness. Many microtheories of play have been proposed, dating back to Aristotle, but a macro, "grand theory" of play has not yet appeared. The greatest obstacle preventing this "grand theory" from being conceptualized is the tendency for research to be either *disciplinary* or *multidisciplinary*. Hence, the theories reviewed in the next section have all been conceived from their own narrow academic perspective. Although each of them, onto themselves, has a strong contribution to make, what is urgently needed is an all-encompassing theory that would subsume the most salient features of these microtheories in order to account for more of the behavior referred to as play.

The play paradigm provides a perspective for the *interdisciplinary* and *transdisciplinary* study of human play behavior and thus transcends the disciplinary and multidisciplinary methodologies and limited perceptions of man.

STUDY SUGGESTIONS

1. Using the format provided, proceed to choose a specific form of play behavior and record information for each of the dimensions. Students are advised to do some specific disciplinary research in developing each of the dimensions (e.g., anthropology, sociology, psychology, physiology, etc.). This form of play analysis would be most useful in counseling individuals, groups, and communities, for it involves a holistic approach to play behavior.

Play Activity _____

(Common Name) _____

_____

Determinants of Play (Why?)

Genetic	Sociocultural	Natural	Artificial

Structure of Play (What? How?)

Elements	Conditions	Processes

Consequences of Play

Biosystem	Ecosystem	Sociosystem	Human System

Conclusions and Recommendations

2. The author has found it convenient to document the literature on play behavior under the headings of the paradigm in Figure 3. Students are asked
to undertake their own review of the literature and sort out their information under the headings of the paradigm.

Category	Author	Year
Determinants of play		
Variable		
Sociocultural	Huizinga	1955
	Eiferman	1968
Genetic	Alderman	1974
Natural environment	Partridge	1975
Artificial environment	Bengtsson	1974
Structure of play		
Elements		
Cognitive	Gallahue, Werner & Luedke	1975
Motoric	Cratty	1970
Social	Singer	1972
Affective	Herron and Sutton-Smith	1971
Conditions		
Symbolic	Bronfenbrenner	1970
Temporal	Csikszentmihalyi	1975a, 1975b
Spatial	Kaplan	1975
Processes		
	Berne	1964
	Goffman	1961
	Sutton-Smith	1967
Characteristics		
Vertigo	Caillois	1961
Flow	Csikszentmihalyi	1974
Suspension of reality	Levy	1976

Consequences of Play

Variable		
Science, philosophy	Huizinga	1955
Mental health	Neulinger	1974
Ascetic	Kenyon	1968
Creativity	Sutton-Smith	1967, 1968
Personality disorientation	Urlick	1975a, 1975b, 1975c
Ecological disruption	Izumi	1972
Conserver society	Berns	1976

5
Classical Theories of Play Behavior

Over the years, there has been a host of explanations to try to account for the enigmatic behavior called play. Each microexplanation of play behavior has been a reflection of the prevalent thinking of that day. These popular and scientific explanations (theories) have most recently been articulated by the following scientists:

1. Britt and Janus (1941
   (a) Biological
   (b) Psychobiological
   (c) Psychological
   (d) Sociological
   (e) Clinical

2. Gilmore (1966)
   (a) Classical
   (b) Recent

3. Ellis (1973)
   (a) Classical
   (b) Recent
   (c) Contemporary

4. Alderman (1974)
   (a) Traditional
   (b) Twentieth century

The purpose of reviewing these theories of play is twofold: first, it will familiarize the student with the theories that have been brought forward, and second, it will permit a discussion of these theories in terms of the play paradigm proposed in Chapter 4.

The recognized classical theories of play have been recapitulated in a contemporary scenario by Beach (1945), Witt and Bishop (1970), Harry (1971),

Kando and Summers (1971), Ellis (1973), and Alderman (1974). Beach (1945) set the tone for the scientific credibility of the classical theories of play when he wrote, "The richness of the observational evidence is in sharp contrast to the poverty of scientific knowledge" (p. 523). Witt and Bishop (1970) expressed an identical scientific pessimism only twenty-five years later:

> Over the years theorists have proposed a variety of explanations of leisure behavior patterns. Classical theories basically center around five main explanations: catharsis, compensation, surplus energy, relaxation and task generalization. Each of these theories purports to predict or explain motivation for leisure behavior. Until recently these theories have usually formed the basis for a philosophy of leisure and recreation and have been accepted as the mainstays of "psychology" of leisure behavior. None of the five theories of leisure, however, has received much, if any, empirical study. Indeed, at times these theories have seemed more burdensome than helpful in understanding the consequences of, or motivation for, participating in certain forms of leisure activity.
>
> (Witt and Bishop, 1970, p. 64)

In reference to the discussion on the scientific approach to the study of play behavior in Chapter 2, we can see that both Beach (1945) and Witt and Bishop (1970) object strenuously to the interpretations of play based upon metaphysical arguments and speculative armchair philosophies that are "deductively derived and completely untested." There is very little evidence that any of the classical theories of play started with a deductive theory and proceeded to test these theories in an empirical fashion, nor did they start with a stable body of empirical data and move inductively to a theoretical explanation. The best-known play theories date back to the nineteenth century or earlier and express notions that are widely current in the literature in education, psychology, sociology, psychiatry, social work, occupational therapy, and recreation.

With specific reference to the play paradigm in Chapter 4, the classical theories of play are mainly concerned with the *determinants* and *consequences* of play. These theories do not directly discuss, in any great depth, the structure or characteristics of play behavior (Gilmore, 1966).

SURPLUS ENERGY THEORY OF PLAY

The surplus energy theory of play is one of the earliest theoretical statements concerning play. It may be attributed to the German poet Schiller (1875) and was also espoused by Spencer (1875).

Theoretical Definition:
Play is the result of a surplus of energy that is no longer needed for basic survival.

Theoretical Concepts

Play Is Motivated by Superabundance of Energy

Play is the result of a surplus of energy that exists because the young are freed from the necessity of self-preservation through the actions of their parents and the society in which they live. The energy surplus finds its release in the aimless, exuberant pursuit of fun and happiness (which we have termed play, for lack of a better word). Thus the earliest theorists predicted that the animal works, that is, is engaged in utilitarian (goal-oriented) forms of behavior, when some *want* is the motive for its activity and plays (not goal-oriented) when the superabundance of energy forms this motive.

Man Is Innately Motivated to Be Active

Another important concept of this theory is based on the premise that man, and other "higher animals" on the phylogenetic scale are, by nature, active organisms. As such, much of their activity is directed toward the preservation of organic needs, namely the maintenance of life. However, life preservation does not expend all the energy, especially in man, who has the capacity to design his environment so that his artifacts make it unnecessary to expend all energy on work and fiber maintenance. Consequently, the early theorists, deduced that since man had to be active and did not expend all his energy, he thus automatically channeled some of his surplus energy into play behavior.

Play Paradigm

The surplus energy theory of play sheds some light on the biological determinants of human play. There is a growing body of knowledge that supports the viewpoint that man is indeed an active organism who is motivated to interact with his environment, even after all his basic survival needs have been satisfied. However, while this theory offers some notions on the biological determinants of play, it fails to identify the impact of specific antecedent environments on play. Witt and Bishop (1970), who have carried out one of the few empirical studies on the classical theories of play, identify the "situational" weakness of this theory.

> Energy proponents of this view hypothesized that the seeking of play or leisure results from an organism having more energy or vitality than is needed for biological maintenance. Today we are less likely to talk of stored or surplus energy, but tend to talk in

> terms of need for activity or stimulation, needs which as yet have no experimental basis. .... The main difficulty with modern versions of the surplus energy theory seems to be the inability to identify the conditions under which a need for activity or stimulation would take place. In most recreation texts high energy activities are assumed to result from situations which allow or force the individual to store surplus energy.
>
> (Witt and Bishop, 1970, p. 65)

With regard to the form of play behavior, the theory fails to distinguish between the structure and characteristics of different forms of play. Thus, it does not help to explain the differences among playing in a sandbox, chess, or climbing a mountain.

The theory's emphasis on play serving as a safety valve for "blowing off steam" has some consequential intuitive appeal in our postindustrial neurotic society. We are now faced with the reality that there will be less and less opportunity to consume energy through our work place, and thus we will have excessive amounts of unused and unneeded energy. The serious question which then follows is: What form of play will the surplus energy take — alcohol, drugs, mass spectator sports, wars?

Critique of Surplus Energy Theory of Play

Play Is Not Aimless (Functionless)

One of the major criticisms of this theory of play stems from Schiller's expression of play as "the aimless expenditure of exhuberant energy." Bearing in mind that Schiller did not define all play as such; but being cognizant that a popular understanding of the theory has been built around this statement. Therefore, it should be pointed out that, based upon inductive observations, it becomes clear that *not all play behavior is aimless.* Skiing, sailing, painting, reading, or attending a rock concert may all be said to fulfill specific functions. These functions may be inherent in the process of the play behavior or in the lead up and pursuit of the play behavior goal. Hence it would appear that future research will have to expand on the relationship between the specific functions of play behavior and its antecedent determinants. This cause-and-effect relationship must be empirically studied if control and prediction are to become important tools of play scientists. For those engaged in the "hygienic" and "therapeutic" use of play, it will become mandatory to have an in-depth understanding of the specific functions (consequences) of different forms of play.

Play Is Not Stored-Up Energy

The need for children to "blow off steam" has long been used as a justification by educators for the provision of play environments (playgrounds, gymnasiums, swimming pools, parks, etc.). The argument states that children store up surplus energy during their sedentary classroom hours and that this surplus energy eventually reaches a bursting point. If the appropriate play facilities are available, it is speculated that the so-called surplus energy can be channeled into socially acceptable and useful behavior.

Beach (1945) confesses that, although physical energy is used for organic functions and stored within the various tissues pending its consumption,

> Present day knowledge of physiology does not support the belief that physical energy is something that can be stored up in the organism like water in a reservoir. There is no known process whereby unexpanded energy "backs up" and creates a pressure, demanding release.
>
> (Beach 1945, p. 528)

Physiologists tell us that certain sources of potential energy, such as liver glycogen, may be accumulated and stored; however, to date, no scientific evidence has been presented to suggest that play occurs because the liver, hypothalamus, kidney, or other organs and cells feel the need to discharge stored glycogen.

We know from direct observations that "young animals can often be seen to play to a point of apparent exhaustion, lie panting with fatigue, and suddenly respond to the advent of a play inducing stimulus with the abrupt resumption of their energy-draining game" (Beach, 1945, p. 529). Needless to say the same observation has been made of children's play behavior. We all know that some children will play to a point where they are not only totally "out of steam" but have also experienced an *oxygen debt*. However, before one can point out to the child that he or she is totally fatigued, the child "appears" to be recharged and ready to play until another episode of exhaustion. The time interval between these episodes of play behavior is certainly not long enough to build up a "surplus reservoir of energy" (Groos, 1901, p. 366).

All Forms of Play Are Not Innate (Drive)

The failure of the surplus energy theory of play to distinguish among different forms of play has made the "play drive" concept of Schiller (1875) difficult to study. Sara Smilansky (1968), in her work in Israel with socioculturally deprived children, found a difference in play forms among various sociocultural groupings. She thus could not accept the universality of the "play drive" motivated by a "surplus reservoir of energy."

Smilansky (1968) made the following criticism of Schiller's (1875) work:

> Schiller's theory cannot satisfactorily account for the fact that "play drive," a phenomenon common to all children, does not provide a basic source of play behavior for under-privileged chil-

dren, as it does for children from high sociocultural background. According to Schiller, children manage, through their "play drive," to free themselves from the shackles of reality. We found no hint in Schiller's theory that could explain why some children (under-privileged) do not achieve this freedom.

(Smilansky, 1968, p. 49)

It must therefore be realized that for a variety of sociocultural, biological, or physiological reasons, the "play drive" may be limited in its expression (Burling-ham, 1961, 1967).

PREEXERCISE THEORY OF PLAY

Many social and psychobiological theorists who have postulated explanations of why man plays have seen it as a form of preparation for adult life. Beach (1945) points out that there have been at least a dozen who have supported this theory of play. Perhaps the most eloquent and informative hypothesis of this theory was formulated by Karl Groos (1901), a professor of philosophy, whose explana-tion came to be known as the preexercise theory of play.

Theoretical Definition:
Play is the impulse to practice incomplete hereditary instincts. Through play, crude instincts are practiced and honed for the struggle to survive.

Theoretical concepts

Instinct Theory of Man
Groos, like many other scientists of the time, was strongly influenced by Dar-win's instinct theory of man. This theory conceptualized man as inheriting some common blueprint of genes, which ultimately accounts for human conduct, as distinct from sociocultural learning (socialization). Those individuals with the best "hereditary equipment" survive. Through a process of natural selection, the evolution of the human species takes place.

Survival of the Fittest
Those individuals survive and perpetuate the species who are best equipped to adapt to their present and future environment. Those unable to adapt and accommodate themselves to the environment will perish.

Play in Order to Survive
Groos went so far as to suggest that children do not play because they are young but that they are young in order to play. Play was the opportunity for the child

to perfect an "insufficient hereditary endowment" in preparation for "coming tasks of life." Groos was greatly influenced by the real-life similarities between playful behavior in young animals and children and occupations that make survival possible.

Play Critical for Evolution of Man

Man has developed through an evolutionary process that has taken thousands of years. While progressing through these various evolutionary stages, he has acquired a unique hereditary endowment. In order for man to adapt these hereditary instincts to his changing environment so that evolution will be achieved, he needs a stage in the developmental process when he can perfect the appropriate responses. This critical stage is characterized by "playful experimentation" (Groos, 1901), where the organism learns to master the senses of survival, that is, smell, touch, hearing, motor kinesthesis, ocular discrimination, and so forth. Since man is the most complex organism in the animal kingdom, he needs the longest childhood to practice and perfect his instincts. Hence, the period of play for man is much longer in both relative and absolute terms than any of the other lower animals.

Play Paradigm

Groos' points out that man has an instinctual need for physical mobility that is rooted in his biological past. Given the emphasis in our society on cognitive tasks and mechanical efficiency, man does not have the same opportunity for physical mobility as did his ancestors. The preexercise theory of play speaks strongly for considering these basic instincts rooted in our ancestor's past and dormant in our genetic makeup as determinants of play behavior. Such a deterministic notion has strong intuitive appeal for explaining children's innate desire to climb, swing, run, swim, and so forth, and adults' compulsion for participation in running, climbing, swinging, pulling, towing and lifting activities. For six million years, man has survived as a result of his affinity for physical expression. How could we be so naive as to assume that this component of his evolutionary heritage can be extinguished in one century?

It must also be pointed out that Groos speculated on the consequences of play through his discussion on the idea of "playful experimentation" in terms of the child's perceptual-motor functioning, that is, balance, visual acuity, ocular pursuit, auditory acuity, and the like. Groos' notions about the growth potential of pleasurable perceptual-motor stimulation has been borne out in the research on the growth problems of blind children who have not been able to engage in play (Burlingham, 1961, 1967; Wills, 1968).

Clearly the literature on the value of play in the development of the child has supported Groos on his "playful experimentation." Groos was again ahead of his time when he emphasized the need for "sensual" play (i.e., water, sand, snow, heat, colors, sound, etc.) in childhood as opposed to cognitive and emotional play. It was Groos' belief that the development of the rudimentary senses is a precursor to the development of the latter cognitive and emotional systems. This hypothesis has also most recently received empirical support from research on the play of children with learning disabilities and emotional problems (Kephart, 1967).

Although Groos proposed many functional consequences of play, there are many people today who will use his play theory to justify the teaching, reinforcing, and monitoring of brutal aggression, hostility, distrust, and a "win-at-all-cost" philosophy. These adult surrogates use play to "perfect" an "insufficient hereditary endowment" through such behaviors as baiting, cheating, fighting, and cursing, which they tell their players are necessary for a successful game (life). One would suppose that if we were interested in creating a world of "stick-swinging goons," then we ought to perpetuate the "sports" that are popular with the masses in North America. However, the preexercise theory of play by Groos should also be looked upon as offering the potential of justifying the promotion of cultural, artistic, and physically competitive activities in which the outcome will not reinforce socially disruptive and physically harmful behavioral patterns. Thus, while Groos' examples of behavioral skills necessary for survival may have been appropriate in the nineteenth-century "survival-conscious" society, they are certainly contraindicated and inappropriate in our twenty-first-century "quality of life-conscious" society.

Critique of Preexercise Theory of Play

Genetic Versus Sociocultural Socialization Determinants

This theory takes a naive approach to the problem, stated earlier, of attributing play behavior to genetic or sociocultural variables. Groos and other "instinct" theorists have been roundly criticized for trying to explain all human conduct by reference to some array of innate instincts common to all individuals. For decades, it became respectable and fashionable for scientists to avoid the term "instinct" and anything that smacked of an innate disposition explanation, favoring instead religious reliance upon a sociocultural–environmental determinism of behavior.

The concern for the overemphasis by Groos for the innate biological determinants of play is expressed by Smilansky (1968), whose research with socioculturally deprived children failed to support the preexercise theory of play.

> In taking issue with this theory our question is this: under-privileged children, too, have instincts; why do they not train and strengthen their instinctual tendencies—clumsy and ill defined as they are in all small animals—through the experience that play activity affords? Where do these children acquire the necessary

> training to strengthen and support their chances of survival in adult
> life? Groos was primarily concerned with the parallelism between
> the play activity of the child and the play behavior of young
> animals in the spirit and under the influence of Darwin. He em-
> phasizes the "biological functionalism" of play, or the common
> destiny of man and beast. Psychological aspects, such as mental
> needs or inner qualities, as factors of play behavior, or the func-
> tion of play in forming psychological processes of the individual
> and society are of secondary significance in his theory.
>
> (Smilansky, 1968, p. 51)

There now appears to be emerging a more interactional viewpoint between
"nativist" and "situationist" explanations of human conduct. Clearly, the work
of Groos would contribute greatly to the "nativist" system of man.

Age of Exploding Knowledge and Change

Another major difficulty with the preexercise theory is its reliance on the past
and present to develop survival skills for the future. We are presently living in a
society that is experiencing an explosion in knowledge, attitudes, philosophies,
life-styles, careers, and so forth (Toffler, 1971). How is one to know what the
survival prerequisites in the year 2100 will be? Furthermore, how can we ever
come to believe that an individual is capable of inheriting the capacity to predict which behavioral responses will be critical in the future. It almost seems as
though the preexercise theory of play is juxtaposed to the premise that man has
the capacity to adjust and adapt to internal and external stimuli on an ad hoc
basis rather than on an a priori basis, which is not only unrealistic but also
impossible and impractical in our day and age when change is the theme of the
times.

RECAPITULATION THEORY OF PLAY

G. Stanley Hall (1906) assumed that play was a recapitulation of the cultural
stages in the evolution of the human race.

Theoretical Definition:

Play is the recapitulation of the various phylogenetic stages that have preceded man on the evolutionary scale, that is, Insectivora, Carnivora,
Hyaendonta, Taeniodonta and so forth.

Theoretical Concepts

Ontogeny Recapitulates Phylogeny

Hall, a professor of psychology and pedagogy at Clark University, stated that
the child is an evolutionary link between present-day man and all cultural stages

that have preceded man on the phylogenetic scale. Through play, man recapitulates the behavioral traits that made survival possible for his ancestors, that is, climbing, swinging, throwing, catching, running, yelling, and so forth.

Atavistic Tendencies of an Earlier State in the Development of the Human Race Are Adapted to the Contemporary Environment

Hall, like Groos and Darwin, linked play to an expression of innate instincts. However, while Groos saw play as a natural human activity for the development of future skills, Hall assigned to play the role of weakening or modifying past skills that have become inappropriate and disruptive (atavistic) for the present stage of development. Thus, through play the primitive instincts find expression and do not interfere with the cultural and social progress of man. Hall explained his recapitulation theory of play as follows:

> I regard play as the motor habits and spirit of the past of the race, persisting in the present, as rudimentary functions, some time of, and always akin to rudimentary organs. The best index and guide to the stated activities of adults in past ages is found in the instinctive, untaught, and nonimitative plays of children which are the most spontaneous and exact expressions of their motor needs. The young grow up into the same forms of motor activity, as did generations that have long preceded them, only to a limited extent. ... Their transformation into later acquired adult forms is progressively later. ... In play every mood and movement is instinct with heredity. Thus we rehearse the activities of our ancestors, back we know not how far, and repeat their life work in summative and adumbrated ways.
>
> (Hall, 1906, p. 379)

In short, just as Groos' postulates on play and man were forward looking (i.e., preexercise for the future), the postulates of Hall were backward looking. Hall saw play as an opportunity to rid the human race of primitive and unnecessary (atavistic) instinctual traits carried over by heredity from past generations.

Play Paradigm

Although Hall's theory may be criticized severely because of its phylogenetic-ontogenetic system, it is this very system that offers fruit for future longitudinal and cross-cultural research. There is some preliminary psychosocial evidence that critical events, environments, and experiences that have taken place during the evolution of a specific organism are encoded for inheritance and passed onto the next generation. Based on this argument, it would seem logical that societies that have experienced violence for several generations would have encoded in their genetic blueprint certain predispositions for violence, crime, aggression, and other antisocial behavior patterns. Subsequent generations would thus require the opportunity to purge themselves directly or vicariously of these atavistic tendencies. This is certainly food for thought in the light of rising antisocial behavior in society, on television, in sports, and in other phases of life. Will we be perpetuating a society of violent, hungry children and adults? Hall's theory opens up some new frontiers on the biocultural determinants of violent and aggressive forms of play.

Taking a more positive approach to Hall's notions, one may interpret the physical aggression manifested in hockey, football, soccer, wrestling, and boxing as an instinctual recapitulation of man's violent phylogenetic struggle for survival. The theory then becomes viable for examining the consequences of play behavior. For example, will children who engage in physical forms of play manifest less aggressive behavior as adults than children who are deprived of the opportunity to be physically aggressive? This type of longitudinal research would provide some empirical data for the cross-sectional observations of Hall.

With regard to the structure and characteristics of play behavior, Hall, like his Darwinian predecessors, only recognized those features of play that were models of survival activities associated with primitive instincts. Little recognition was given to distinguishing between the structures of play as determined by sociocultural and environmental factors.

Critique of Recapitulation Theory of Play

Ontogenetic Recapitulation of Phylogenetic Evolution Questioned

Hall's Lamarckian view of evolution, upon which he formulated the concept that each child passes through a series of play stages corresponding to, and recapitulating, the cultural epochs of the particular race, has been severely criticized.

It has been pointed out by developmental psychologists that although there may be a uniform neuromuscular and cognitive developmental sequence followed by all children, there is no evidence for the unvarying order for this development with respect to the unique structure of play. The structure of play depends, to a great degree, on what a child has been exposed to in his or her environment. For example, if a child has reached a stage of development where his or her neuromuscular system has a need to climb and pull, the form that this neuromuscular mastery will take will vary depending on the environment surrounding the child as well as his or her genotypical and phenotypical background. For example, rural children may leap across narrow rivers and brooks, drive tractors, or jump from hay lofts, while urban children may ride on top of elevators, climb on playground apparatus, steal batteries, or flirt with death in traffic as their way of satisfying some basic neuromuscular needs.

Recently, Smilansky (1968) questioned the structural relevancy of the phylogenetic theory of play. Smilansky clearly makes a case for environmental and sociocultural input:

In our extensive observations of children at play in Israel (children from both high and low sociocultural backgrounds) we did not witness games played on the themes of the wandering tribes, hunters after prey, and so on. As we described earlier, the themes chosen by the children for their games were taken from the everyday life of the adults in their immediate environment.

(Smilansky, 1968, pp. 51–52)

Atavistic Traits Do Not Manifest Themselves in Contemporary Play

A more obvious criticism of the "ontogeny recapitulates phylogeny" thesis of Hall may be reached when one observes contemporary children playing games with computers, rocketships, modular dolls, submarines, and a host of other contemporary and future-oriented artifacts of play. Surely these can hardly be interpreted as vestiges representing "atavistic tendencies of an earlier epoch in the development of man." Ellis (1973) reinforces this criticism when he writes:

The theory does not explain the intense interest of man in toys that utilize contemporary technology, such as slot cars, dirt bikes, chemistry sets, and talking dolls. Nor does it explain sports and games that are concerned with the competitive application of technology to improving control of the environment in such sports as sailing, car racing, and gliding.

(Ellis, 1973, p. 44)

RECREATION THEORY OF PLAY

Diametrically juxtaposed to the surplus energy theory of play and somewhat unsupportive of the instinct theory of play is the recreation theory of play proposed by Lazarus (1883), a professor at the University of Berlin.

Theoretical Definition:
Play is the result of the individual's need to overcome a deficit of energy.

Theoretical Concepts

Play Motivated by Deficiency of Energy

Play is the result of fatigue brought about by the overuse or inappropriate use of body organs. Alderman (1974), in his review of the "traditional theories of play," summarized the recreation theory of play in the following conceptual terms:

This is an "energy" theory in reverse-rather than looking at play as the result of a surplus of energy, play is seen as the means to

> revive one's energy stores. Playing tennis or golf after a hard day
> in the office is seen as "relaxation" for the person, which not only
> alleviates boredom and psychological tension but also seems to
> replenish one's physical stores.
>
> (Alderman, 1974, p. 30)

The recreation theory of play is not easy to reconcile with the surplus energy of play, since it implies that play comes from depletion rather than from excess of available energy.

Characteristics and Consequences Different for Work and Play

Lazarus defined play by contrasing it with work. Play, for Lazarus, implied fun, self-selection, activity for the sake of, but divorced from, itself, and an illusion of reality. Work, on the other hand, is serious; causes undesired physical and mental strain; has an explicit purpose, goal, and measurable end product; and is externally imposed. In total, Lazarus claimed that work caused a physical and psychological strain on man, whereas play produced the freedom and recreation of man's various human systems.

This contrast between work and play causes the recreation theory to be somewhat discongruent with the preexercise theory of play, since, according to the recreation theory, play is apparently most conducive to recovery when it contrasts with the antecedent activity that has led to fatigue. In other words, play leads to improvement not in the instincts that the individual uses in everyday life (e.g., work, school, family life, etc.), but in the activities that would contrast with these real-world survival activities.

Play Paradigm

Lazarus' recreation theory of play has its greatest intuitive appeal for the consequences of play behavior. The need for a contrast of behavior from the modern work place is strongly advocated by those in the various branches of mental health.

This theory makes a start at identifying the possible characteristics and consequences of play. It does not distinguish between the structural dimensions of various forms of play, which one would have to take into account for any meaningful research of the work–play continuum.

Critique of the Recreation Theory of Play

Person by Environment Interaction Essential

Intuitively and experientially, it can hardly be denied that play experiences often make people feel better prepared for a renewed bout of work, but it remains to be scientifically demonstrated which kind of play recreates which individual following which kind of work experience. One must keep in mind that the interaction between the individual and the environment (determinants) will produce different individual states. It is these individual states that the person seeks to deal with in play behavior. The fact that similar environments (work, school, home, play, etc.) have different impacts for various individuals or, conversely that different environmental situations may have the same impact must be considered in the design of any research on play behavior. This critical model is schematically represented in Figure 4. This paradigm has also been discussed by Kando and Summers (1971) and Harry (1971), with implications for work and leisure.

It thus appears that the major criticism of the recreation theory of play is a result of its emphasis on the need to experience a recreative activity widely different from the previous activity. Theory and practice would seem to indicate that this may not be an invariant theorem. It may be that four students will experience four different results (individual state) from the same two-hour university lecture. Thus the same environment would produce a need for four different kinds of play experiences. One student may go home and do crossword puzzles (bored), another may simply go home and watch television (anxious), a third may decide to attend a guest lecture on his favorite hobby (satisfied), and the fourth may decide to do some further readings on the material covered in the class discussion because he found the class very enjoyable (satisfied.)

RELAXATION THEORY OF PLAY

1. W. Patrick (1916), a professor of philosophy at the University of Iowa, extended the recreation theory of Lazarus (1883) to speculate that play stems from a need for relaxation.

Theoretical Definition:
Play is the result of man's need for gross motor activities that are not being exercised because of man's high reliance upon small-muscle activities.

Theoretical Concepts

Play Motivated by Strain of More Recently Developed Fine Motor and Cerebral Activities

Patrick, like his predecessor Lazarus, defined play by juxtaposing it to work: fun versus seriousness, intrinsic versus extrinsic-motivation, process-oriented versus goal-oriented. However, Patrick, who felt the need for a true psychology of play, was very articulate in pointing out that modern technology requires concentrated, cognitive, and abstract thinking, which puts an excess amount of strain on the cerebral cortex (brain) as well as on the smallest muscles

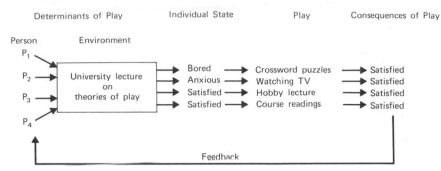

Figure 4   A Schematic Representation of the Different Individual States Resulting from Exposure to the Same Environment.

of the body required for fine motor dexterity tasks. According to Patrick, the mechanisms for highly sophisticated cerebral tasks demanded in most contemporary jobs have only recently been acquired by the human race. Consequently, these modern skills put an excess amount of strain on the brain tracts and on the smallest muscles of the body. Patrick did not conceive of play as providing excitement ". . . but release from those forms of mental activity which are fatigued in our daily life of grind" (Patrick, 1916, p. 351). The following quote from Patrick reflects the recapitulation and instinctual Darwinian notions of his time, which were critical to most formulations of the essence of man during the late nineteenth and early twentieth centuries:

> There is a striking similarity between the plays of children and the sports of man on the one hand and the pursuits of primitive man on the other. This similarity is due to the fact that those mental powers upon which advancing civilization depends, especially voluntary and sustained attention, concentration, analysis, and abstraction, are undeveloped in the child and subject to rapid fatigue in the adult. Hence the child's activities and the play activities of the adult tend always to take the form of old racial pursuits.
>
> (Patrick, 1916, p. 280)

Play Motivated by Man's Need to Exercise Racially Old Instincts

Following the argument that man has a natural ability for certain racially older pursuits, it was thus proposed by Patrick that certain forms of play behavior, such as outdoor gross motor activities, are more wholesome than quiet, small-muscle activities. Patrick did much to apply his theory of play to the education of children, in whom he believed the higher abilities of the brain are underdeveloped. As a result, concentrated work and monotonous repetition, which required sustained use of the small muscles, is impossible.

As has been already pointed out, Patrick, whose theory is reminiscent of Groos' instinct theory, writes that the child's natural activity is play developed in "deep-rooted race habits." It thus follows that Patrick advocated participation in physically active games of football, wrestling, swimming, gymnastics, running, and the like. These games are supposed to be satisfying and relaxing because they offer satisfaction of racially old instincts and furnish an adequate way of escaping from an artificial life made up of human artifacts. Patrick stated that the body becomes physically relaxed from participation in activities using large muscles and originating in "racially old co-ordinates."

Play Paradigm

Patrick's theory of relaxation is most appropriate for the postindustrial computer age. Whether the adult works as a bank clerk, consulting engineer, assembly line worker, or sales manager, the work usually involves little gross motor activity or extreme uses of energy. It is only through play that modern man can overcome the extreme effects of mental fatigue and engage in the relaxing use of bodily muscles. The term "relaxation" has become a common way of describing the recuperative and restorative effects of leisure-time behavior (Levy, 1977).

Critique of the Relaxation Theory of Play

Racially Older Habits are Better Learned Skills

Like some of the other classical theories of play, Patrick's theory is stimulating and thought-provoking, and it contributes some support for school recess periods and leisure services to cope with life in the postindustrial computer age where the push of a button produces "instant coffee," "instant love," "instant youth," and even "instant life." However, Patrick's theory is less satisfactory in explaining the motivation of play behavior in terms of "race habits" and "racial memory." There does not appear to be scientific evidence for any sort of "racial memory," in that most human behavior appears to be learned or adapted to suit one's genetic makeup. It would seem more tenable that the so-called "racially old co-ordinates" are learned in early childhood and practiced in later life, and this would mean that they are likely to be less physically fatiguing (Mason and Mitchell, 1948) than more recently learned mental skills.

All Children's or Adults' Play Is Not Motoric

There are many examples of play behavior in both adults and children that require cognitive skills. By stating that children play because they cannot work since their cerebral skills are in a neophyte stage, Patrick eliminates any mental content or cognitive component from children's play. Yet the work by Piaget (1962) and other cognitive psychologists would suggest that an important function of play is mental development.

In the case of adult play, it is impossible to exclude the cognitive component of those activities we would classify as motoric. Thus, while playing squash may be classified by some as motoric, it also becomes apparent when observing a game of squash that there are clear-cut cognitive inputs that determine the style of play. Man is a product of his advanced technological work, and as such, his recently developed cerebral skills are part of all his motoric activities − play included.

SUMMARY OF THE CLASSICAL THEORIES OF PLAY

Despite the claim by some (Ellis, 1973) that "classical theories are not a very promising group of theories" (p. 48), the author strongly contends that these theories offer great promise for future empirical research on play behavior. It would almost appear as though the classical theories have acted as the foundation for any future theoretical developments on the study of play. This view has recently been reiterated by Alderman (1974):

> It is obvious that these traditional (classical) theories of play tend to be quite consistent with modern thought, in many cases as we will see, actually predating a great deal of current thinking. Though lacking in the orderly study of details and the important recognition that a large part of the meaning of play lies in a person's subconscious, these turn-of-the-century views provided a solid, pragmatic base for later theorizing.
>
> (Alderman, 1974, p. 31)

It was exactly this type of theorizing that Witt and Bishop (1970) engaged in when they carried out their research on the classical theories of play. As a result of their research findings, they proposed that the relaxation theory be subdivided into two theories (diversionary and restoration), and that monotony, fatigue, and the like, as antecedent conditions, be interpreted differently under the two classical theories of play: the surplus energy theory and the relaxation theory. Witt and Bishop discuss their interpretation of these two theories based on empirical research:

> The relaxation theory, which is also referred to as both the recreation theory . . . and the restoration theory . . . stands in marked contrast to the surplus energy theory. This theory implies that intensive involvement in or preoccupation with any activity demands a period of respite during which the person relaxes or re-creates himself. Monotonous conditions provide a point of inter-

section for the surplus energy and relaxation theories. The difference is that for the surplus energy theory, monotony induces boredom; but for the relaxation theory it can induce fatigue. . . .

In addition, the relaxation theory seems to have two distinct aspects, relaxation after one is fatigued (restoration–relaxation), and relaxation after one has been involved in activity that is not necessarily fatiguing but has left little time for escape (diversionary–relaxation).

(Witt and Bishop, 1970, p. 65)

Represented in Figure 5 are the critical theoretical tangents introduced by Witt and Bishop (1970).

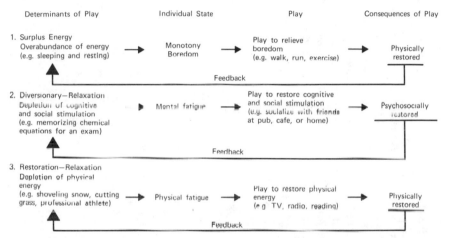

Figure 5   A Schematic Representation of the Surplus Energy and Relaxation Theories of Play Studied by Witt and Bishop (1970).

STUDY SUGGESTIONS

1. Perhaps the most meaningful way to get an appreciation of the classical theories of play is to actually examine human behavior and determine the degree to which these theories are valid in explaining antecedent-play-consequent relationships. Using the format provided on the next page, analyze your own play behavior in order to determine the degree to which the classical theories explain play behavior.

Think back to the last three times that you were involved in a play activity (e.g., playing golf, watching television, reading, walking, etc.). For each of these activities, fill in the information requested below.

First Activity	Antecedent Situation	Play Behavior	Consequence of Play Behavior
(E.G., playing bridge)	Describe what you were involved in and your experiences *prior* to engaging in play (e.g., studying at the library all afternoon; feeling *exhausted mentally* and *physically*; library *insulates* you from *social contact* with people)	Describe the characteristics of the activity (e.g. opportunity to demonstrate *skill* to *friends*; *emotional involvement*, not overly concerned about *outcome*; *self-pacing* and *internal control* over decisions)	Describe how you felt shortly *after* the termination of the activity (e.g., *mentally* and *physically* alert; *self-awareness* increased as a result of being with friends; feeling of *personal satisfaction* as a result of having played several good hands)
Second Activity			
Third Activity			

6
Psychoanalytic Theories of Play Behavior

In light of the criticism that has been directed toward the psychoanalytic theories by contemporary scholars interested in studying the phenomena of play (Ellis, 1973), it would seem most appropriate to point out that the dynamic psychology of play developed by Sigmund Freud was an outgrowth of the scientific period in which Freud was immersed. Let us very briefly review the highlights of this historical period of science, which has provided the basis for so many of our social and physical disciplines.

When Freud was three years old (1859), Charles Darwin published the *Origin of Species*. This book was destined to revolutionize man's conception of man. Before Darwin, man was set apart from the rest of the animal kingdom by virtue of being allocated a soul. The evolutionary doctrine of Darwin made man a part of nature, an animal among other animals. The acceptance of this radical view meant that the study of man could proceed along naturalistic lines. Man became an object of scientific inquiry, no different, save in complexity, from other forms of life.

The year following the publication of the *Origin of Species,* Gustav Fechner founded the "science of psychology." This great German scientist and philosopher of the nineteenth century demonstrated in 1860 that man's mind could be studied scientifically and measured quantitatively. These two scientists, Darwin and Fechner, had a tremendous impact upon the intellectual development and theoretical formulation of Freud, as they did upon so many other young scientists of that period.

The life sciences were also on a creative rampage, and needless to say they influenced Freud's conceptual development of play. Louis Pasteur and Robert Koch, by their fundamental work of the germ theory of disease, established the science of bacteriology; and Gregor Mendel, by his investigation on the garden pea, founded the modern science of genetics.

There were other scientific influences that affected Freud even more profoundly. One of the most important came from physics. In the middle of the nineteenth century, the great German physicist Hermann von Helmholtz formulated the principle of "conservation of energy." This principle stated, in effect, that energy is a quantity just as mass is a quantity. It can be transformed, but it cannot be destroyed. This deductive theory was totally incorporated by Freud in the formulation of the psychic energy theory of man, which he hypothesized can be transformed into play, work, dreams, sex, and so forth (to date, a reductionistic hypothesis void of empirical evidence).

The fifty years between Helmholtz's principle of the conservation of energy and Albert Einstein's theory of relativity has been termed the "golden age of energy." Most of the labor-saving devices that make our lives so much easier today flowed from the vast abundance of nineteenth-century physics. We are still reaping the benefits of this golden age of energy, as the latest exploits of the lunar space program bears witness.

But the age of energy and dynamics did more than provide us with appliances, go-carts, color televisions, automobiles, jet planes, and the hydrogen bomb. It has   ed us to formulate a new conception of man. Darwin conceived of man as an animal. Fechner proved that the mind of man did not stand outside of scientific inquiry but that it could be brought into the laboratory and accurately measured. The new physics, however, made possible an even more radical deductive view of man — that man is an energy system and that he obeys the same physical laws that regulate the steam engine, the combustion engine, and the movement of ions. Thus, Freud's greatest achievement, and one of the greatest achievements in modern scientific inquiry, was the discovery of a dynamic psychology based on the premise that within man's personality there takes place the transformation and exchange of energy.

PSYCHOANALYTIC THEORY

As has been indicated above, the psychoanalytic theory of man is a scientific explanation developed by Sigmund Freud and revised and extended by post-Freudians, notably Erik Erikson. Central to the psychoanalytic theory are a number of major concepts.

Unconscious Wishes

Memories, wishes, needs, or other mental elaborations are omitted from conscious awareness when they become questionable, objectionable, or painful to the conscious self.

Freud observed that these inner wishes are not completely omitted from one's behavioral repertoire, but are manifested in some other form or disguise. An oft-cited example is that of the parent of an outstanding child athlete, actor, musician, or criminal, who subconsciously may be gratifying his or her own needs for recognition, power, success, or revenge. Similarly, the woman who, in the course of her work, becomes angry at her boss and would like to tell him off but realizes the consequences of such aggressive behavior. This angry woman would unconsciously take out her aggressive and hostile wishes on her dog, husband, or children; on subway passengers; or her paddle ball opponent at the gym. More recently, it has become obvious that those who take on the do-gooder role in order to protect the morality of society by reviewing obscene books and pornographic movies for censorship may be hiding from themselves their tremendous need for such erotic material while at the same time receiving a strong exposure to it in an acceptable way.

Theory Based on Instincts and Drives

The psychoanalytic theory is based on two major instincts or drives: sex and aggression. Unfortunately for the study of play, the psychoanalytic theory of aggression is not well elaborated and is usually restricted to children's play therapy. The literature on the sexual libidinal drives is extensive and dates back to Freud's earliest works. Based upon Freud's clinical observations of himself and others, he discovered, contrary to professional views, that sexuality does not begin in adolescence but that sexual drives are evident during the initial years of life (zero to five years of age). Freud, unlike popular interpretation, did not restrict the term "sexuality" to adult sexual intercourse but applied it to a wide spectrum of interpersonal and intrapersonal behavior (same-sex friendships, parent–child relationships, and pleasant bodily sensations originating from three major erotogenetic zones — mouth, anus, and genital organs). Immediately after birth the newborn infant demonstrates interest in its bodily organs and derives sensual or sexual gratification from playing with these newly discovered toys. Early childhood sexual gratifications differ from adulthood sexual gratifications in that the child's sexual behavior is independent of the need to love another person. Hence they are autoerotic. A salient symptom of regression to an early stage of play is the adult's reliance upon primitive forms of autoerotic sexual gratification.

Psychosexual Conflict Resolution Phases

Freud conceived of man as biologically unfolding through three major phases. It is through the resolution of these sexual drives in the real world that the individual matures into a healthy, functioning organism. If the experiences during any of these phases is too disruptive, the individual may become fixated at one of the levels and subsequently most of his or her personality would reflect this fixation syndrome.

The first phase to be worked through for sexual conflict is the oral area of the body. The infant soon learns to use its mouth not only for intake of food but also for sensuous stimulation. Thus the infant uses its mouth for breast-feeding as well as for thumb sucking. Fixation at this phase may occur as a result of difficulties related to feeding and oral stimulation. Freud and his contemporary psychoanalysts have documented case studies of adults who, as a result of fixation at this sexual stage, have developed pathological sexual patterns, eating patterns, drinking patterns, and leisure life-styles. Some of the clinical literature suggests that fixation at this level becomes associated with a narcissistic personality profile, that is, a chronic need to satisfy their own needs without consideration of their impact on others and the environment. The orally fixated person appears to have an insatiable need for love and affection but is incapable of returning it.

Sometime around the second year of life, the anal phase emerges, and the anal area becomes the critical erotogenetic zone. The first anal accomplishments are purely autoerotic but shortly become environment- and person-directed as the infant begins to learn the antecedent–consequent relationships of its anal powers. The withholding of feces, as well as the planned and timely discharge of them, gives the child a lever for manipulation as well as sexual gratification. Problems around this sexual stage arise from too strict or too lenient toilet-training procedures. Adult characteristics such as messiness, disorderliness, irresponsibility, as well as the extremes of being excessively neat, clean, frugal, fastidious, and a preoccupation with objectivity (money, time, space, etc.) have all been attributed to an anal fixation.

The final psychosexual stage of development is the phallic phase. Here, for the first time, Freud made a distinction between boys and girls. In boys, the penis becomes the dominant zone for erotic pleasure. For girls, Freud contended that the clitoris is the erotic zone. During this stage the boy tries to resolve his sexual conflicts revolving around his mother and father. This conflict is referred to as the Oedipus complex. Conflict resolution takes place when the boy realizes that he cannot possess his mother, and he begins to identify with his father. This identification is manifested through the child's wish to be grown up and active like his father and to someday love someone like his mother.

Freud was not as logical in his explanation of the Oedipal struggle (sometimes called the Electra complex) for girls. His emphasis on the girl's penis envy has been severely criticized as being a male chauvinistic theory. However, despite this criticism, some still support the theory that the girl resolves her Oedipal conflict when she realizes that she cannot possess her father and finds it appropriate to identify with her mother. Like boys, most young girls initially make efforts to model themselves after their mothers or other appropriate female surrogates. The basis of all forms of neuroses is viewed by psychoanalysts as being the failure to resolve the Oedipal struggle.

Structure of Personality

In addition to the phases of conflict resolution, Freud also described man in terms of three levels of interaction. These levels of personality interaction were termed the id, ego, and superego. It is these three dynamic components that have played such a major role in the explanation of all human phenomena. They have not only influenced all the social sciences and humanities but they have also become household communication symbols for the modern world.

The first dynamic system is the id, the genesis of all the instincts with which man is born. The id is the most primitive and uncultured of all the systems. It is demanding, spoiled, and requires immediate gratification. When the world of reality gets in its way it turns to vicarious and very primitive ways of satisfying its urges. When direct sexual gratification is not possible during the waking hours, the id satisfies its sexual needs through primary process dreams, hallucinations, and even unconscious activities such as painting, writing poetry, or climbing a mountain. The id always operates on the pleasure principle — maximum pleasure and minimum pain. At no time does the id ever stop to examine the consequences of its behavior. Some habitual criminals, sexual offenders, and psychopaths have been described as being under the control of their id; however, most individuals have learned to control or sublimate their primitive instincts of sex and aggression.

In order to bring the individual in touch with reality, the personality develops a coordinating or executive branch called the ego. In the optimally functioning person the ego is responsible for negotiating between the id and the real world as well as with the person's conscience (superego). The ego acts as a judge, determining what is best for the overall situation. Being too strict with the id or superego may be as deleterious as being too lenient. Hence, the ego has the delicate and critical job of maintaining an equitable balance between a person's needs and the real world. The ego maintains this balance by continually testing out different solutions and strategies in the real world, and in this way appeases the id, ego, and superego (guilt).

The ego, in order to maintain the sanity of the individual, that is, not to permit the individual to become guilt-ridden, and in order to satisfy the most basic needs of man within the confines of the real world, has developed a set of defensive strategies, or defense mechanisms. Every time that the ego fears the psychosocial or physical consequences of an unchecked instinct (id), it sets in motion these defense mechanisms. When used appropriately and in moderation, these defense mechanisms provide for a healthy satisfaction of instincts and a badly needed emotional outlet. Peller (1952), in a classic paper, discusses how children use these models (defense mechanisms) in play to resolve some traumatic events in real life. These defense mechanisms permit the individual to achieve one of the prime goals of the psychoanalytic model of man — to change one's stance from a passive to an active role. As Peller pointed out, instead of assuming the position of the person being threatened, hurt, or laughed at, the individual becomes the person making the threat, inflicting the pain, and doing the laughing.

The third personality system, in addition to the id and the ego, is the superego. The superego becomes the repository and data bank of all primary (parents, siblings, relatives, etc.) and secondary (school, church, army, etc.) socialization agents. The superego internalizes all of the mores, norms, standards, and philosophies of these socializing agents. The superego is our moral and idealistic, rather than our realistic system. Most mentally healthy people have some form of conscious guilt about a variety of events — smoking, crossing a red light, stealing, cheating, not working hard enough, sexual promiscuity, and the like. However, this guilt can be controlled through the use of the defense mechanisms. Individuals who are subjected to severe socialization models often develop a harsh and perfectionistic superego. This kind of superego finds it difficult to bestow praise upon the person and is continually driving the person to unrealistic goals. The result is an individual with low self-esteem, a severe conscience, and an inability to enjoy the pleasures of life. It is this system that contributes more to a playful and leisurely attitude toward life than any of the other systems.

EXTENSIONS OF THE PSYCHOANALYTIC THEORY

Many neo-Freudians have recognized the limitations of the original psychoanalytic theory and have attempted to modify it. The major extension of concern to the study of play is the work of Erik Erikson, the American psychoanalyst, educator and artist from Harvard University (department of human development and psychiatry). Through the publication of such works as *Childhood and Society* (1950) and *Identity, Youth and Crisis* (1968), Erikson has extended the classical psychoanalytic theory to include several significant aspects. Whereas Freud, like his peers, emphasized the biological and instinctual determinants of behavior, Erikson emphasized the interactive role of the human social environment with the biological makeup of the individual. Erikson's theories, unlike Freud's, span the whole life cycle. He thus shows how human beings continue to grow and develop beyond the resolution of the Oedipus complex.

Theoretical Definition:
Play provides the opportunity to fulfill two major needs of man: (1) the need to be grown up and (2) the need to assume an active role.

Theoretical Concepts

Need to Be Grown Up
Freud's early statements concerning the powerful need to grow up were clearly enunciated in *Beyond the Pleasure Principle* (1948). This wish, said Freud, may be seen to have two component parts that are somewhat related: first, the internal biological maturational pressures that push the individual to grow up, and second, the wish to be grown up as it is experienced sociologically and psychologically through the observation and imitation of parents and others by the child. Between the biological push and the psychosocial pull, the child deals

with these two forces in play behavior. Gilmore (1966) and, more recently, Alderman (1974) both discuss the wish to be grown up as a primordial drive behind the child's play behavior.

> There are the wishes a child has to be big, grownup, or in the shoes of someone more fortunate. Thus, in accordance with an inherited tendency to seek immediate pleasure, even if this pleasure must be in part hallucinated, the child phantasises some situations he would like to see exist.
>
> (Gilmore, 1966, p. 351)

Alderman (1974) writes:

> Play, then, for the child is the seeking of pleasurable experiences and the avoiding of painful ones. Play is determined by the wishes of the individual, not by the hard facts of reality, even though objects and situations are borrowed from reality in order to create a play world which is familiar to the child. The child distinguishes play from reality by creating a world of his own, in which he can order and alter events in such a way as to derive only pleasure. The child wishes to be grownup and do what adults do. In play he can structure his activity so as to accomplish this. The little girl who is bossy to her dolls is wielding an authority denied her in real life, while the little boy who plays Little League baseball can achieve a status and recognition that would normally be years in the future for him.
>
> (Alderman, 1974, p. 34)

Play then becomes the child's own world where he or she can vicariously, symbolically, or realistically structure it so that the need to feel grown up is there.

Need to Assume an Active Role

Freud also conceived of play as providing an arena for the child to allay the anxiety precipitated by conflicts aroused in real-life interactions. This seeking of a "sense of mastery," which was "necessarily restricted to play . . . serves to reverse a previous painful experience" (Gilmore, 1966, p. 351). Thus Erikson (1968) writes, that play

> often proves to be the infantile way of thinking over difficult experiences and of restoring a sense of mastery, comparable to the way in which we repeat, in ruminations and in endless talk, in daydreams and in dreams during sleep, experiences which have been too much for us.
>
> (Erikson, 1968, p. 85)

Table 1 Summary of Symbolic Models of Children's Play Proposed by Peller (1952)

Symbolic Model	Role Play	Consequences of Role Playing
1. Role assigned to an inanimate object	Player assigns the status of a child or baby to inanimate object such as a doll, chair, broom, ball, etc. Some players "suddenly" acquire imaginary brothers, sisters, pets, angels, etc.	This role of having someone or something dependent on the player, gives the player status, control, and security. For the first time, the player is in control of someone else.
2. Choice based on fear	Player takes on the role of someone he or she has feared or has been told fearful things about. The child who assumes the role of the dentist or doctor after visiting their offices is playing this role.	This role mitigates any traumatic experiences associated with these roles and leaves the player better prepared to resume the passive role. Assuming an active role also permits the player to inflict upon another inanimate object or person (brother, sister, mother, friend, etc.) the same pain and discomfort that has been inflicted upon the child. Important role in helping children adjust to situations that cause some discomfort (school, hospital, barbershop, etc.)
3. Incognito indulgence	Player assumes roles and status that are inferior to present level of functioning. For example, the player may pretend to be an animal or a baby, with all the incumbent traits—crawling, thumb sucking, cuddling, etc. The player may explicitly confess that he or she is a puppy dog who is crawling around in the sandbox.	This role permits the player to assume a set of behaviors that is not acceptable to the player or to parents and friends. Thus, an older child who pretends to be a baby can crawl into the crib and insist on being rocked to sleep just like the baby in the family. This allows the player to satisfy various critical needs while at the same time being protected from any internal (ego and (conscience) and external (parents, friends, etc.) retributions.

4. Clowning

Player deliberately repeats a mishap (tripping, putting on clothes the wrong way, verbal slips, etc.) in an exaggerated form and draws everyone's attention to it. Player pretends that the mishap purposely occurred.

Player switches an embarrasing situation from the passive to the active. Primary result is avoidance of being controlled by an event. Secondary result is the attention derived from the behavior.

Peller (1952), in an article entitled "Models of Children's Play," identified ten symbolic models that a child might utilize in play to assume an active role and overcome emotional conflicts. Table I summarizes some of the critical symbolic models of play and the consequences of their enactment. It should be pointed out that all these models may be experienced either directly or vicariously. These models reflect the emotional values of permitting and encouraging children to engage in symbolic play.

Waelder (1933) summarized the traditional psychoanalytic theory of play in the following terms:

> The psychoanalytic contributions of the problem of play may be indicated by the following phrases: instinct of mastery; wish fulfillment, assimilation of over-powering experiences according to the mechanism of the repetition compulsion; transformation from passivity to activity; leave of absence from reality and from superego; fantasies about real objects.
>
> (Waelder, 1933, p. 224)

As was discussed at the beginning of this chapter, the Freudian concept of man's need to assume an active role has been extended beyond the biological realms by a number of neo-Freudians. These ego psychologists view play as an opportunity for the development of the ego through its interaction and adaptation to the real world. This adaptation takes place throughout man's life cycle. Erikson discussed these human developments through two major paradigms that have not as yet been explored by play theorists or those concerned with planning for play. The first paradigm deals with the whole of man's life cycle.

Erikson conceived of a set of universal stages through which all human beings pass. Within each stage, man is vulnerable to conflicts, anxieties, and guilt that may arise from an interaction between the biological needs of the organism and the environmental contingencies. Furthermore, Erikson has strongly indicated that the experiences of one generation would be clearly imprinted on the next generation. The stages of life and the corresponding psychosocial crises for each of these stages are listed below:

Life Cycle	Psychosocial Crises		
1. Infancy	Basic trust	versus	Basic mistrust
2. Early childhood	Autonomy	versus	Shame, doubt
3. Play age	Initiative	versus	Guilt
4. School age	Industry	versus	Inferiority
5. Adolescence	Identity	versus	Confusion
6. Young adulthood	Intimacy	versus	Isolation
7. Adulthood	Generativity	versus	Stagnation
8. Old age	Integrity	versus	Despair

With specific reference to planning for children's play in an urban environment, Erikson (1973) cautions against reinforcing "inhibitory guilt in the child," as a result of the child's need to assume an active role in a constricting physical environment. Erikson writes:

> If the infant's relation to his maternal caretakers must establish a certain ratio of trust over mistrust, then a mother's mistrust of her own environment and her disgust with her own placement within the spatial scheme, obviously will curtail her capacity to convey trust. Where this is the rule in a whole neighborhood or type of city, not only individuals but also communities will suffer some lasting consequences. Correspondingly, if, in the "initiative versus guilt" stage, a child is habitually made to feel that he is a bad child because he uses space in a playful and exploratory way and ignores warnings he has not understood, this represents a particular environmental reinforcement of the way in which parents establish inhibitory guilt in the child, instead of making the world—as far as they can—both safe and explainable. Thus, with each stage, some aspect of the architectural environment is "built into" the next generation; becomes part of its tensions and conflicts, and contributes to the disturbances to which individuals and groups are prone.
>
> (Erikson, 1973, p. 216)

Recognizing the limitations of the life cycle conflict model of man proposed by Erikson, his concern regarding the play deprivation of our contemporary communities must be given serious consideration in terms of planning for play. It may be shortly recognized that the popularity and advocacy of creative types of playgrounds in small urban spaces may be totally inadequate for dealing with the psychosocial crises arising during early childhood.

The second major interactive paradigm proposed by Erikson, which sheds light on the play of man, includes his distinct developmental stages of infantile maturity. There are three developmental stages proposed by Erikson: autocosmic, microcosmic, and macrocosmic. Each of these stages brings the child into contact with a greater radius of interpersonal contacts. The autocosmic stage is the first and most primitive phase of human development. In this stage the child is egocentric and has not yet learned to distinguish self from the rest of the world. All play at this stage is focused on the body and is more appropriately referred to as exploration and reflexive in nature.

The microcosmic stage is the second stage of infant development. At this stage the child begins to appreciate distinctions between self and the real world and begins to search for play models of the real world. The radius of the child's play has greatly increased, and now the child is ready to interact with miniature replicas of family members in an environment removed from surrogates.

The macrocosmic stage is the third stage of infant development. At this stage the child begins to share the real world with adults. The child has come to appreciate the consequences of his or her actions and has also learned to accommodate to the rules and demands of the social and environmental systems.

Each of these stages is described by Erikson as being endowed with crises and resolutions which, if resolved, form the basis for a creative, productive, and healthy life. Based upon this view that childhood involves one mastery after another, Erikson viewed play as fulfilling a major function in the development of man (ontogenesis) and the human race (phylogenesis).

Play Paradigm

The psychoanalytic theory of play is mainly concerned with the determinants and consequences of play behavior. The determinants of play are explained in terms of anxiety and various forms of conflict resolution. The homeostatic model of man proposed by Freud and his followers viewed the organism as constantly attempting to reduce the level of nervous tension generated by various biological–psychological–sociological interactions.

Play performs its greatest function when it facilitates the mastering of anxiety-provoking conflicts. It is only through conflict resolution that man progresses in his ontogenetic development. The growth and positive aspects of play result when man is able to utilize his libidinal energy for creative and human progress rather than for defense mechanisms and other conflict-resolution strategies.

Critique of the Psychoanalytic Theory of Play

Psychoanalytic Theories Lack Empirical Support

The universal psychosexual and psychosocial stages of Freud and Erikson both lack the empirical rigor of a strictly scientific delineation of stages, and their appeal to a host of social disciplines must be thought of as literary unless more precise evidence in support of them is forthcoming. Since the substantive support for the psychoanalytic theories of play is subsumed under the above models of man, their validity is also questionable (as are all explanations until duly tested).

Ellis (1973), in his criticism of the psychoanalytic theories of play behavior, condemns the authors of these theories for their "subjective" approach and lack of "scientific" data. Ellis states:

> Psychoanalytic aspects of play have not been treated extensively here. The reason is simply my inability to grasp any essential and rigorous thread to the arguments of the psychoanalysts. The orientation of this book to play is a behavioral one dealing with theo-

retical formulations and data bearing on them. In contrast to this thrust the essence of psychoanalysis seems subjective rather than scientific. Having revealed my biases, it seems that psychoanalytic theories have been ill-formulated and that there has been almost no attempt to establish ways of testing them.

The psychoanalytic writings and reports are essentially subjec-
tive interpretations of what the analyst thought the motives for play behavior of the patient might be.

(Ellis, 1973, p. 63)

Psychoanalytic Theories Were Derived from Work with Emotionally Disturbed Individuals

Smilansky (1968) expressed serious reservations about the populations that were initially studied by the psychoanalysts in order to formulate their conflict reduction models. Her research findings would seem to shed some serious doubt on the appropriateness of these theories in populations that do not suffer from any emotional dysfunctions.

STUDY SUGGESTIONS

Despite the scarcity of rigorous empirical research on the psychoanalytic theories of play, there exists a wealth of professional literature on the clinical application of the theories of play, as well as on the psychological dynamics behind leisure, recreation, and sports. Listed below are some suggested classical readings that will help students to expand their knowledge of the psychoanalytic theories of play.

Adatto, C. On play and the psychopathology of golf. *Journal of the American Psychoanalytic Association*, October 1964, *12*, 826-841.
Axline, V. M. *Dibs in search of self*. Boston: Houghton Mifflin, 1965.
Axline, V. M. *Play therapy*. New York: Ballantine Books, 1969.
Beisser, A. R. Psychodynamic observations of a sport. *Psychoanalysis and Psychological Review*, 1961, *48* (1), 69-76.
Fine, R. *The psychology of the chess player*. New York: Dover, 1967.
Greenacre, P. Play in relation to creative imagination. *Psychoanalytic Study of the Child*, 1959, *14*, 61-80.
Haun, P. Pathological play. *Bulletin of the North Carolina Recreation Commission*, 1961, *30*, 22-29.
Haun, P. *Recreation: A medical viewpoint*. New York: Columbia University Press, 1965.
Herron, R. E., and Sutton-Smith, B. *Child's play*. New York: John Wiley and Sons, 1971, chapters 9-11.

Levin, H., and Wardwell, E. The research uses of doll play. *Psychological Bulletin,* 1962, *59* (1), 27-56.

Martin, A. R. The fear of relaxation and leisure. *American Journal of Psychoanalysis,* 1951, *11,* 42-50.

Martin, P. A. *Leisure and mental health: A psychiatric viewpoint.* New York: American Psychiatric Association, 1967.

7
Developmental Theories of Play Behavior

Following the classical biological models of play behavior and the Freudian character and personality conflict resolution models, we are ready to discuss the developmental theories of play. Perhaps the first exponent of a human developmental process was the British playwright Shakespeare. Shakespeare's stages, although not age-specific, were certainly indicative of his era. They were:

1. Infant
2. Schoolboy
3. Lover (or adolescent)
4. Soldier (or young adult)
5. Justice (or middle-aged man)
6. Old age, and
7. Second childhood (or senility)

Since the days of Shakespeare, we have made some progress in developing more inclusive human developmental models. The preceding chapter discussed the conflict resolution models of Freud and the neo-Freudians. In this chapter, we examine the most heuristic and grand developmental system proposed to date. We are referring to Piaget's (1952, 1962) cognitive developmental model.

PIAGET'S DEVELOPMENTAL THEORY OF PLAY

Dr. Jean Piaget, the world-renowned Swiss child psychologist who altered the educational world's schemas on human intelligence, writes that cognitive development is a product of the interactions between heredity and the environment and that it is not possible to draw a sharp demarcation between biologically inborn and socioculturally learned patterns of behavior. To Piaget the growth of intelligence is accomplished through interaction with the environment vis-à-vis two complementary processes: *assimilation* and *accommodation*. Furthermore, as the individual vascillates between these two poles of behavior, he or she is also progressing through four major bio-social-cognitive stages of development: sensorimotor, preoperational, concrete operational, and formal operational.

Theoretical Definition:
Play is the act of bending reality ("taking in") to fit one's existing level of cognitive functioning.

Theoretical Concepts

Accommodation–Assimilation

Accommodation involves the process whereby the organism is trying to alter and update its own memory bank so that it can negotiate the novel demands of the situation. For example, the infant accommodates the rudimentary inherited grasping reflex to the shape of the novel object to be grasped by curving the fingers in one way for a round, soft object (e.g., mother's breast) and in a different way for a plastic pull toy. This looking and grasping is initially a crude trial-and-error process; that is, the child is continually modifying and altering behavior in order to fit the specifications of the environment. Piaget postulated a tendency in all healthy living organisms to make repeated efforts to interact with slightly novel stimuli; this constant interaction creates greater awareness, greater expectations, and new distinctions regarding the environment as a whole. The infant gradually learns to act by "habit" and to act less and less by trial and error. Thus, accommodation is concerned with mastery of the environment through self-modifying aspects of behavior that bends the self to fit reality.

Assimilation is the cognitive act of imposing upon reality certain limitations and modifications, which would make accommodation possible within the individual's unique functioning level. During assimilation, the individual bends the external environment to fit its currently existing cognitive level. It is during the assimilation process that the individual has the greatest flexibility in terms of dealing with social, emotional, and motoric difficulties. Despite the obvious subordinate role[1] of assimilation in the learning process, Flavell (1963) cites Piaget, who points out that the organism vascillates between accommodation and assimilation as a unitary interrelated action.

> From the beginning assimilation and accommodation are indissociable from each other. Accommodations of mental structures

[1] This subordinate assignment has caused Sutton-Smith (1966) to criticize Piaget for his discussions which have assigned accommodation the major role in cognitive development.

to reality implies the existence of assimilatory schemata apart from which any structure would be impossible. Inversely, the formation of schemata through assimilation entails the utilization of external realities to which the former must accommodate, however crudely.
. . .

Assimilation can never be pure because by incorporating new elements into its earlier schemata the intelligence constantly modified the latter in order to adjust them to new elements. Conversely, things are never known by themselves, since this work of accommodation is only possible as a function of the inverse process of assimilation.

(Flavell, 1963, p. 49)

The crucial factors for cognitive development are the qualitative and quantitive nature of the assimilation–accommodation interactions with the environment. As the complexity of these reciprocal interaction experiences increases, so does the cognitive capacity (schematas) of the organism. Flavell points out that individuals are not always ready to assimilate or accommodate all the internal and external stimuli bombarding them at any one time. This concept has obvious implications for "play readiness" as well as "cognitive readiness."

In summary, the functional characteristics of the assimilatory and accommodatory mechanisms are such that the possibility of cognitive change is insured, but the magnitude of any given change is always limited. The organism adapts repeatedly, and each adaptation necessarily paves the way for its successor. Structures are not infinitely modifiable however, and not everything which is potentially assimilable can in fact be assimilated by an organism at point X in his development. On the contrary, the subject can incorporate only those components of reality which its ongoing structure can assimilate without drastic change.

(Flavell, 1963, p. 50)

Following the accommodation–assimilation paradigm, one can see why Piaget stated that the newborn infant shows no play and that play reaches its apex during childhood and drops off toward adulthood. In short, play drops off as children mature because they gradually acquire a sophisticated repertoire for responding to unfamiliar environments without resorting to assimilation (play). Following this paradigm to its theoretical limits, one could speculate that with complete mastery of the environment, adults have a greatly reduced need to rely upon altering reality to fit their sophisticated intellectual schemas. However, there is a strong body of evidence that seems to be indicating that man will not allow himself to reach a point of intellectual saturation, that is, he is continually

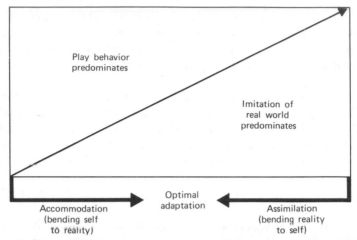

Figure 6 Piaget's Assimilation-Adaptation-Accommodation Model of Play

looking to bend reality in order to experience and expand his perception of himself and his environment. Thus, through progressive assimilations and accommodations, optimal adaptation proceeds, and adaptation is achieved at a higher level of functioning. Adaptation is not a static state but a dynamic continuous process resulting from interaction of the individual in response to novel internal and external stimuli. It is thus not surprising to see children using "traditional" play equipment in novel and inappropriate ways in order to create an assimilation-accommodation interaction at a higher adaptation (optimal) level. Too often, parents and educators misinterpret the search for optimal levels of adaptation as asocial and destructive behavior (e.g., setting fires, turning slides upside down, climbing high fences, etc.).

Play, in Piaget's terms, takes on a critical assimilatory function. It is only through assimilation that the developing child can proceed to accommodation of novel situations. Flavell (1963) summarizes the meaning of play for Piaget:

> In play the primary object is to mold reality to the whim of the cognizer, in other words, to assimilate reality to various schemas with little concern for precise accommodation to that reality. Thus, as Piaget put it, in play there is "primacy of assimilation over accommodation."
>
> (Flavell, 1963, p. 65)

Schematically presented in Figure 6 is the interactive relationship between assimilation, adaptation, and accommodation.

Ontogenetic Stages of Cognitive Development

According to Piaget, a child passes through four major age-related, but not age-determined stages. Summarized in Table 2 are Piaget's stages of cognitive development and their implications for play behavior.

Table 2   Piaget's Stages of Cognitive Development and Their Implications for Play Behavior

Piaget's Stages of Cognitive Development	Implications for the Study of Play Behavior
1. Sensorimotor Stage (0–2 years)	1. Sensorimotor Play (0–2 years)

The utilization of rudimentary inherited reflexes and sensorimotor systems (e.g., sucking, grasping, Moro, Babinski, etc.). This stage is characterized by sensorimotor exploration, development of motor control, development of speech, and the beginning of mental experimentation and problem solving. It is at this stage that the child begins to look for varied ways of doing things and solving problems. Normal infants first develop control of their eyes, then of their head, and gradually, of their arms, trunk, and legs. At about 6 weeks of age, infants begin to notice things and follow them with their eyes. By the age of 3 or 4 months, they can begin to grasp an object such as a rattle, and soon after they can begin both to reach for an object and to grasp it. At about 6 to 8 months, they will grasp and hold objects such as a ball, plastic blocks, and boxes. At 10 to 12 months, they learn to walk. This orderly sequence of sensorimotor development takes place as a result of normal maturation and environmental support. It is essential for later development that the infant has opportunities to practice (accommodation) and experiment (assimilation) with each newly acquired skill.

Summary: The sensorimotor stage is

Playthings that provide opportunities for seeing, feeling, and hearing; toys and environments that provide opportunities for reaching, grasping, pushing, and pulling

Suggested toys for *Hearing:* bells, radio, record player, sound rugs, rubber bumps, voice toys, music boxes

Feeling: rubber beads, plastic teether, touch toys, furry animals, sucking–biting doll (oral toys)

Crawling: opportunities to hide, peek-a-boo houses, push and pull toys, seeking and hiding

Coordination: rocking horse, merry-go-round, stacking toys, blocks, pegs, balancing beam

Shape–Size: blocks, jigsaw puzzles, shape sorting

Discrimination: toys, nesting toys

Problem solving: take-apart toys; matching, sequencing, and re-creating of sizes, shapes, and weights.

Socialization: pat-a-cake, teddy bear, solitary and parallel play, people for egotistical play.

generally characterized by pure assimilation of environment to self; the child understands the environment only in terms of the basic needs for survival. Until about age two, the child makes no distinction between fact (reality) and fiction (imagined). Following Freud's "pleasure principle," the child reshapes and perceives the world to fit his or her needs.

2. Preoperational Stage (2–7 years)	2. Preoperational Play (2–7 years)		

Language and symbolic thought have their beginnings. Children can internalize and represent in thought process that which was first developed in the sensorimotor stage. During the early part of this stage (18 mo. – 4 yr.), language is developing at a fantastically rapid pace. Thought and language are becoming interrelated; from thinking only in images, they move to thinking in words. They can express their ideas in words and can understand the communication of others. Three major features of thinking: (1) They are perceptually oriented, i.e., they make judgments in terms of how things look to them. For example, the child at this level is likely to think that the number of objects in a set changes if the objects are bunched together rather than spread out. (2) They center on one variable only, usually one that stands out visually. They lack the ability to coordinate variables. For example, if one of two identical balls of clay is elongated while the child looks on, the child will think that the elongated shape now has more "stuff" in it and weighs more. This centering is confounded by the child's inability to carry on a mental operation called reversibility—reversing a process mentally to compare what is now with what was. (3) The child has difficulty in

Gross Motor and Fine Motor Play	Creative Play	Imitative Play
Tricycle	Sand toys	Dress-up
Climbing equip.	Tinker toys	Doll-house play
Push-pull toys	Hammer and nail sets	Dramatic play
Climbing ropes	Clay	Toy animals
Graduated size boxes	Finger paints	House-keeping toys
Jungle gym	Pegs	Let's pretend we're. . .
Walking boards	Collage material	
Skipping ropes	Paste	

realizing that an object or person can possess more than one property and thus belong to several classes at the same time. A baseball player can belong to the class of baseball players; the class of men; to the class of fathers; to the class of neighbors; and so on. One can live in Toronto and in Canada at the same time. This property of a class is referred to as multiple classification.

Summary: This preoperational second stage is the first time in which Piaget admits to play. Two separate but equal realities appear to the child— play and the perceived real world. For the child, unlike adults, the world of play and reality are juxtaposed rather than arranged in a hierarchy as with adults, i.e., the child move (vascillate) from play to reality with no recognition of the fact that they are different worlds.

Social Play	Cognitive Play
Sandbox (cereal)	Jigsaw puzzles
Records	Number games
Sesame Street	Letter games
Child-sized cooking utensils	Correspondence games
Child-sized dressing	
Play groups	Running a store
Cooperative play	Science kit

3. Operational Stage (7–12 years)	3. Operational Play (7–12 years)

Beginning of the child's desire for a system of thought, rules, prediction and noncontradiction. Children begin the mental operations of classifications. They know that if all the birds in the world died, there would be no ducks left, but that if all the ducks died, there would still be some birds. They now learn that the same goal can be reached by different paths, e.g., $3 + (4 + 2) = 9$, or $(3 + 4) + 2 = 9$. At this stage, they still need concrete data to make decisions; they are not able to think abstractly or hypothetically about a problem.

Summary: The operational stage marks the beginning of the child's wish for a system of thought and for noncontradiction. Only after age 7, according to Piaget can the child be-

Games and play with rules and order appear. Play and games that manipulate numbers, weight, volumes, and temporal and spatial orders—toy scales, magnet sets, collection books, stamps, albums, etc. Fine motor skills grow rapidly—beanbag, ring toss, croquet sets, marbles, ball and jack sets, tool chest, skates, bicycle, etc. Group play takes on more social and emotional bonds — organized sports, clubs, parties, card games, etc. Egocentricism is sacrificed for group goals and cohesion. Moral development seen in play when there is a search for consistent rules and officiating. Child's moral conscience will be greatly effected by the degree of moral consistency between play and the real world, i.e., cheating on the ice becomes generalized to

gin an observation of the external environment and become aware of the implications of reasoning based upon these inductive observations. Logical reasoning ("if . . . then") is possible, but formal reasoning ("let us say that . . . ") is not.

cheating at home, community, and school. Gradual integration of the child into the immediate real environment. Less and less utilization of make-believe play.

4. Formal Operations Stage (12 years and on)	4. Formal Operations Play (12 years and on)

The crowning achievement of man's intelligence is the ability to engage in abstract thinking. Adolescents begin to reason in terms of propositions, and they can make logical combinations of these propositions. They can compare by conjunction, as when one says, "Both eating and sleeping make a difference on my running." They can combine by disjunction, as when one says, "It's got to be my shoes or shorts that. . . ." They can combine by implication, "If its my shoes, then I can't run. . . ." Or they can combine by incompatibility, "When my shoes hurt, then that doesn't happen. . . ." Their thinking is in terms of possible combinations and not with objects or events necessarily.

Summary: The fourth stage is characterized by the introduction of formal thought and logical assumptions. Necessity and possibility are now tools used for reasoning, for formal reasoning connects assumptions, propositions, hypotheses, i.e., relationships in which one does not necessarily believe, but which one admits in order to see where the consequences lead.

Problem-solving games, stories, movies, plays, cartoons, etc. The "what" and "why" of events is important. Arts and crafts become more exact, realistic, and detailed. Attempts to win social approval for peers overshadow parental approval. Teamwork, group cohesion, and skill in sports become increasingly important. Most appropriate type for assigning responsibility and accountability through play. Adventure playgrounds, youth farms, camping, and other self-initiated and "effectance" activities should be promoted. Sense of community responsibility and conscience can be developed through voluntary projects involving the disabled, aged, socially disenfranchised, and younger ages — brotherhood through play.

Recently, the original play categories developed by Piaget (1962) have been modified by Smilansky into four stages of play: (1) functional play (sensorimotor); (2) constructive play (manipulation of environment and objects to create something); (3) dramatic play (let's pretend); and (4) play with rules of conduct and procedure. Using these play categories elaborated by Smilansky

(1968), Rubin and Maioni (1975) provided empirical evidence for the ontogenetic developmental theory of play proposed by Piaget (1962). These researchers reported that the least mature form of play (sensorimotor) was negatively correlated to more advanced cognitive and social skills. However, as Piaget's theory would predict, the more mature forms of play (let's pretend) were positively correlated with advanced cognitive and social skills.

Play Paradigm

Piaget's developmental theory has ramifications for every dimension of the play paradigm. His stages of development clearly indicate the need to consider the ontogenetic functioning level of the child and the quality of the physical and sociocultural environment in which the child was reared.

The assimilation–accommodation process, which leads to a higher level of human functioning, is clearly reflective of the characteristics of play–suspension of reality, intrinsic motivation, and internal locus of control. To be in a state of extreme assimilation is play behavior par excellence. And to be in a state of extreme accommodation is extrinsic motivation, reality, and external locus of control. Assimilation, like play, is the transformation of reality to self, whereas accommodation, like nonplay, is the transformation of self to reality.

Piaget's theories also strongly relate to the effects and consequences of play behavior. There are two germane by-products of play behavior according to the Piagetian formulation. The first is pleasure, joy, euphoria, satisfaction, efficacy, or some closely related affective existential state. This deep satisfaction is clearest in the young child who will spend hours playing with blocks or a pull toy while showing the most obvious signs of deep satisfaction. For Piaget, like Groos (1901), play interactions bring with them a feeling of "Funktionlust," that is, "the functional pleasure of use." As the child gets older, play takes on a more utilitarian function that becomes strongly determined by the environment. However, despite this concern for reality, pleasure is still apparent throughout the various stages of play.

The second critical consequence attributed to play by Piaget is the adaptive role. Through play the child is given the opportunity to test out new social, physical, cognitive, and emotional patterns that cannot be accommodated in the real world. Thus, through play the child undergoes a buffered form of learning. Play provides the opportunity to be wrong, sad, confused, uncoordinated, and aggressive. Once the patterns have been tested out through play, they become incorporated in the memory bank. Hence, from a cognitive perspective, play permits the development of intelligence. From an emotional perspective, play provides for the release of emotional stress and the assuaging of interpersonal and intrapersonal conflicts, and from a physical perspective, it permits the testing out of new physical roles, situations, and the like. Play also assures the child of the opportunity to practice and expand on existing behavioral repertoires so that they will not be lost as a result of disuse.

Critique of Piaget's Theory of Play

To date, the most definitive criticisms of Piaget's developmental theory of play behavior have come from three major works: Sutton-Smith (1966), Smilansky (1968), and Eifermann (1971).

Assimilation Secondary to Accommodation

Sutton-Smith (1966) has expressed strong objection to Piaget's conceptualization of assimilation as not being as critical in intellectual development as accommodation. Sutton-Smith voiced his criticism of Piaget in the following terms:

> As "reproductive assimilation," or "assimilation of reality to the ego," play can merely repeat; it can never originate." We thus have a situation in which the symbols of play are merely the reproductions of images preestablished through the copyist activity of imitation following accommodation. On this interpretation then, imitation is an essential factor in the constitution of representative activity, whereas play is not. It has no essential role in the structure of intellect as conceived by Piaget. Intelligence cannot proceed without imitation. It can proceed without play.
>
> (Sutton-Smith, 1966, p. 107)

It would thus appear that play (assimilation) according to Piaget, is merely a buffer for the development of intelligence through imitation.

Developmental Play Stages

A second major criticism levied by Sutton-Smith (1966) deals with the progression of play behavior from sensorimotor to symbolic to games with rules. Sutton-Smith rejects Piaget's (1951) unilinear developmental statements of play, which state that

> progress in socialization instead of leading to an increase symbolism transforms it more or less rapidly into an objective imitation of reality. . . .
>
> (Piaget, 1951, p. 139)

> Rule games . . . mark the decline of children's games and the transition to adult play, which ceases to be a vital function of the mind when the individual is socialized.
>
> (Piaget, 1951, p. 168)

Sutton-Smith (1966) reacts very strongly to this invariant veiw of the ontogenesis of play behavior by writing:

> On the basis of the evidence about play several objections can be raised to the view that the symbolic games of childhood are

simply replaced by more realism with age, and that play which is "vital" in childhood ceases to be vital in adulthood. In general it can be maintained with equal cogency that, rather than a decrease in the symbolic play function with age, what we actually find is a shift in the applications and the differentiation of this function. First, the early rule games of children continue to be heavily loaded with symbolic elements which play a part in determining outcomes equal in importance to skill. In the host of singing games of young girls, for example, it is the one who is arbitrarily chosen as Punchinello or as Farmer-in-the-Dell who determines the outcome. Similarly, in the great group of central-person games of early childhood which model the family drama, it is the player chosen by the arbitrary counting-out processes or the player with the role vestments of Caesar or Red Rover who decides by fiat when the game will start, when the players will run, etc. . . . Here the play symbolism has been collectivized, but it has hardly been decreased, or given way to greater realism. . . . .

There is, after all, little that is precisely rational about a game of football or a game of basketball. In fact, there is support for the point of view that such sports are best conceived as modern ritualized dramas of success and failure . . . and as such have little that is either rational or real about them. . . .

Though preschool egocentric symbolic play may decrease with age, play nevertheless finds expression in the midst of a variety of other cultural and social forms. It is thus not displaced by realism or by greater rationality, nor does it cease to be a vital function with age. Instead it becomes more differentiated and more representative in its contents of the other forms of human development. Without such a point of view it is difficult to understand the verbal play of adults, their social and sexual play, their rituals and their carnivals, their festivals and fairs, and their widespread and diversified playfulness.

(Sutton-Smith, 1966, p. 108–109)

In summary, it may be said that Sutton-Smith (1966) does not support Piaget's (1951) view that children's play gives way to intelligent, rational behavior but that, instead, the early infantile play becomes transformed and differentiated into more sophisticated and varied symbolic play (e.g., drama, costume parties, Mardi Gras, uniformed athletes, etc.).

The next major work that offers valid criticism of Piaget's hypotheses regarding the developmental aspects of play behavior, is Smilansky's (1968) extensive research with culturally deprived and culturally enriched Israeli children. Smilansky's major contribution for purposes of our discussion is that:

> culturally deprived children from five to six years in the kindergarten groups under our observation readily engaged themselves in a large number of competitive games and games-with-rules without ever having engaged in sociodramatic play. It seems feasible, therefore, that the developmental stage of sociodramatic play is not a prerequisite for the later stages of competitive games and games-with-rules. Children who do pass through the earlier stage are, perhaps, better players and are able to engage in more complicated forms of competitive games and games-with-rules.
>
> (Smilansky, 1968, p. 58)

Smilansky's research with culturally deprived children would seem to provide strong evidence that Piaget's invariant sequential developmental stages of play may not be a universal phenomena. Thus, it would appear that environmental factors (e.g., culture, child-rearing practices, etc.) have a great influence on the quality and sequencing of the developmental stages of play. Smilansky (1968) makes her case very well when she discusses the failure of culturally deprived children to engage in symbolic play despite their adequate language development, a prerequisite for symbolic play according to Piaget (1951).

> Piaget links symbolic play with general intellectual growth. He states that real symbolic play develops rapidly when the child learns language, and is characteristic of the period between two and four years.
>
> Our observations indicate that culturally deprived children aged from three to seven years, in spite of their development in the language-learning process, do not develop the ability to engage in symbolic play. We are aware that culturally deprived children are inferior verbally, but they have, at age five to seven, at least the verbal ability of other three-to-four-year-olds. It seems to us, therefore, that this ability does not necessarily develop automatically along with language development, in the way that Piaget states in his theory. Other factors in a child's development are apparently prerequisites for the development of his ability for symbolic play. . . .
>
> Our observations confirm this process of make-believe in regard to objects, and this ability to identify, in the play of A (culturally advantaged) children. Piaget, however, does not provide us with any adequate explanation for the lack of these phenomena in the play of the D (culturally disadvantaged) children.
>
> (Smilansky, 1968, p. 58)

Smilansky (1968) also interpreted the function of symbolism in children's play somewhat differently than Piaget (1951), and like Sutton-Smith (1966), she empirically discovered that symbolic play, rather than declining with age, takes on a more elaborate form. On these two matters, she writes-

> But our contention is that the symbolism in the child's play, before his integration in the real world of his surroundings at the age of seven to nine, does not serve to bend reality to egocentric needs and wishes, but rather to overcome the material limitations that prevent him from behaving as in real life. Make-believe is for him the means to the end of active participation in the world of reality. We did not observe in the play of (culturally advantaged) children any decline in symbolism at the age of six. We found rather that the technique of make-believe becomes more elaborate with age. It extends from make-believe objects and roles to pretended activities and imaginary situations. These components are present until the age at which the child stops playing altogether.
>
> (Smilansky, 1968, p. 59)

The last major critique of Piaget's developmental theories on play is provided by Eifermann (1971), whose extensive scientific investigations in Israel on children's play has become a modern research classic. Eifermann summarized her findings, which both confirmed and rejected some of the major tenets of Piaget's developmental theory of play behavior.

> Piaget's claim to the effect that games with rules increase in number both relatively and absolutely, with age, replacing the earlier "practice" and "symbolic" play, has to a considerable extent been disconfirmed by our findings. We have found that: (a) on the contrary, an absolute decline in participation in games with rules sets in at a certain age, around 11 on the average; (b) at a somewhat later age, a relative decline in participation in games with rules set in; this was confirmed by observations conducted at school as well as in streets and improvised playfields; and (c) the corresponding rise in participation in unstructured play is due, at least in part, to a return to some forms of practice play.
>
> On the other hand, we have verified, in accord with Piaget's general statements (though he is not concerned here with differences due to socioeconomic level), that symbolic play, in the one "high" school that was tested for this purpose, is already rare at the age of 6 to 8 — and remains steadily so throughout school — while in the corresponding "low" school, there was still some noticeable symbolic play in the two first grades, with a significant decline thereafter.
>
> Piaget's explicit assumption that all rule-governed games are competitive has been found lacking, both in theory and in ob-

> servation. There is a point in playing multiperson rule-governed but noncompetitive games, e.g., of the cooperative type, and there is a definite sense in which a single person can play a game with rules. Children have been observed to play such games.
>
> (Eifermann, 1971, pp. 292–296)

Based on the criticisms offered by Sutton-Smith (1966), Smilansky (1968), and Eifermann (1971), it may be stated with some degree of confidence that beyond the age of seven years, Piaget's developmental theory of play behavior contains to great a degree too much of unverifiable variability and error.

SUMMARY

Piaget represents the most comprehensive developmental play theorist of our times. He has been referred to as "Mr. Child Psychology" (Flavell, 1963, p. 250). His thoery of play behavior is logically elegant, has a great deal of heuristic power, and has generated prolific research. Many of the criticisms of Piaget's developmental theory of play are moot at this point, since very little scientific evidence is aviable for all the theories of play behavior.

Piaget has been criticized by research methodologists for his analysis of data, the lack of random sampling in his use of intensive behavioral observations of single subjects, and for the almost exclusive use of Swiss middle-class subjects. One ought to be reminded, however, that Piaget, like Hebb (1958), never assumed his epistemological theory to be final. Instead, like the children with whom he interacted, his theories on play are in a continuing, flowing, assumptive, and dynamic state of development. Thus, Piaget's theory of play behavior must be viewed as being provisional, to be used as long as it is useful and then discarded for a more appropriate theory or hypothesis. His theory should be looked upon as the best working assumption on the developmental perspective of play behavior available today.

STUDY SUGGESTIONS

1. Using the four ontogenetic stages of play originally proposed by Piaget (1962) and elaborated upon by Smilansky (1968), observe young children (zero to seven years) playing and describe the structure, conditions, processes, and consequences of the play episode. A brief example is provided for the functional play category.

Play Episode	Play Categories	Structure	Conditions	Processes	Consequences
Climbing a cargo net	Functional play (sensorimotor)	Climbing, pulling, holding, balance, flexibility visual cues, kinesthetic cues, etc.	Nursery school playground, crowded, windy, teacher supervised, 45° angle.	Taking turns, safe appropriate use of net	Muscular endurance, agility, rhythm, synchrony, social recognition, etc.
	Constructive play				
	Dramatic play				
	Play with rules				

8
Ecological Theories of Play Behavior: Behavior Settings

Thus far the major focus of the discussion on play has been to explain differences in play behavior based upon individual differences ("states"). The individual differences have traditionally been used to describe the psychosocial composition or life space of the individual. More recently there has been a recognition by social scientists that play behavior can only be described in terms of person X situation interactions—hence the need for the development of a suitable taxonomy of play ecological environments.

In order to study play environment–play behavior relations, the play environment and the play behavior must be described and measured independently; otherwise one becomes entangled in a tautological argumentive circle. The socioculturally shaped individual's play behavior cannot be used as the only reference point for explaining the various unique play environments. This is true, not because scientists find it impossible to observe all the human behavior that occurs, but because the infinite number of possible ecological environments comprise their own class of phenomenon and should only be described independently of the behavior that it may elicit.

The ecological theories of play deal with the structure and conditions of play behavior. Hence the spatial, temporal, physical, behavioral, and symbolic discriminable parts are used to generate ecological taxonomies of play. Since the early 1930s, a small number of play researchers have attempted to work toward developing a taxonomy of ecologically defined play situations (Hurlock, 1934; Parten, 1932, 1933; Johnson, 1935; Gump and Sutton-Smith, 1955a; Gump, Schoggen, and Redl, 1963).

Definition of Play:
Play settings possessing similar attributes will elicit similar play behavior responses from different individuals.

124

ECOLOGICAL RESEARCH

Parten (1933), employing the observational sampling technique that has become the methodological trademark of ecological research, reported the following findings:

1. The most frequently evolving play group among preschool children has two children in it.
2. Group size increases with age of play group.
3. House and dolls generated the most highly cooperative form of play, whereas clay and beads elicited the most parallel form of play.
4. There is an interaction between age and play environment, with sand play the most often chosen by the two- to two-and-a-half-year-old group, and family, house, and dolls play the most chosen by the three-year-old group.
5. By assigning a social[1] participation quotient to each transaction of play behavior, she was able to determine that playhouse equipment (house and dolls) elicited the most complex social responses; whereas train play elicited the least complex social responses.

Building upon the work of Parten in the 1930s and the classical ecological research of Barker and Wright (1955), Gump and Sutton-Smith (1955a) carried out their study entitled "Activity-Setting and Social Interaction: A Field Study." Their study proposed to examine the effects of two independent ecological variables — physical setting and standard performances — upon a dependent variable conceptually described as "social interactions." With regard to the play paradigm, the "physical setting" would be subsumed under the conditions of play behavior, and the "standard performances" would be subsumed under the elements of play behavior. Continuing with the play paradigm, Gump and Sutton-Smith's dependent variable would be subsumed under the consequences of play behavior. Gump and Sutton-Smith introduce their study with a strong ecological rationale for studying play; that is, they were interested in identifying those features of the activity, independent of the individual, that mold behavior to its shape or quality. Notwithstanding the extent to which variables other than ecological ones operate to determine the final person–environment unit, Gump and Sutton-Smith's ecological study on play was introduced in the following terms:

---

[1] Parten's (1933) classical categories of play were assigned a quotient score directly related to the amount of social participation inherent within the category: (a) unoccupied behavior, −3; (b) solitary play, −2; (c) onlooker behavior, −1; parallel, 1; associative play, 2; cooperative play, 3.

When the relationship between children and their activities is investigated, interest usually centers upon the question of how children select and use various activities to express their personal and social needs. The present study, and the larger research project from which it derives, attempts to reverse the direction of this interest and ask the question: How do activities limit, provoke, or coerce the expression of children's needs and problems? This form of consideration is based upon the general hypothesis that activities have a reality and a behavior-influencing power in their own right. An activity, once entered, will exclude some potential behaviors, necessitate other behaviors, and, finally, encourage or discourage still other behaviors. This coercive and provocative power of an activity rests upon two subaspects: the behavioral limitations and possibilities in the physical setting and its objects, and in the "standard patterns of performance" which constitute the activity. Thus, the activity-setting identified as "making a boat in craft shop" includes the physical objects of shop, wood, saws, etc., and the performances of hammering, sawing, attending to materials, etc. Beyond the performances which are standard in boat making, are behaviors which may become more or less likely because a child has entered this particular activity-setting. For example, if the setting should provide one saw and the standard performance should require sawing, conflict interaction may be more likely in such an activity-setting than in one in which tools are plentiful or in which boys are not pressed to use the same tool at the same time.

Those behaviors which are made more likely, although not required, by the physical setting and its standard performances may be labeled respondent behaviors. In the present study, the respondent behaviors under investigation were social interactions. The hypothesis tested was that the amount and kind of social interaction is significantly affected by variation of activity settings.

(Gump and Sutton-Smith, 1955a, pp. 755–756)

Gump and Sutton-Smith defined their independent ecological variables— crafts and swimming—in terms that indicate the structure, conditions, and processes of play:

With crafts as a baseline, some of the hypothesized characteristics of the two settings may be compared and contrasted.

1. The materials and the standard performances of crafts involve "difficult" goals.

In crafts one is supposed to "make something." This has several subsidiary effects. Interest and effort tend to go from the child to his project; he is "too busy" to seek interaction. This tends to reduce interaction in crafts. In swim, on the other hand, most of the standard performances are easily accomplished and one has freedom to seek and to respond to interaction. A second effect of the difficult goal is that it leads to need for technical assistance and to need for validation of one's efforts. The latter need is more subtle but important. Boys often ask counselors to approve (not just admire) their progress, although no "real" help is necessary. Thus, the predominance of the help type of interaction in crafts. In swim, the boys need little help or validation for the simple motor acts they accomplish.

2. The materials and the standard performances of crafts are re-
   strictive of the gross motor actions and of "bodily expansive-
   ness."

In crafts, boys have to be careful; running, falling, jumping, etc., are, of course, not a part of the usual craft activity. Swim, how-ever, provides a physical setting with elevations (docks and diving boards) and water (which can break a fall); these, together with standard performances of leaping and diving, lead to novel and "gravity-defying" acts. Cries of "Look at me!" are a likely part of such acts. As one experienced counselor puts it, "They want you to watch the darnedest things — little silly things that wouldn't be possible on land." Protocol material shows that this freedom of bodily action apparently leads to the display reflected by the high incidence of assortive interaction in the swim activity-setting. For some boys, the freedom of bodily actions also seems to lead to a need to test one's physical prowess in competitive or combative interaction; this would account for the high number of conflict interactions in swim.

(Gump and Sutton-Smith, 1955a, pp. 759–760)

The dependent respondent variable—social interaction—was operationalized by using six major categories:

I. Sharing — The subject either makes or receives an interaction with the quality of mutuality. Neither the
subject nor his associate asks or is asked to serve
the purposes of the other but to share an experience or an activity, e.g.: "Hey, look at the boat
coming in." "Let's make a submarine."

II. Helping — The subject asks, or is asked for help (material, information, effort). The subject gives or receives assistance. The interaction is not one of mutuality as in sharing, e.g.: "How do you make lanyard?" The counselor gives swimming or craft instruction, etc.

III. Asserting — The subject is involved in an interaction attempt, the intent of which is to gain admiration or interested attention, e.g.: "Hey look at me! I'm a drunk!" "I know how to do that — that's easy!"

IV. Blocking — The subject is involved in a deliberate "stopping" interaction. The blocker may refuse, ignore, etc., e.g.: "I will not!"

V. Demanding — The subject makes or receives a forceful request. No autonomy implied to the associate, e.g.: "You give me that!" "Get outa here!"

VI. Attacking — The subject is involved in an interaction attempt, the purpose of which is to "hurt" the recipient — to reduce him, or beat him, e.g.: "You S.O.B.!" One boy physically attacks another or takes something from him.
(Gump and Sutton-Smith, 1955a, p. 756)

The research by Gump and Sutton-Smith reported statistically significant "respondent social behavior" differences between the two "behavior settings." For example, results indicated that more help interactions were elicited in the crafts and that more assertion and attacking interactions were elicited in the swim setting. With regard to play-setting-generated camper–counselor interactions, the study reported that more interactions (forty-six percent) transpired in the craft than in the swim setting (twenty-six percent).

Based upon the findings of their research, Gump and Sutton-Smith point out the therapeutic and prescriptive value of being able to assess the specific consequences of the spatial, temporal, behavioral, and symbolic settings of the play activity.

The preceding data demonstrate that activity-settings determine more than the specific activity engaged in by a child. The properties of the activity-setting produce significant and general effects upon the respondent social behavior of its participants. In the settings investigated, these effects were noticeable in the amount and kind of interaction, in the type of person (boy or counselor) involved, and in the types of interaction sought from or offered by these different persons. The results do not seem explicable on the basis of differences in groups or in adult personnel involved—these were similar in each setting.[2]

The general implication for recreational and therapeutic work with children is that choice of activities per se is very important; this choice will markedly affect the children's relations to one another and to the leader or therapist. Specifically, the above results indicate that in the swim setting, the counselor often will be called upon to admire and recognize assertive actions and to settle or supervise conflict interactions; he will be involved in relatively few helping interactions. In crafts, the opposite tends to be true; here the counselor's role involves less admiration and conflict supervision and more helping. Related to setting-produced variations in counselor's role, are the variations in kinds of peer social experiences of the child participants. The counselor learns from such data that a "prescription" of swimming will send a child to a "robust" social climate in which total interaction is high and in which assertion and attacking are highly likely. A crafts "prescription," on the other hand, will place a child in a "mild" social climate in which total interaction is low, assertive and conflict interaction minimal, and dependency (helping-being helped) interaction high.

(Gump and Sutton-Smith, 1955a, p. 759)

Gump and Sutton-Smith conclude their research by identifying the need to develop an ecological taxonomy of play settings. The ultimate function of this taxonomy would be to facilitate the "fit" between individual needs and the inherent makeup of the activity.

In the final analysis, the basic characteristics of the activity setting—not the activity-settings as such—determine the impact upon participants. The problem for research is the delineation of these characteristics and the discovery of their relationship to the participant's respondent behavior and experience. This problem may be approached by determining what are the major behavioral limitations and opportunities presented by typical settings [conditions] and by their standard patterns of performances [Elements]. Then

[2] Another way of stating this finding is in terms of variability; that is, the ecological setting accounted for more respondent behavior variability than the possible individual (camper or counselor) or group influence. Their findings support the viewpoint that in some ecological settings, the external forces overshadow any internal organismic determinants of behavior. Extreme examples of this were manifested in World War II and in Vietnam, where battle shock was common to all personalities and socioeconomic groups.

one is in a position to ask what respondent behaviors [processes and consequences] become more or less likely because children engage in activity-settings with these characteristics.

From here on, the problem may be followed up in two ways: the modal or average effects of certain characteristics can be investigated (as was attempted in the discussion of this study); or, the particular effects upon participants with known personality needs and organizations [determinants] can be assessed. The first approach [study of structure of play behavior] is merely a step toward the second [interaction between person and setting] ; as the second is developed, it becomes feasible to prescribe strategically activities for specific children and groups; it becomes possible to make activity-settings congruent with diagnostic knowledge and with therapeutic aims.

(Gump and Sutton-Smith, 1955a, pp. 760)

The most recent research to demonstrate the ecological potential of certain behavioral settings has been the work carried out by survival-oriented wilderness programs (Barcus and Bergeson, 1972; Bernstein, 1972; Hanson, 1973; Kaplan, 1973, 1974). One such program, the "Outdoor Challenge Program" (Kaplan, (1974), is sponsored by the Community Mental Health Center in Marquette, in Michigan's Upper Peninsula. Dr. Robert Hanson, the center's chief of Psychological Services, is in charge of the program. Dr. Hanson implements his survival programs in a 17,000-acre tract, which has minimal road access and is maintained in a primitive state for purposes of maximum environmental impact on the participants. Some of the behavioral goals of survival training programs such as the one operated by Dr. Hanson were discussed by Barcus and Bergeson (1972):

Outdoor survival training pits a person against the natural environment with a minimum of artifacts in the struggle for survival. Programs emphasize learning to deal with nature both alone and as a member of a group. Strong emphasis is placed on learning interdependence with other group members. A common goal of survival training programs is development of better social relationship behaviors that will generalize back to normal life. Relationships are explored through group discussions and decision making, relating with instructors, and living under stress with peers.

Survival training emphasizes stress experiences-experiences that push the person beyond his usual performance. Such tasks as mountain climbing, white water river running, living off the land alone for a number of days, and difficult search and rescue missions are common. These experiences are designed to force people to stretch their perceived potentials to broader boundaries.

(Barcus and Bergeson, 1972)

Of all the survival training programs presently operating, the most well known is the "Outward Bound" program operated in Colorado. This program has been used with teenagers, businessmen, delinquents, college dropouts, and potential leaders in all fields. Outward Bound claims six behavioral goals for these programs:

1. To establish relationships between the student and the instructor in a neutral environment. To confront and solve problems together.

2. To create a group identity, a reference group, and to learn to work together and to help one another.

3. To enhance the student's self image by helping him overcome a graded set of physical and mental challenges. Resulting self confidence would enable the youth to contribute to the total group.

4. To provide the youth with an acceptable male image.

5. To promote communication through group discussion. Better understanding of own and others' needs and thereby better human relations.

6. To provide legitimate adventure as an acceptable release, resulting in a better appreciation of recreation and leisure time activities.

(Barcus and Bergeson, 1972, p. 4)

Survival training programs offer great promise for a new and badly needed behavioral setting. However, despite claims of survival training as being the panacea for human potential and mental health, the amount of rigorous research supporting these claims is rather meager (Kaplan, 1974). Barcus and Bergeson raise some of the substantive and methodological weaknesses in survival training studies.

There are few studies evaluating the effects of survival training on personal functioning. . . . Investigation of which existing personality measures are appropriate for evaluation of survival training is essential. In the broader picture, the question of what types of criteria-tests, interviews, behavior measures-at best must be answered.

Another weakness evident in these studies is the lack of clear definition of variables defining survival training. Taxonomies of environments, instructions, experiences, and behaviors comprising survival training are needed.

(Barcus and Bergeson, 1972, p. 6)

Almost twenty years have passed since Gump and Sutton-Smith (1955a) carried out their classical behavioral setting research. The recent popularity of survival training only brings to our attention the urgent need to compile a taxonomy of behavioral settings that will include natural and artificial settings. Sells (1963), while not intending his comments exclusively for play research, neatly captures the present state of affairs regarding behavioral play settings.

> The most obvious need in evaluating the manifold encounter of organism and environment is a more satisfactory and systematic conceptualization of the environment. This implies a taxonomic, dimensional analysis of stimulus variables comparable to the trait systems that have been developed for individual differences variables. . . . While work proceeds actively to extend the exploration of individual differences . . . the equally important frontier of situational dimensions is virtually ignored. . . . Experimenters must have systematic information about relevant dimensions of the environment beyond the piecemeal, concrete, immediate variables customarily observed on the basis of experience.
>
> (Sells, 1963, p. 700)

Play Paradigm

The ecological research that demonstrated that play behavior of the same children changed markedly as they left one play setting and entered another offers further support for the need to develop a taxonomy of play structures, conditions, and processes. The findings by the classical ecological play studies showed not only that play behavior of the same children differed markedly from setting to setting but also that different personality dispositions in the same setting displayed high similarity in play behavior. Although the findings indicated moderate child-to-child play variability for any isolated moment, over the long run, play settings molded their inhabitants. A concerted effort to determine which structures, processes, and conditions lead to which type of behavioral consequences would contribute greatly to the prescriptive application of play.

Another major consideration in terms of the play paradigm is the fact that Gump and his colleagues established that "personality differences" were not the major determinants of at least some kinds of behavioral dimensions. This major change in scientific thinking has meant that the objective environment (not simply the psychosocial environment), operationalized in terms of space, color, texture, light, sound, and the like, would be influencing and shaping critical behaviors. This has led to some serious scientific research on the impact of ecology on man. The consequences of play settings cannot be understood without an analysis of its relationship and coupling to the preceding objective environmental units.

Critique of the Ecological Theories of Play

The ecological theories of play strongly reinforce and bolster the need to incorporate the impact or contribution of the play setting. However, to advocate that it is the play setting that accounts for the major variance in play behavior is to ignore fifty years of social science research. Behavioral science has unequivocally demonstrated the impact of personality dispositions and acute traits on all human behavior, play included. It is the failure to incorporate the unique life space of the human organism that leaves the ecological theories open to criticism. To say that creative or adventure playgrounds will elicit socially appropriate behaviors from all children is to remiss and ignore the variability in personality dispositions and preceding environmental stimuli.

The ecological elements of the play setting, be it the theater, shopping mall, or bedroom, must be interpreted within an interaction framework of human play behavior. Such a framework is proposed for purposes of discussion in Figure 7.

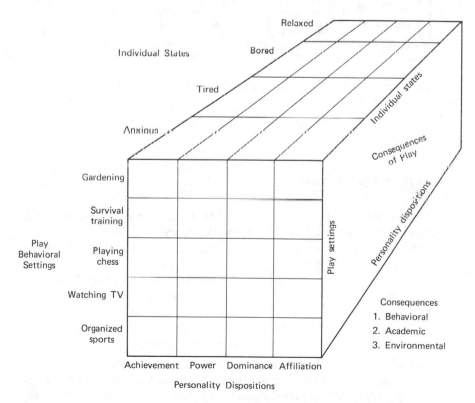

Figure 7 A Personality X Individual States X Behavioral Settings Interaction Model of Play

From Figure 7, it should become evident that only through the simultaneous interactions of the individual states X personality dispositions X play settings will it become possible to study the effects of all these independent variables on the dependent variable — consequences. Thus, future research could be planned to determine what the consequences of gardening are on individuals with different personality dispositions after experiencing an anxiety provoking situation prior to play. This antecedent–consequence paradigm is presented below.

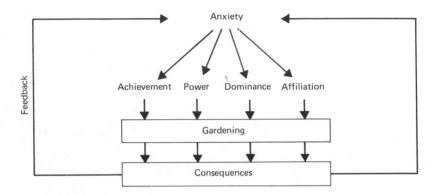

The same experimental paradigm could be designed for each of the possible permutations identified in Figure 7. Only this way could it be determined to what degree the variance in the consequences may be attributed to ecological or individual difference variables.

STUDY SUGGESTIONS

1. Select three different behavioral play settings (e.g., swimming pool, library, tennis court, park, lake, sidewalk, etc.) and:
   (a) Describe its unique ecological characteristics (e.g., space, equipment, location, colors, noise, etc.),
   (b) Using an observational procedure, describe the major behavioral activities elicited in each of the behavioral settings. To do this, specific operational definitions of behavior will have to be identified (e.g., verbal communication, cooperation, competition, physical aggression, etc.,) in order to permit comparisons across settings.
2. At some point in your professional career you will be asked to prescribe play activities that will generate certain desired behavioral goals. Based upon your personal experience (intuition), the professional literature (authority), and scientific research in the area of play behavior, construct a

taxonomy of play settings with their concomitant behavioral components. For example, canoeing would be one of the natural behavioral settings that could elicit cooperative, verbal, and group interactions, while a visit to the library could elicit a host of individual and independent behaviors.

A very critical goal must be achieved by those individuals wishing to use play behavior as a means to other ends (e.g., socialization, cognitive skills, personality development, etc.). This goal involves three major steps.

(a) *Description* (taxonomies) of play structure, conditions, and processes
(b) *Prescription* of specific client goals
(c) *Evaluation* of consequences of play behavior

The above two study suggestions should further the description-prescription-evaluation professional process.

9

Ecological Theories of Play Behavior: Arousal Properties in the Environment

As has become clear in our discussions on the theories of play behavior, it is virtually impossible to discuss the phenomena of play without a discussion on the nature of man. In the classical and psychoanalytic theories of play behavior discussed previously, man was assumed to emit all his behaviors in response to the primary utilitarian biological drives of survival (hunger, thirst, sex, warmth, shelter, reproduction, territoriality, etc.). Thus, by implication, the early play theorists, viewed all play behavior as connected to biological gratification or relief. However, beginning in 1949 with Hebb's influential book, *The Organization of Behavior,* followed by the works of Berlyne (1960) and Fiske and Maddi (1961), a new motivational theory for human behavior, heretofore misrepresented by the drive-reductionist internal theorists, was developed. This new motivational theory is formulated on the premise that man often seeks stimulation from the environment for the sake of stimulation alone and not necessarily to reduce biological needs.

Berlyne (1966), in one of his many outstanding discussions on the stimulation model of man, captures the essence of this concept, through his discussions on "curiosity and exploration."

> Higher animals spend a substantial portion of their time and energy on activities to which terms like curiosity and play seem applicable. An even more conspicuous part of human behavior, especially in highly organized societies, is classifiable as "recreation," "entertainment," "art," or "science." In all of these activities sense organs are brought into contact with biologically neutral or "indifferent" stimulus patterns—that is, with objects or events that do

not seem to be inherently beneficial or noxious. Stimulus patterns encountered in this way are sometimes used to guide subsequent action aimed at achieving some immediate practical advantage. An animal looking and sniffing around may stumble upon a clue to the whereabouts of food. A scientist's discovery may contribute to public amenity and to his own enrichment or fame. Much of the time, however, organisms do nothing in particular about the stimulus patterns that they pursue with such avidity. They appear to seek them "for their own sake."

Until about 15 years ago these forms of behavior were overlooked in the theoretical and experimental literature, except for a few scattered investigations. Recently they have been winning more and more interest among psychologists. They constitute what is generally known in Western countries as "exploratory behavior". . . .

Early demonstrations of the prevalence and strength of these activities in higher animals were rather embarassing to then current motivation theories. Animals are, of course, most likely to explore and play when they have no emergencies to deal with, but there are times when these behaviors will even override what one would expect to be more urgent considerations. A hungry rat may spend time investigating a novel feature of the environment before settling down to eat. A bird may approach a strange and potentially threatening object at the risk of its life. Even human beings are reported to have played the lyre while Rome was burning and to have insisted on completing a game of bowls after an invading armada was sighted.

(Berlyne, 1966, pp. 25-26)

Theoretical Definition:
Play is the behavior that maintains an optimal flow of stimulation for the individual.

Theoretical Concepts

Man the Stimulus Seeker

Traditional biological drive-reduction models of man are unable to explain why people go out to climb mountains, paint sunsets, drive golf balls, and jog at 5:00 A.M. The classical and psychoanalytic theories of play are based on the assumption that man plays in order to reduce the disequilibrium caused by some drive-reductionist need. Thus, we play in order to release some excess energy. And once we have completed playing, the drive is reduced, and equilibrium has been reached. However, such is not the case with many individuals who appear to play beyond the stage of biological or need reduction. Some individuals appear to be activated or motivated by external and internal stimuli divorced from any classical tension reduction paradigms. Recently Berlyne (1960, 1966, 1968) and Fiske and Maddi (1961) have proposed that man seeks tension and varied experiences and maintains his stimuli input at a level suitable to his unique biological and sociocultural makeup.

Fiske and Maddi delineated the functions of varied experience for human beings:

> First, variations in stimulation contributes to the normal development and also to the functioning of organisms.
> A second function of varied experience is that it is oriented toward and sought for its own sake.
> Finally, varied experience is one factor contributing to the affective state of human beings.
>
> (Fiske and Maddi, 1961, p. 12)

Dimensions of Stimulation

What are the salient dimensions of stimulation that activate man to play? Those most frequently discussed by psychologists as having an impact on man include simple intensity, meaningfulness, variation, novelty, complexity, surprisingness, and incongruity. Fiske and Maddi (1961) have described the impact that stimulation has on one's level of activation in terms of its *dimensions* and *sources*. Figure 8 is a schematic representation of the stimulation impact model proposed by Fiske and Maddi.

The *stimulation sources* are threefold: exteroceptive (stimuli from external sources); interoceptive (stimuli from internal sources); and cortical (stimuli from the cortex of the brain).

There are also three *stimulation dimensions*. *Intensity of stimulation* can refer to levels of noise and visual intensity. What is the stimulation impact of playing a game of chess in a crowded airport waiting room as opposed to a quiet and serene private boudoir? *Meaningfulness* is the dimension of stimulation that refers to significance or importance that that stimulation has for the individual. A national flag may have degrees of meaningfulness for individuals, depending on their degree of chauvinism and patriotism. A clenched fist at the 1972 Munich Olympics was clearly a meaningful response to the American flag. *Variation,* as a stimuli dimension, is operationalized in terms of change, novelty, and unexpectedness. A walk through a shopping mall in which each store window display (stimulus) is different would be an example of a change in stimulus. The importance of novelty is well documented by observers of that favorite pastime, sightseeing, a facet of human behavior beginning to play an important role in problems of urban design (e.g., historical landmarks such as streetcars, old homes, churches, etc.), as well as in the administration of our natural wilder-

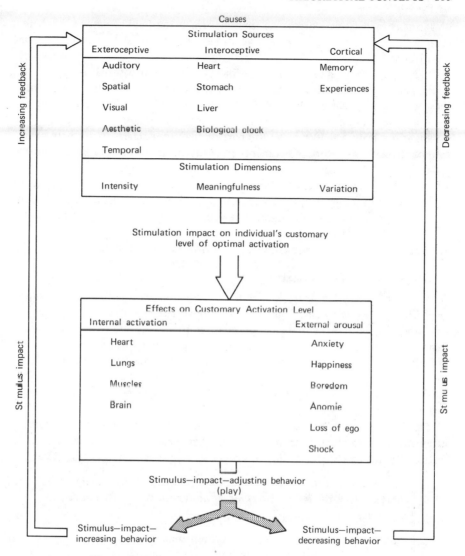

Figure 8 Play: Stimulus-Impact-Adjusting Behavior

ness recreation areas (how do you maintain novelty when a stimulus is over-used?). Unexpectedness refers to stimulation that deviates from what is expected, such as the typical, wary reaction if one is suddenly stopped by a police-man while taking a Sunday drive through the local park.

Thus the *activation level* that exists at any point in time is a function of the *total stimulation impact*. The *interval activation level* gets translated into an *external arousal level,* which leads to a change in *stimulus impact*. Hence, if a stimulus impact increase is in order, the stimulus dimensions will be activated, whereas if a stimulus impact decrease is in order, the stimulus dimensions will be deactivated.

Berlyne has called all the stimulus dimensions "collative variables." To date, while many play theorists have had a tendency to associate their work with these collative variables (Ellis, 1973; Alderman, 1974), systematic research on the operational definitions and measurement of these variables is badly lacking.

There has been a tendency on the part of play researchers to strongly advocate controlled laboratory experiments to study these collative variables. Unfortunately, play behavior can never be realistically simulated in the laboratory setting. The actual physical environment, such as the theater, mountain, lake, landscape, or urban ghetto, must be researched, even at the cost of sacrificing to a certain extent our scientific rigor. If it becomes impossible to experimentally manipulate variables independently, their relative stimulation impact can be assessed through techniques of statistical control and multivariate analysis.

Optimal Level of Arousal

A number of psychologists working in the arousal area have proposed an optimal level of arousal hypothesis. This hypothesis postulates an inverted-U-shaped relationship between magnitude of stimulation along the dimensions discussed above and the arousal value of, interest in, or preference for a given stimulus. The optimal arousal level theory has been most systematically investigated by Fiske and Maddi (1961), who proposed a number of theoretical hypotheses. The most critical hypotheses by Fiske and Maddi are discussed below, with direct reference to the study of play behavior.

The fact that man is an arousal-seeking animal who does not stop exploring, inventing, and creating when his basic survival needs are met is clearly manifested by Fiske and Maddi in the following major propositions and discussions.

> *In the absence of specific tasks, the behavior of an organism is directed toward the maintenance of activation at the characteristic or normal level.*
>
> Organisms manifest a need to maintain their normal level of activation. This motive is nonspecific in the sense that any of a wide range of behaviors may be utilized to furnish stimulation with appropriate impact. When no specific motive is present, the organism commonly attempts to sustain activation by seeking or producing stimulation with variation; it may attend to complex stimulation, it may explore, or it may play.
>
> (Fiske and Maddi, 1961, pp. 42–46)

The above hypothesis would seem to suggest that for every individual, there is a unique, normal, and adaptive optimal level of activation. It is hypothesized by Fiske and Maddi that, at any particular point in time, a discrepancy may exist between one's normal customary level of activation and one's actual level of activation. This discrepancy between activation level and psychological affect is presented in the following terms:

> *Negative affect is ordinarily experienced when activation level differs markedly from normal level; positive affect is associated with shifts of activation toward normal level.*
>
> Through experience, the organism learns to avoid markedly high or low levels of activation under most circumstances, because they are accompanied by unpleasantness. An extremely high level of activation is typically unpleasant because it is associated with such states as inability to concentrate, anxiety, rapid heart beat, or a sinking feeling in the stomach. The decrements in the effectiveness of performance associated with high levels of activation may also be a factor in the negative affective tone. Affect is also likely to be negative when the impact of stimulation is low, as in reading a dull book. Some manifestations of the concomitant low level of activation may be boredom, drowsiness, and apathy.
>
> (Fiske and Maddi, 1961, pp. 46–47)

The relationship between stimulation impact, activation level, and affective state is presented in Figure 9.

Let us try to apply this hypothesis to a person's choice of a holiday spot. To this end, let us conceive of an individual whose optimal activation level is reached during interaction with cultural and social play service systems (theater, art gallery, zoo, library, park, playground, etc.). For purposes of discussion, we can label this hybrid play dimension, "sociocultural affinity," which probably represents a composite of stimulus dimensions proposed by Fiske and Maddi, Berlyne, and others — intensity, meaningfulness, variation, complexity, novelty, and so forth. We shall further assume that this person's optimal arousal level is somewhere in the middle of this "sociocultural affinity" play dimension. Now, the research question: Where will this person go for a vacation? One possibility is the kaleidoscopic sociocultural attractions of a big megolopolis like New York or, alternatively, the peaceful and serene sociocultural atmosphere of eastern Quebec and the Maritime Provinces of Canada. However, in keeping with the hypothesis that beyond a certain deviation (discrepancy) from the optimal activation level, behavior begins to have negative affect, we may hypothesize that our vacationer will tend to avoid or experience negative affect from holiday spots representing the more extreme levels of stimulation impact. Hence the person is more likely to avoid the extreme levels of stimulation found in New York City and to choose the more peaceful eastern part of Canada. However, in

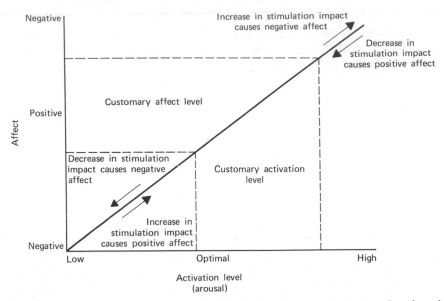

Figure 9 The Relationship Between Stimulation Impact, Activation Level, and Affective State for Each Person

keeping with his or her optimal stimulation needs, the person is more likely to vacation in the more "civilized" parts of the country, where it would be possible and acceptable to engage in stimulus impact-increasing behavior if it became necessary. The models in Figures 8 and 9 offer some plausible explanations of why wilderness campers would be least likely to come from the larger metropolitan urban cities, and conversely, why those most strongly attracted to the manifold excitement of the large metropolis would not, in most cases, be from small, quiet, and serene hamlets and towns.

What happens when one experiences a discrepancy between one's customary level of activation and the actual level of activation. As was indicated by Fiske and Maddi in Figure 8, the individual engages in impact-modifying behavior, which makes the individual activation level congruent with task or situational demands.

> *The behavior of an organism tends to modify its activation level toward the optimal zone for the task at hand.*
>
> This proposition introduces the notion of a different type of instrumental behavior. While it is well known that an organism will behave so as to relieve certain tissue needs (for example, those associated with hunger or thirst), it appears that the organism's be-

havior can also be instrumental in preparing the organism for performing specific goal-oriented activity. . . .

This proposition suggests that classes of tasks can be characterized by the level or band of activation which they require for maximally effective performance. The present proposition indicates that when a discrepancy exists between activation level and this optimal activation for the task, the organism will ordinarily attempt to decrease the discrepancy by engaging in impact-modifying behavior. . . .

Running a foot race to the best of one's ability is an example of a task which requires a rather high level of activation. From our point of view it is not mere accident or superstition that runners warm up for such a remarkably long time before the race. One function of this procedure is to increase the amount of impact from stimulation, and hence, to increase activation level.

Sometimes the existing level of activation will be too high for optimal performance. By comparison with running, a task requiring less energy output but more precise movements and considerable concentration (for example, surgery) is probably best performed with a somewhat lower level of activation. If the surgeon's activation level is too high, there are a number of things he can do in an attempt to reduce it. He can seek a place free of extraneous stimulation in which to rest. In an attempt to relax, he may try listening to soothing music or lying still for a period of time before working.

One implication of this proposition is clear: when the organism is unable to modify its level of activation toward the optimal zone for the task at hand, its efficiency or effectiveness will be reduced. Thus, if the individual in the example above is not successful in lowering his level of activation to within the optimal range, he may not be able to carry out a surgical operation which demonstrates maximal utilization of his abilities. This holds not only for excessive degrees of activation but also for deficient levels.

(Fiske and Maddi, 1961, pp. 35-37)

Fiske and Maddi have thus far clearly indicated that individual differences exist in customary activation levels. Thus, while one individual or group of individuals may perceive and experience reading "Peanuts" boring and require an increase in stimulus impact, another individual or group of individuals may find reading "Peanuts" too stimulating and consequently gravitate toward less stimulating reading material, which is congruent with their customary level of activation.

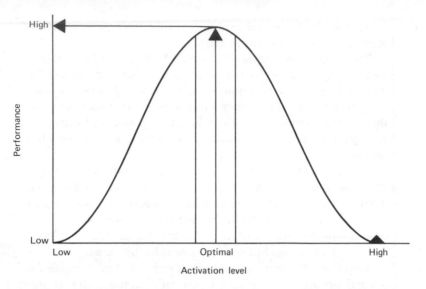

Figure 10 Performance as an Inverted-U Function of Activation Level

Of critical importance here is the recognition that some individuals have extremely high customary activation levels and will seek out play opportunities to satiate these activation levels, even at the risk of death — skydiving, mountain climbing, skiing, automobile racing, and the like. At the other extreme are individuals who suffer from trauma and anxiety reactions when forced to "play" in activities that are at extreme variance to the individual's customary activation level — children "forced" by their parents, teachers, or peers to compete in minor league sports in which one dare not make a mistake for fear of serious repercussions.

Moving from individual differences in customary activation levels, Fiske and Maddi proposed a number of hypotheses related to tasks and activation level. The first hypothesis deals with performance and activation level.

> *For any task, there is a level of activation which is necessary for maximally effective performance.*
>
> It is currently fairly well accepted that activation level is an important determinant of effectiveness of performance. The function relating the two variables is typically considered to be an inverted U.
>
> (Fiske and Maddi, 1961, p. 31)

Figure 10 depicts the inverted-U function relating performance effectiveness to activation level (arousal level) discussed by Fiske and Maddi.

Fiske and Maddi continue to discuss the relationship between performance and activation level:

> The significance for performance of the U-shaped relationship mentioned above is as follows: at low levels of activation, the organism may be inattentive, easily distracted, and not concentrating fully on the task. At somewhat higher levels, the organism is alert and attentive; it mobilizes its resources and is oriented toward coping with the situation. It performs to the best of its abilities. Still higher levels of activation are associated with excessive tension or hyperactivity. Anxiety and other strong emotional states appear, and behavior is less efficient.
>
> (Fiske and Maddi, 1961, p. 32)

This hypothesis has direct application to such play activities as mountain climbing, alpine skiing, parachute jumping, and a host of other similar activities in which the individual must be optimally activated in order to perform the activity at a satisfactory and safe level. Most recently Csikszentmihalyi (1974) has documented the increase in arousal level that accompanies mountain climbers. Furthermore, if the arousal level was lacking, the mountain climbers were reported to have modified their style of climbing in order to raise the level of activation, which in turn assured the climber of performing at an adequate and safe level.

The next proposition by Fiske and Maddi deals with the relationship between activation levels and differential tasks.

> ### The activation requirements of different tasks
>
> While the exact function relating performance to level of activation must be worked out empirically for each task, some preliminary indications are available, such as the narrowness of the plateau for difficult tasks. It is likely that a given level of activation will often be within the optimal zone for several easy tasks and for one or more difficult ones.
>
> It is also probable that different types of tasks have different activation requirements, that is, that there are different ranges of activation which are optimal for the effective performance of different tasks. While this possibility is by no means conclusively supported by everyday experience. A routine, repetitive task requiring no thought may be performed better at a relatively low level of activation; a challenging intellectual problem may best be solved at a higher level; maximum exertion of physical energy, as in running a fast race, would appear to call for a still higher level.
>
> (Fiske and Maddi, 1961, p. 34)

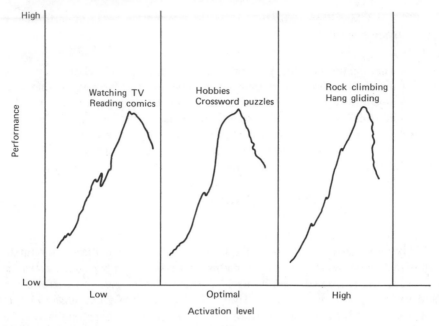

Figure 11 The Relationship Between Activation Level and Performance across Differential Play Activities

The above inverted-U relationship between different tasks and absolute activation level alluded to by Fiske and Maddi is schematically displayed in Figure 11. The figure is to be only considered for its descriptive and deductive power, since no empirical research exists on the stimulus impact of each unique activity; that is, does one really have to have a higher activation level to climb a mountain or run a foot race than to write a poem or read *Playboy* magazine? These kinds of theoretical questions have not as yet been tested.

Combining the activation hypothesis for individuals and tasks brings us to an interactionist model of play behavior proposed in Figure 12. Let us expand on the three individuals depicted in Figure 12. P_1 represents the low-arousal seeker, whose optimal customary play activity is reading *Playboy*. This individual would be most uncomfortable and anxious engaging in the activities that provide optimal levels of arousal for P_2 and P_3. P_2 is our average everyday arousal seeker, whose most customary and optimally arousing activity is sightseeing. This individual would not be attracted by activities T_1, T_2, T_3, and T_4. To be more explicit, these four activities would bore him, and T_6, T_7, T_8, and T_9 would create too great a stimulation impact, forcing him to engage in stimulus-impact decreasing behavior. P_3 is our high arousal seeker whose need for stimulation impact is above the average person in society. She goes to great efforts to generate high activation levels. Although Figure 12 has used socially accepted forms

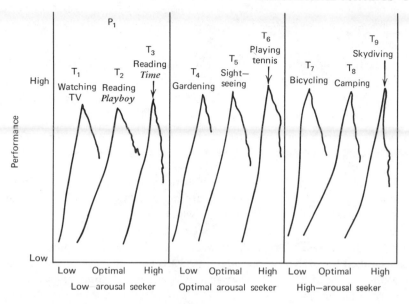

Figure 12 The Relationship Between Task Activation Level and Individual Activation Level

of behavior for satisfying activation levels one must be prepared to interpret such socially unacceptable behavior as crime, drug addiction, promiscuity, extreme forms of risk, and spiritual cults as manifestations of attempts to raise or lower the activation levels.

There has been no more exciting and observant discussion of man's attempt to cope with the stimulation impact in his environment than the *Human Zoo* by Desmond Morris (1969), the British zoologist recently turned popular writer and critic. In Chapter Six, entitled the "Stimulus Struggle," Morris discusses at great length six ways that man had adopted to cope with both boring and over-arousing stimuli present in the "human zoo." These six propositions have been reported below, since the author feels they provide tremendous insight into man's coping mechanisms and the potential role of play service systems, at all age levels.

1. If stimulation is too weak, you may increase your behavior output by creating unnecessary problems which you can then solve.
2. If stimulation is too weak, you may increase your behavior output by overreacting to a normal stimulus.
3. If stimulation is too weak, you may increase your behavior output by inventing novel activities.
4. If stimulation is too weak, you may increase your behavior

> output by performing normal responses to subnormal stimuli.
>
> 5. If stimulation is too weak, you may increase your behavior by artificially magnifying selected stimuli.
>
> 6. If stimulation is too strong, you may reduce your behavior output by damping down responsiveness to incoming sensations.
>
> (Morris, 1969, pp. 185–225)

The concept of optimal level of stimulation has been discussed by Berlyne (1960, 1968) in terms of man's need to process information or knowledge. Berlyne termed man's need to process information, the *epistemic theory* of behavior. Berlyne (1960) hypothesized a relationship among uncertainty, surprisingness, incongruity (all the collative variables), and information flow. It is this relationship between information flow and the dimensions of uncertainty that has been used by Berlyne to develop his own theory of play. According to the epistemic theory of behavior, when man is faced with a stimulus (a building, a highway, interpersonal communication, a game, etc.) where he is unable to predict the outcome of the event, he is thrown into conflict (i.e., a deviation from the customary activation level causes negative affect). This conflict motivates man to process information, and the processing of information reduces uncertainty and conflict. Berlyne defines "uncertainty" as

> situations where events have probabilities other than 1 or 0.
>
> Two intuitively recognizable characteristics of uncertainty are thus exemplified by these two approaches. One is that when uncertainty is greater, the greater the range of values that a variable may have or, in other words, the greater the range of alternative possibilities. The other is that when uncertainty is greater, the further probabilities diverge from 0 and 1, so that the maximum of uncertainty is reached when an event has an equal chance of materializing and not materializing.
>
> (Berlyne, 1960, p. 25)

For each individual, there theoretically exists an optimal information-seeking level for each stimuli. Conflict (uncertainty) is precipitated when the individual does not have sufficient knowledge to predict the consequences of his or her behavior. When the individual has had the opportunity to overcome the deficiencies of knowledge about the stimuli, the conflict is reduced as a result of the flow of information.

Most recently, Ellis (1973) has incorporated the work of Berlyne and the other arousal psychologists into his definition of play behavior:

Play is an artificial category. It is merely that part of stimulus-seeking behavior to which we cannot ascribe a prepotent motive. In trying to set it apart as a watertight category our understanding is clouded with the efforts necessary to seek the discriminants that differentiate work from play. We are led into an artificial dichotomization of the behavior into work and play, when clearly some behavior can be both. Any juxtaposition of work and play must be along a continuum with serious or critical behavior at one pole and behavior that serves only to maintain arousal and no other effect at the other.

It is more simple to adopt a view of animals as driven to interact with their environments by their needs to maintain their separate integrity as organisms. Activity is intimately tied to the processes of growth and maintenance. One of the drives serving these processes is the need to process information to maintain optimal arousal levels. The animal will indulge in interactions that lead to the elevation of arousal level when possible.

In the normal environment of a neophilic animal the opportunities for stimulus-seeking are good and the exigencies of change encourage its practice. However, stimulus-seeking may not occur for a variety of reasons. Stimulus-seeking activity may be preempted by stronger incentives to emit responses that are tied to other needs, or the contingencies may be such that it is punished. Alternatively, there may be no opportunities to indulge in stimulus-seeking because the environment is so simple and well known that there may be no interactions available which carry information or arousal potential.

A definition for play then becomes: *play is that behavior that is motivated by the need to elevate the level of arousal towards the optimal.*

It seems that pure play can occur only when all extrinsic consequences are eliminated and the behavior is driven on solely intrinsic motivation.

(Ellis, 1973, pp. 109–110)

Dr. H. I. Day, a psychologist at York University in Toronto and a leading authority on intrinsic motivation (1971), who was once a student of Berlyne, defines play in terms of uncertainty as

a type of activity that includes information search, skill training, and repetitious practice, motivated by lack of information. Un-

> certainty about the conceptualization of a precept and the choice of an appropriate response in a situation of high ambiguity, etc., induces exploration of the source of uncertainty. Exploration often takes the form of locomotion, manipulation, and testing of various solutions. Play includes these exploratory responses in any combination, is initiated in the presence of uncertainty, and may be abandoned either when all the uncertainty is resolved or when other environmental stimuli with higher levels of uncertainty become more attractive and interesting to the individual and are seen as more conducive to exploration. Children play more than adults, probably because they are more at liberty to choose to react to interesting environments and can move among various alternatives with greater ease.
>
> (Day, 1971, p. 6)

Although the psychological literature on arousal, optimal level of stimulation, and information processing dates back to the 1940s, there have been few documented studies on the application of these theories to real-life settings, particularly play settings. This finding is most disturbing, since so much of play behavior manifests elements of risk, tension, conflict, anxiety, novelty, uncertainty, and the like. It would thus appear that the professions of recreation, education, architecture, planning, and so forth could make wide use of the arousal theories of man. One researcher who has taken advantage of the uncertainty dimension of play has been Senters (1971). Senters, using the participant observation technique of social anthropologists, set out to investigate "uncertainty and stakes . . . as they related to a theoretical orientation toward recreation." Senters operationalized "uncertainty" and "stakes" in the following terms:

> Moderately uncertain outcome means that the probability of an event occurring is about 0.5. This condition is realized when winning or losing in an activity is nearly equal, such as the case where opponents are similar in ability or subject to the same chance conditions. This meaning of uncertainty is dependent on the performer's assessment; uncertainty is assumed to be a cognitive state reflecting current communication from the environment, past experiences, and perception.
>
> Stakes refer to the consequences of an event occurring. While simply winning or losing may be the sole outcome (consequence) of a game, there may be others, such as payment on a bet.
>
> (Senters, 1971, p. 260)

Senters made the following comment regarding the function of uncertainty and stakes in recreational activities:

> It is submitted here that moderate uncertainty and stakes both serve to increase the value of a recreational activity and, further, that a "maturation phenomenon" occurs such that in the course of engaging in an activity persons alter their behavior to ensure that the conditions of play (uncertainty) and the outcome (stakes) continue to add value. Such an approach to recreation permits the presence of excitement, tension, and extreme effort, unlike the premise that recreation serves primarily as tension relaxation and the absence of anxiety.
>
> (Senters, 1971, p. 261)

Following a year and a half of observation of six men engaged in a game of shuffleboard at a tavern, Senters concluded her study with a comment on how the players developed stimulus-impact increasing behaviors (e.g., betting, competition, and adjusting performance level).

> It is concluded . . . that the players . . . engaged in shuffleboard for the pleasure of the game itself until they became relatively skilled. Then, essentially, they rejected the previous sole stakes (win or loss) by demanding that this group activity be conducted only when stakes were increased through a competitive league structure or through betting.
>
> The players continually adjusted their performances to ensure an ongoing level of uncertainty in the final outcomes of the league games. They developed patterns of interaction (the norm of carrying a player) and communication (jargon) relating to examination of their progress according to the score sheets.
>
> These findings suggest that man requires a certain level of uncertainty with which to test his own talents and responses, and that changing the consequences or outcome of behavior is interdependent with uncertainty. If this is valid, then where men have a choice of activities, as in recreation, they will seek opportunities for consequent challenge. . . If persons individually or in groups prefer certain levels of uncertainty, they will be motivated to maintain it where present, and seek it where it is absent through the examination of alternatives.
>
> (Senters, 1971, p. 266)

Long-Term Stimulus Adaptation Effects

The concept of optimal stimulation level raises a major question for play theorists: What are the long-range play effects of exposure to a given environment that has a very unique level of intensity, complexity, surprisingness, or incongruity of stimulation dimensions? Dubos (1968) points out that in spite of man's capacity to adapt to an astonishingly wide range of environmental conditions, such prolonged exposure to stimulus environments falling near the extreme of the complexity or intensity dimension, for instance, may leave serious long-term effects on the individual. Clearly, it is recognized that individuals have the capacity to adapt to environmental stimuli on a short-term basis; yet more subtle and critical long-term effects on behavior may nevertheless occur. For example, the Wall Street executive who lives in the suburbs and commutes to work each day on the railroad or subway may come to experience the morning and evening rush-hour traffic conditions as no more arousing than would someone taking a peaceful, relaxed, and uncrowded bus trip in the same suburb. From a short-term perspective, the commuter develops all sorts of stop-gap behaviors to deal with a negative stimulation impact. Such popular subway pastimes as sleeping in a standing position, reading, daydreaming, or working, which on the surface appear incongruent with the noise, shoving, crowding, and other typical subway characteristics, must be examined in terms of their cumulative long-term effect. Will these forms of surface stimulation adaptations create a society with inflated arousal thresholds that is addicted to high levels of noise? What will these forms of adaptation levels mean in terms of the play arousal needs of future generations? Will they find the quiet, serene, and picturesque countryside too boring and unstimulating? Is it any wonder that the most popular behavioral setting for family play has become the highly stimulating and ever-changing shopping mall? It is not surprising that the citizens of tomorrow find the playgrounds designed by the citizens of today boring, uncreative, and far less preferable to watching some of the highly arousing television shows. When one begins to notice that the children of today are operating at an extremely high level of stimulation impact, at the expense of shutting out or not being interested in those human accomplishments that operate at lower stimulation levels (e.g., forms of art, literature, architecture, music, drama, philosophy, etc.), it is conceivable that many of our aesthetic and artistic traits are in danger of being replaced by highly stimulating modes of expression in the form of light, sound, speed, drugs, and the like. One only has to attend a junior high school dance to see these extreme forms of stimulation impact operating. Is it any wonder that these same twelve-year-olds could not bear to be in an art gallery for more than fifteen minutes without causing some form of mischief?

Admittedly, many of our long-term behavioral effects of exposure to particular levels of stimulation impact are still open to scientific investigations; however, researchers such as Milgram (1970) who have made extensive studies on the urban experiences of man have provided strong evidence on the deleterious psychosocial and physiological effects of particular levels of stimulation.

Play theorists and professionals concerned with the delivery of play services will have to identify the role of play in helping man adapt to the various levels of stimulation impact. And perhaps more critical is the need to have input into the design of behavior-shaping environments, such as schools, homes, communi-

Table 3 A Hypothetical Intensity Play Scale

Stimulation Source: Noise
Operational Definition of Noise: Decibels

Play Behavior	Decibels
Hunting	150
Flying a jet plane	140
	130 (human pain threshold)
Loud discotheque	120
Motorcycle, powerboat, stock cars, etc.	110
Spectator sports (football, baseball, etc.)	100
Loud movie theatre	80
Outdoor shopping	70
Indoor shopping	60
Conversation	40
Camping	30
Fishing	20
Reading	5
Meditating	4

ties, subways, and highways, so that they do not condition and addict man to deleterious stimulation dimension levels.

Play Paradigm

The arousal explanations of play behavior focus on the need to examine the stimulus properties of individuals as they interact with their environment. While the literature has made some progress on identifying the social, cultural, and interpersonal determinants of play, it has not as yet examined the stimulus dimensions of play. A child's choice to play with blocks instead of listening to a "loud" record should be as explainable from a stimulus impact framework as from the more prevalent sociocultural drive motivation framework. The description and prescription of play activities will someday be carried out in terms of stimulus dimensions as well as interpersonal, psychosocial, and cultural dimensions. For purposes of discussion, a hypothetical stimulus dimension play scale (Table 3) has been compiled. It is hoped that through concerted interdisciplinary and transdisciplinary research, valid and reliable play taxonomies, defined in relation to stimulus sources and dimensions, will evolve.

The consequences of not considering the stimulus properties of play settings are evident in our human and nonhuman systems. For example, the failure to take into account the behavioral and physiological consequences on man of continual and enforced crowding in the planning of play service systems (as well as education, housing, shopping, etc.) is most unfortunate. In light of the overwhelming evidence (e.g., Hall, 1966; Byrne, 1969; Griffith, 1970) of gross behavioral aberrations attributed to "crowding," it is little wonder that crowded urban playgrounds induce vandalism, racism, and aggression; it is little wonder that crowded soccer, baseball, football, and hockey arenas elicit feelings of discomfort, hostility, and other manifestations of negative affect from a population already living under conditions of "high density" prior to entering the crowded play behavioral setting.

Critique of Arousal Theories of Play

The major criticism of this model of man is its lack of real-life research. To date, the majority of the research on man's affective response to the qualitative and quantitative stimulus dimensions of natural and artificial environments have been simulated in laboratories of the type used by Fiske and Maddi (1961) in their "stimulus deprivation" research. The actual interaction between man and environment may be radically different from that observed in an artificial and preempted situation. This is not to diminish the value and need of laboratory-type studies. Quite the contrary, some research, can only be validly carried out under rigorous controls. However, once the laboratory evidence is available, the research should progress toward the most realistic field situation.

STUDY SUGGESTIONS

1. In order to give students the opportunity to test out the degree to which the "collative" stimulation dimensions are operative in various forms of play behavior, the Activity Arousal Analysis chart is provided on the next page. The student should interview a variety of people and compare how different individuals respond to the same activity. Activity arousal comparisons across a number of respondents will reveal the degree to which these collative variables are operative.

2. Play settings for children have, for too many years, been taken for granted and not examined in terms of their arousal dimensions. Using the stimulus properties proposed in Exercise 1, evaluate individual play settings that are available to children in your community. This sort of evaluation will permit you to interpret some of the behavioral and ecological reasons for the preference of the more adventurous and natural playgrounds over the more traditional and sterile playgrounds.

Activity Arousal Analysis

Activity Name:

Stimulus Properties of Play Activity	Always Present	Often Present	Sometimes Present	Rarely Present	Never Present
High risk					
Moderate risk					
Low risk					
High information					
Moderate information					
Low information					
High novelty					
Moderate novelty					
Low novelty					
High variation					
Moderate variation					
Low variation					
High predictability					
Moderate predictability					
Low predictability					
High meaningfulness					
Moderate meaningfulness					
Low meaningfulness					

10
Socialization Theories of Play Behavior

One of the clearest documented scientific lessons learned in the twentieth century is the fact that through a process of *socialization,* individuals become *acculturated* into a mold made up of motives, needs, values, desires, and incentives valued in their culture or subculture. The word *"socialization"* is used here to refer to the process by which individuals learn the values of their society and are ultimately acculturated.

SOCIAL LEARNING THEORY

The theory of human behavior that most strongly[1] supports the socialization process as a determinant of behavior is the *social learning theory* or, more specifically, *stimulus-response* (S-R) theory.

Ivan Pavlov (1927), the distinguished Russian physiologist and Nobel Prize winner, discovered the techniques that have become the hallmarks of S-R theory. Pavlov's classic experiment with dogs showed how, through repeated simultaneous exposure to the stimulus (S) of a bell followed by food, a given response (R) of salivation could be produced by ringing the bell alone. In America, J. B. Watson, the father of social learning, expanded on Pavlov's work by demonstrating that a given stimulus could produce a certain response in human beings as well as in animals. His famous experiment based on Pavlovian theory demonstrated emotional conditioning in an infant boy. From these original classical and famous experiments grew a body of knowledge that has been generated by such famous psychologists as Hull, Spence, Dollard, Miller, Woodworth, Thorndike, Tolman, and Guthrie. What are the basic tenets of the S-R theory of socialization?

---

[1] The term "most strongly" is used, since there have been several theories of socialization that have not considered socialization as a major product of social learning but have viewed socialization as a secondary result of primary conflict resolution. Thus, according to the psychoanalytic school of psychology, socialization involves dealing with one's libidinal drives through appropriate and conflict-reducing social interactions.

The first is that man is a living organism whose *biological needs are the ultimate springs of action:*

> The major primary needs or drives are so ubiquitous that they require little more than to be mentioned. They include the need for foods of various sorts (hunger), the need for water (thirst), the need for air, the need to avoid tissue injury (pain), the need to maintain an optimal temperature, the need to defecate, the need to micturate, the need for rest (after protracted exertion), the need for sleep (after protracted inaction). The drives concerned with the maintenance of the species are those which lead to sexual intercourse and the need represented by nest building and care of the young. . .
>
> (Atkinson, 1964, p. 163)

Second, man derives *primary reinforcement* from the reduction of biological needs:

> Whenever a reaction (R) takes place in temporal contiguity with a stimulus (S), and this conjunction is followed closely by the diminution in a need . . . there will be an increment in the tendency for that stimulus on subsequent occasions to evoke that reaction.
>
> (Atkinson, 1964, p. 164)

The third basic tenet is that man's socialization (learning) is accomplished through a process of *secondary reinforcement:* man has been observed to undergo a great deal of learning in the absence of *primary reinforcement.* It is thus speculated by learning theorists that stimuli that have in the past been closely and consistently followed ("associated") by primary reinforcement take on the capacity to serve as *secondary reinforcers.* The classical work by Pavlov clearly demonstrates the association valence assumed by *secondary reinforcers.* Pavlov had first presented food to a dog immediately after the sounding of a ticking metronome, producing the usual conditioned salivary response to the ticking metronome on subsequent occasions. Following this, the dog was exposed to a stimulus of a black square in its line of vision. Initially, the black square had no effect (no association) on the dog's behavior, but then the black square was presented and followed, after an interval of fifteen seconds, by the ticking of a metronome for thirty seconds, with no food being given. On the tenth exposure (association) of the black square by itself for twenty-five seconds, a total of 5.5 drops of saliva were secreted. This meant that the sound of the metronome, a stimulus that had earlier been associated with the ingestion of food, had acquired the capacity to act as a reinforcing agent. This has been referred to by S-R psychologists as *secondary reinforcement.*

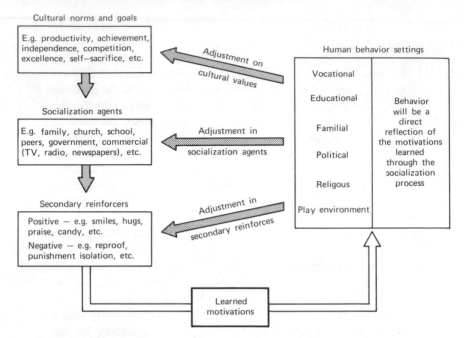

Figure 13 The Socialization Process at the Macrosystem Level

> Whenever a reaction (R) in temporal contintuity with a stimulus (S) and this conjunction is closely followed in time with the diminution of need ... or with a stimulus situation which has been closely and consistently associated with such a need diminution, there will result an increment to the tendency for that stimulus to evoke that reaction. ...
>
> (Atkinson, 1964, p. 166)

S-R experimental data show that a stimulus loses its capacity to serve as a secondary reinforcement if not consistently followed by primary need satisfaction (law of effect).

It is the secondary reinforcers in our society that shape the critical goals, decisions, and priorities of the individual. Our society is structured so that the ethos of our cultural heritage filters down to our smaller units (e.g., family, school, church, etc.), which in turn administer the secondary reinforcers to these cultural values. Presented in Figure 13 is a schematic representation of the socialization process from a macrosystem viewpoint.

Figure 13 points out the important fact that the impact of socialization is evident in all spheres of life. A need for achievement and status in our society is as clearly evident on the tennis court as it is in law courts, schools, vocations, churches, and synagogues. However, while some would be inclined to interpret the socialization process as a closed loop or a self-fulfilling prophesy, man's ability to transcend beyond his own hedonistic needs permits him to adjust to the socialization process despite the extreme conditioning he has been subjected to in his formative years. This is demonstrated by the reluctance on the part of some and the outright rebellion on the part of others to support extreme, Vince Lombardi[2] dehumanizing forms of competition in schools, playgrounds, and vocations. The same situation has developed around the use of corporal punishment in schools.

How does socialization work at the microsystem level? With particular application to play behavior, Figure 14 schematically demonstrates the socialization process that is most evident in a number of competitive play situations. From Figure 14, it may be seen why the aggressive and violent forms of play behavior, as well as the humane and respectful manifestations of play, at times appear no different than the act of salivating to the sound of the bell by Pavlov's dog. It is important for play theorists to recognize that play behavior should also be viewed as a learned (conditioned) connection or association between stimuli and responses. Thus, play behavior should be examined as a function of reinforcement (socialization) contingencies and incentives.

Learned motivations are the fourth basic tenet of S-R theory. Motivation as a determinant of human behavior is a product of the twentieth century. Although it has antecedents that date much further back, its modern character as an empirical science began to emerge near the turn of the century. William MacDougall (1918), early in the century became fascinated with the empirical analysis of the factors that initiate individual action and then direct it toward particular goal states. MacDougall, like all behavioral scientists following him, was concerned with a search for *why* man behaves the way he does. Alderman (1974), in his thorough view of the "underlying motivational dimensions of sport," reports that "fully one-third of all psychological literature is either directly or indirectly related to the topic of motivation" (p. 186). However, while Alderman carries out an extensive review of the nature and role of motivation in athletics and physical activity, to date, with the exception of some isolated efforts (Ellis, 1973; Neulinger, 1974; Csikszentmihalyi, 1974), such an extensive review of play behavior could not be brought to fruition because of the paucity of literature.

What is encompassed in the concept of motivation? Essentially, motives are learned stable personality dispositions of an individual toward all possible direct or vicarious experiences. In essence, one's motives will determine how one goes about satisfying all of one's needs, be they primary (food, excretion, warmth, sex, etc.) or secondary (creativity, affiliation, esteem, self-identity, etc.). Hence, one could theoretically assume that two individuals have the same need

---

[2] The late Vince Lombardi, former coach of the Green Bay Packers, had a poster painted for his players' dressing room that read, "Winning isn't everything, its the only thing."

160

Biological need
e.g., hunger

Stimulus ———————→

Hunger pains .... →

Parents with food ...... **Primary reinforcement** .... →

Parents with smiles and kisses, etc. .. **Secondary reinforcement** ...... →

Parents and other human beings become critical secondary reinforcement agents in the socialization process

Response

Searching for food

Reduce hunger pains

Comfort, satisfaction, acceptance, etc.

Social need
e.g., to be
accepted and
needed

Stimulus ———————→

Hits home runs .... →

Parents, coach, fans, peers cheer .. **Secondary reinforcement** ....→
agents

Response

Happy, secure, satisfied as a result of the positive reinforcement

From secondary reinforcement agency

Play activity:
baseball team

Play activity:
hockey team

Stimulus ———————→

Victorious in a fight with opponent .... →

Parents, coach, fans, peers cheer .. **Secondary reinforcement** ....→
agents

Response

Happy, secure, satisfied as a result of the positive reinforcement

From secondary reinforcement agency

Figure 14 The Socialization Process at the Microsystem Level

for creativity. However, if their personality dispositions are distinctly different, they are very likely to approach the satisfaction of that need differently. Alderman describes a motive as

> the tendency within him either *to do* that something or *not to do it*. A tendency is a psychological entity that determines a person's thoughts, feelings, and actions directed toward goals and/or certain kinds of behavior. A motive, then, can be defined as a latent, relatively stable personality characteristic which causes a person to be either attracted or repulsed by the consequences of particular courses of action; it is a tendency within the person directing his thoughts, feelings, and actions toward the service of goals or functions.
>
> (Alderman, 1974, p. 199–200)

While Atkinson (1964) reviews a plethora of motivational determinants of behavior, very few of these theories, with the exception of *achievement motivation,* have progressed beyond the MacDougall (1918), Murray (1938), Hull (1943), and Freud (1943) stage of conceptualization.

With the above background on the socialization model of human behavior, a number of major S-R theories of play will now be reviewed.

COMPENSATION THEORY OF PLAY

The compensation theory of play is an extension of the psychological defense mechanisms intended to explain how man has learned to deal with repeated or continuing conflict and frustration. Defense mechanisms are supposed to be learned modes of behavior intended to protect the individual's self-esteem and ego from excessive onslaught by the primitive *id* and social *superego*.

Hilgard and Atkinson (1967) ascribe two functions to defense mechanisms:

> Positively, they seek to maintain or enhance self-esteem; negatively, they seek to escape or defend against anxiety.
>
> (Hilgard and Atkinson, 1967, p. 515)

The defense mechanism commonly referred to as *compensation* is

> a strenuous effort to make up for failure or weakness in one activity through excelling in either a different or an allied activity. The boy who fails at games may compensate for the failure by excessive study in order to gain recognition in the classroom. Here a completely different activity substitutes for the athletic ineffectiveness.
>
> (Hilgard and Atkinson, 1967, p. 520)

Theoretical Definition:

People are motivated to play in order to compensate for a disability that delimits their behavior in other important spheres of life.

Often individuals are observed to use play behavior to excel in an area of endeavor where their performance is indeed unexpected, for example, the club-footed professional football goal kicker. Hilgard and Atkinson (1967) discuss this defense mechanism in the following terms:

> Overcompensation comes in an attempt to deny a weakness by trying to excel where one is weakest. The weakness thus acts as a goad to superior performance.... Illustrations are not hard to find. The power-driven dictators of recent times have been mostly men of short stature, who may have suffered a sense of physical powerlessness for which they overcompensated by a struggle for political might. Mussolini, Hitler, and Stalin were short, as was Napoleon before them. Roosevelt, a frail boy with weak eyes, took up boxing at Harvard and later led the Rough Riders during the Spanish-American War. Overcompensation is an energetic and effective way of meeting weakness.
>
> (Hilgard and Atkinson, 1967, p. 520)

Despite the articulation of the compensation theory of play as early as 1934 by Mitchell and Mason (cited in Witt and Bishop, 1970), it was Witt and Bishop (1970) who reworked the theory in social-psychological terms. They described the compensation theory of play as

> overcoming, by a specific displacement activity, a frustration induced by blockage of specific goal. According to the compensation theory, the individual would seek leisure activities that compensate for blocked goals in other spheres of endeavor.
>
> (Witt and Bishop, 1970, p. 66)

Kando and Summers (1971) discuss the common and traditional interpretation of the compensatory theory of play with reference to the juxtaposition of work and leisure:

> Compensatory hypotheses are implicitly employed in the suggestion that workers on automated assembly lines may require less recuperation as their work demand less physical effort, that they may seek creative nonwork outlets because their work is noncreative, and that job isolation may lead to increased leisure time spent with others; we find it also in the argument that for white-collar

workers, "leisure time . . . [may come] to mean an unserious freedom from the authoritarian seriousness of the Job."

(Kando and Summers, 1971, p. 314)

Recognizing the fact that the same preceding environmental situation may
cause different individual states and, conversely, that different preceding environmental situations may cause similar individual states, Kando and Summers
(1971) proposed two types of compensatory play theories.

1. Supplemental Compensatory Theory of Play

Supplemental compensation is comparable to the "motivation factors"
identified by industrial psychologists in the early 1950s, or the "growth
needs" discussed by Maslow (1955), or the "expressive needs" discussed
by the author (Levy 1971b). In *supplemental compensation,* man is
striving for "higher-order" need dissatisfaction. Today, Western society is
slowly approaching a state where man's survival is assured both on and off
the job. Thus his energy and focus is toward attaining the true expression
and definition of being human. Man in the *postindustrial age of leisure*
is concerned with optimizing his creativity, unique subjectivity, self-actualization, and several *secondary needs* associated with a higher degree of
human functioning. It is these goals that are the cathexes of man's concern
when engaged in supplemental compensatory play.

Kando and Summers (1971) summarize the supplemental compensation
theory of play in the following terms:

In supplemental compensation, desirable experiences, behavior,
psychological states (for example, autonomy, self-expression,
status) that are insufficiently present in the work situation are
pursued in a nonwork context.

(Kando and Summers, 1971, p. 314)

2. Reactive Compensatory Theory of Play

This form of compensation is an attempt to come to grips with the "hygiene factors" discussed by industrial psychologists in the early 1950s, or
the "deficiency motives" discussed by Maslow (1955), or the "instrumental needs" discussed by the author (Levy 1971b). In the process called *reactive compensation,* man is striving to overcome primary survival dissatis-
factions such as health hazards, physical fatigue, tension, and anxiety.
These are all elements which, if not brought under control, will ultimately
lead to the destruction of man or, if not to total destruction, to some serious physical or psychosocial deterioration. Thus, through play and recrea-

tion activities, man is attempting to regenerate his battery so that he can face the onslaught of dissatisfiers, again, the next day.

Kando and Summers (1971) summarize the reactive compensation theory of play by stating that

> in reactive compensation, undesirable work experiences are re-dressed in a nonwork setting. Examples would include "letting off steam" in response to job tension, resting from fatiguing work; in a word, all forms of recreation.
>
> (Kando and Summers, 1971, p. 314)

Critique of the Compensation Theory of Play

Psychologists tell us that whenever a person's progress toward a desired goal is blocked or otherwise interfered with, that person encounters *frustration* (Hilgard and Atkinson, 1967). How individuals have learned to respond to this frustration is critical to the theoretical posture of the compensation theory of play. If an individual has experienced a long history of frustrations (failures) in different human behavioral settings (school, work, family, etc.), that individual is very likely to have developed an avoidance-oriented type of personality disposition (avoidance motivated). Hence it is very unlikely that this individual will voluntarily seek out further potentially frustrating behavioral settings, such as the gymnasium, arts and crafts program, or library, to compensate for the long history of failure socialization. Recreators, social workers, and planners often express puzzlement and frustration at the "lack of motivation" on the part of avoidance-oriented citizens, who avoid participating in innovative and highly expensive play service systems. This has clearly been the experience with urban-oriented recreation and leisure systems whose success has been minimal to say the least.

Goal-seeking behavior in play will only be sought by those individuals who have experienced a greater degree of goal satisfaction than failure satisfaction. Thus, there appears to be a very important intervening variable between the experience of failure (blocked goals) in one situation and the compensation for that blocked goal in a play situation.

There now appears to be an overwhelming amount of scientific evidence that many individuals who have experienced long histories of failure, rejection, and incongruency with the norms of society will resort to behaviors such as *aggression, destructiveness, apathy, fantasy, stereotype* (abnormal fixation) and *regression* rather than to the more socially acceptable and positively reinforcing compensatory behavior. It thus appears that man's social learning history pre-empts his behavior across a number of environments as a result of the similarity of stimuli in these situations. This "generalization principle" brings us to our last S-R theory of play.

THE GENERALIZATION THEORY OF PLAY

Theoretical Definition:

Learned play behavior responses to one set of stimuli, will also be evoked to other stimuli closely associated with the original set of stimuli.

If a child learns to enjoy sliding down a small slide, that child will also enjoy sliding down the dangerous fire escape railing at the back of an apartment house. The more nearly alike the new stimuli are to the original, the more completely they will substitute for it. The psychological principle, called *generalization,* accounts for our ability to react to novel play situations in accordance with their similarities to familiar cues. Psychological experiments have shown that the amount of generalization drops off in a curvilinear function as the second stimulus becomes more and more dissimilar to the original conditioned stimulus.

Although the generalization theory is an old mainstay in the social learning psychology literature, it has only recently been applied to the investigation of play behavior (Kando and Summers, 1971; Harry, 1971; Witt and Bishop, 1970). Witt and Bishop (1970), who have been two of the most comprehensive researchers on the phenomenon of leisure, discuss the generalization theory of play:

> The concept of task generalization has only recently been applied to the investigation of leisure behavior... The idea behind task generalization is essentially the same as the older psychological concept of response generalization—the tendency for a stimulus, to which a particular response has been learned, to evoke similar responses. . . .
>
> The concept of task generalization has been applied primarily in the comparison of work and leisure to account for some people's tendency to choose leisure activities that are the same as, or similar to, the activities in their work. An example would be a college professor who uses his "leisure" time to read professional magazines or to attend special lectures. Presumably, such similarity in behavior is based on certain reinforcing events, but no attempt has been made to identify what they are, except to assume that somehow one's work is intrinsically motivating and rewarding. The task generalization concept is still somewhat vague, but might be useful for describing certain situation-leisure response sequences in which the leisure responses are similar to the responses observed in an antecedent situation.
>
> (Witt and Bishop, 1970, p. 66)

More recently, Harry (1971) stated that "it remains possible that attitudes generated at the workplace may be generalized to nonwork situations" (p. 302).

Citing Hendee (1969), Harry summarizes Hendee's research, which examined the effect of different occupations on outdoor recreation:

> Since rural occupations such as farming, mining, and logging are typically based on the exploitation and consumption of natural resources, they might encourage an exploitation attitude toward natural resources, thus allowing a generalization of workplace attitudes to outdoor recreational leisure situations. Urban occupations, on the other hand, are typically in manufacturing or service industries far removed from the natural environment. Urban residence may thus allow the development of appreciative attitudes toward nature. . . . A utilitarian attitude toward nature may thus be associated with "harvesting" recreational activities—fishing, hunting, and the like—whereas an appreciative orientation is more closely linked to the realization of aesthetic and social values in outdoor activities.
>
> (Hendee, 1969, p. 33, in Harry, 1971, p. 302)

In light of the above discussion by Hendee (1969) on the types of occupations associated with rural and urban residence, Harry (1971) put forth the following hypotheses:

> 1. Persons having occupations which required the direct exploitation of natural resources—farming, mining, logging—will have more exploitative attitudes toward nature than those having other occupations. This hypothesis covers those cases in which work and leisure situations have important aspects in common—as with nature-exploitative occupations and outdoor recreation—and as such asserts that these individuals will have a more extractive and manipulatory attitude toward natural resources in their leisure situations.
>
> 2. Persons having nature-exploitative occupations will look upon outdoor recreational situations as being less appropriate for the expression of social and aesthetic values than those having non-nature-exploitative occupations. This hypothesis argues that, by virtue of its status within the workplace as a resource, the natural environment will serve less as a vehicle for the expression of the social and aesthetic values which are customarily expressed in leisure situations.
>
> (Harry, 1971, p. 303)

Although Harry's (1971) research design is open to some criticism because of his failure to control and partial out the effects of many intervening variables, his findings did support the generalization theory of play. He found "that there is some direct transfer of occupational culture to the leisure situation" (Harry, 1971, p. 308).

Kando and Summers (1971), who were responsible for proposing a distinction between two types of compensation theories of play (supplemental and reactive compensation), have described the generalization theory of play in terms of "spillover hypotheses":

> The spillover hypotheses are equally common. For example, jobs requiring constant disciplined activity may lead some workers to compulsive leisure patterns of being "busy-occupied" and "passing time" since "attitudes acquired during work become so deeply ingrained that they are often carried into the life off the job". . . . Katz . . . observes that "work habits and interests of the white-collar worker will spill over into his family and community life," while Gerstl . . . has shown that, for some occupations, the presence of specific occupational skills and interests influence the choice of leisure pursuits.
>
> Thus spillover occurs when styles of behavior or of psychological functioning suitable for, or acquired in, the performance of work are transferred to a nonwork context.
>
> (Kando and Summers, 1971, pp. 314–315)

Kando and Summers have pointed out a very serious possible limitation in the generalization theory of play discussed by Witt and Bishop (1970). They caution against assuming that all behaviors learned in the work place will be generalized to play behavior settings. There may indeed only be selective generalizations from work to play. Kando and Summers express this selective spillover characteristic in the following terms:

> Two recent articles . . . have referred to this process as *generalization* rather than *spillover*. We prefer the descriptive if somewhat inelegant term spillover to generalization, however, since it avoids the implication that behavioral or psychological traits acquired in work will be applied generally to many leisure activities rather than specifically to few, an issue which is still problematic.
>
> (Kando and Summers, 1971, p. 314)

Kando and Summers reiterate a need to interpret the compensation and generalization theories of play vis-à-vis a paradigm that examines the individual and environmental determinants of play:

> Despite their wide use and strong appeal, with few exceptions (Witt and Bishop, 1970), writers have applied compensatory and spillover hypotheses speculatively ad hoc; there has been little systematic effort to specify the conditions under which compensation or spillover is likely to occur, or to explicate the underlying mechanisms involved.
>
> (Kando and Summers, 1971, p. 315)

Critique of the Generalization Theory of Play

The major criticism of the generalization theory of play is very similar to that levied against the compensation theory of play, that is, the difficulty of explaining the relationship between antecedent environmental impacts and resulting individual states that play behavior may seek to satisfy. Kando and Summers (1971) summarize the difficulty of empirically validating the compensation and generalization theories of play as follows:

> The compensatory and spillover mechanisms are not mutually exclusive, and both may operate at the same time for the same individual. For example, managers and blue-collar workers who both experience their work as insufficiently creative may seek compensation in leisure pursuits. But the manager may compensate by writing, whereas, the blue-collar worker might seek creative outlets requiring the use of tools. But the fact that compensation and spillover are alternative modes of explanation has some potentially serious pitfalls. For unless one can specify the conditions under which compensation or spillover are likely to occur, one or the other hypothesis may be used to explain any relationship between work and nonwork. For example, if we find isolation at work associated with a high degree of sociability in leisure, this can be accounted for by compensation. Clearly, a theory which permits anything to be explained after the fact is completely lacking in predictive power. The situation is further complicated by the possibility that some workers may respond to a work situation by compensating whereas for other workers the identical situation might produce an opposite spillover response. Thus, while dull, repetitive jobs may lead some workers to compensate by seeking stimulating or creative nonwork alternatives, for others the same job might produce habits of passive mindlessness that would reflect in their leisure.

Where such dual patterns occurred in nearly equal proportions there would be no discernible effect of work on nonwork.

Difficulties such as these, resulting from the overlap and potential contradictions, can be resolved only by theoretically specifying the precise conditions under which compensation or spillover is likely, or by utilizing research techniques that discriminate between instances of spillover and those of compensation.

(Kando and Summers, 1971, pp. 315-316)

CONFLICT-ENCULTURATION THEORIES OF PLAY

To date, the most articulate and scientific undertaking utilizing the S-R learning model to study the socialization theories of play has been accomplished by Roberts and Sutton-Smith (1962), Sutton-Smith, Roberts, and Kozelka (1963), Sutton-Smith, Rosenberg, and Morgan (1963) and Sutton-Smith and Roberts (1964).

Theoretical Definition:
Play gives the individual the opportunity to engage in social learning without the fear of experiencing serious repercussions that would be incurred if the same learning attempts met with failure in the real world. Sutton-Smith (1968) views play as the exercise of voluntary social learning. Through play the child learns the motivation to control or master his or her environment in a safe and optimal level of anxiety.

Based upon extensive cross-cultural research, as well as research in the United States, it was clearly documented that there exists a strong relationship between child-rearing practices of various cultures and the dominant games played by those societies. According to these authors, different child-rearing patterns produce a host of anxieties, and children would attempt to assuage their stress by playing games at a microscopic level that were models of the macroscopic society. Taking part in these forms of play would better prepare and socialize (teach) the child to deal with society's goals. This relationship was termed the "conflict-enculturation hypothesis."

Variations in the distributions of games among cultures throughout the world, and in the game playing of American children and adults, are related to variations in child training. It is held that these relationships can be viewed in terms of psychological conflicts which lead people to become involved in games and other models.

(Roberts and Sutton-Smith, 1962, p. 166)

These relationships suggested a conflict-enculturation hypothesis of model involvement which stated that conflicts induced by

Table 4 Expressive Game Model

Outcome Determined by:	Skill	Strategy	Chance
Skill	Must	Must not	Must not
Strategy	May	Must	Must not
Chance	May	May	Must

> social learning in childhood and later . . . lead to involvement in expressive models, such as games, through which these conflicts are assuaged and as a result of which a process of buffered learning occurs, which has enculturative value for the competences required in the culture. . . .
>
> Sutton-Smith, Roberts, and Kozelka, 1963, p. 26)

Roberts and Sutton-Smith (1962) grouped games into three classes on the basis of elements determining outcome. Table 4 schematically represents the Roberts and Sutton-Smith specifications of game types with a clarification made by Ball (1972). They then went on to study the association with specific child-training variables (responsibility, obedience, self-reliance, achievement, nurturance, and independence) in 111 different societies. Following extensive secondary analysis of the 1959 Cross-Cultural Survey Files and Human Relations Area Files at Yale University, the following major findings were reported:

> *Games of Strategy*
>
> Tribes possessing games of strategy were found more likely to have high ratings on child-training procedures which involved rewarding children for being obedient, punishing for being disobedient, anxiety about nonperformance of obedience, conflict over obedience, and high frequency of obedient behaviors. . . .
>
> *Games of Chance*
>
> When tribes with games of chance were compared with those lacking such games, relationships were noted with reward for responsibility, frequency of responsibility, and anxiety about the performance of achievement. . . .
>
> *Games of Physical Skill*
>
> Games of physical skill, whether considered separately as pure physical skill or as physical skill and strategy jointly, show significant relationships with reward for achievement and frequency of achievement.
>
> (Roberts and Sutton-Smith, 1962, pp. 170–174)

Table 5 Game Models and Play Behavior

Expressive Game Models	Macrocosmic Scale (Real World)	Microcosmic Scale	
		Direct Play Behavior	Vicarious Play Behavior
Physical skill	Building a house	Building a model house	Reading about great builders
Strategy	Investing in the stock market	Bridge, monopoly, poker	Watching a TV program emphasizing strategy—prize programs, detective programs, etc.
Chance	Lotteries, gold and oil finds	Horse racing, dice games, roulette games	Reading books and watching films that emphasize chance outcomes

In order to demonstrate the potential use of their ethnographic research for those engaged in play service systems, Roberts and Sutton-Smith proceeded to discuss games as being manifested at different scales of participation. Table 5 is an elaboration of that presented by Roberts and Sutton-Smith (1962) to demonstrate the relationship between game models and play behaviors.

Roberts and Sutton-Smith (1964) summarize their conflict-enculturation theory with the following three implications:

1. That there is an overall process of cultural patterning whereby society induces conflict in children through its child-training processes.

2. That society seeks through appropriate arrays and varieties of ludic models to provide an assuagement of these conflicts by an adequate representation of their emotional and cognitive polarities in ludic structure.

3. That through these models society tries to provide a form of buffered learning through which the child can make enculturative step-by-step progress toward adult behavior.

The cross-cultural research by Roberts and Sutton-Smith (1962) was extended to include differences in play behavior as a result of sex–child-rearing interactions (Sutton-Smith, Rosenberg, and Morgan, 1963; Sutton-Smith, 1965) and to include adults and children in different socioeconomic classes in the United States. Sutton-Smith, Roberts, and Kozelka (1963) put forth the following adult game predictions based upon the earlier discussed conflict-enculturation hypothesis:

1. Because games of strategy are associated with severe primary socialization, psychological discipline, high obedience training and complex cultures, they will be preferred in this culture by the persons who have had greater experience of such a child training pattern, that is, the higher status groups as compared with the lower, and women as compared with men.

2. Because games of chance are associated cross-culturally with high routine responsibility training, punishment for the display of initiative, and belief in the benevolence of the gods, they will be preferred in this culture by members of the lower status groups as compared with the higher and by women as compared with men.

3. Because games of physical skill are associated cross-culturally with high achievement training, they will be preferred in this culture by the upper as compared with the lower status groups and by men as compared with women.

(Sutton-Smith, Roberts and Kozelka, 1963, p. 16)

As would be exptected, Sutton-Smith and his colleagues strongly confirmed their *conflict-enculturation* hypothesis with the American adult sample. These authors present four major propositions that are directed at explaining their *conflict-enculturation* hypothesis. The first two propositions explain the *conflict* part of their hypothesis and the latter two propositions discuss the *enculturation* ("social learning" and "personality adjustment") aspect.

Conflict (assuaged through expressive game models)

1. *Conflict induced in children or adults by achievement training arouses in them curiosity about those expressive models that contain a representation of winning and losing as a result of the application of power and skill.*

The hypothesis holds that learning can produce conflicts (a balance of approach and avoidance tendencies), which heighten an individual's interest in the variables which are involved in his conflict. . . . Thus playing games of physical skill was found in tribal cultures with a high frequency of achievement training, a high reward for achievement, but at the same time high punishment for nonperformance of achievement. It would seem that children, seriously limited in size, skill and power, yet motivated to achieve and anxious about being able to do so, can seldom find in full scale cultural participation sufficient behavioral opportunities to match adequately both their desire and their anxious incompetence. . . .

2. *Persons who are made curious about achievement by their conflict over it readily become involved in achievement as represented in expressive models.*

Desiring to beat opponents but frightened to lose, the child is motivated to explore and to be curious about opportunities to deal with his conflict in a more manageable fashion. He is attracted to a variety of culturally provided expressive models. Some of these may be vicarious as in folktales, comics, and television and may suggest that the small participant can win (Jack and the Giant Killer, Mighty Mouse), or that the central figure may have powers to overcome insuperable odds (Superman). Or the expressive models may be of the participant variety like physical skill games in which the consequences of winning and losing are drastically reduced. Noticeably, in the earliest forms of physical skill and strategy games such as tagging and hide-and-seek, both winning and losing are episodic and their intensity is decreased by the instability of the sides. There is, in addition, no final explicit outcome so that there is a lack of clarity about which players have actually won or lost. This reduction in the objective clarity of winning and losing, however, permits rather than prevents subjective estimates of success to assume relatively egocentric proportions. Thus Piaget has shown very young children all imagine they have won in the games that they play. And Maccoby has demonstrated that six-year-olds anticipate success with their peers in a way far exceeding the limits of possibility. With the passage of chronological age there is a developmental change in the models in which children can find a statement for their problems of winning and losing. The diffuse skill models of the earlier years give way to games in which the requirements for winning are more rigorous and the penalties for losing more obvious (marbles, football). Children of different maturity levels, therefore, can find a matching for the maturity of their achievement conflicts somewhere in each of the many series to be found in the cultural model array of tales and games, etc.

Enculturation ("social learning" and "personality adjustment")

a. Social Learning

3. *In the case of children, and to a lesser extent adults, participation in achievement games contributes to physical, intellectual and social learning, each of which in due course may contribute to the participant's ability to survive in the full scale success system of the larger systems of the larger culture. . . .*

The argument is, that because games reduce the scale on which the competition occurs, then winning and losing as complex interpersonal events become more readily assimilable by the child. Even loss is more acceptable when it is known that victory may occur in a second episode. The dangers and threats associated with both winning and losing are thus much reduced, while the gratification in winning is not. Furthermore, losers are defended by the play convention that the game is for "fun" anyway. . . . The view that expressive models . . . exist for the very reason that they can convey to participants information which cannot be assimilated more simply nor without overwhelming anxiety in large-scale cultural participation.

b. Personality Adjustment

4. *Expressive models contribute to a player's adjustment to the cultural pressures which have given rise to his conflict (child training pressures for children, current success pressures for adults), because they are exercises in mastery.*

By scaling down the conflict dimensions the games give their participants the confidence that winning and losing as complex interpersonal processes and anxiety inducing ones can be mastered. It is in this sense that the game is a mechanism of personality adjustment. It is legitimate to call this an enculturative function, however, because the adjustment involved means that the underlying process of achievement training adopted by the parents has greater assurance of success, and that the pressures put upon children to achieve and be concerned about achievement will not lead to overwhelming dispair and inferiority. Likewise the adults' contemporary pressures towards success may be similarly reduced to assimilable proportions.
(Sutton-Smith, Roberts, and Kozelka, 1963, pp. 24–27)

The social learning model of play behavior may also be used to explain differences that exist between male and female children's play patterns. Rosenberg and Sutton-Smith (1960) stated this problem in the following terms:

It is commonly assumed that children's games are one of the ways in which boys and girls learn appropriate sex role behavior in their

> own society. It follows that differences in the games chosen by
> boys and girls will reflect their perceptions of behaviors appropri-
> ate to their own sex.
>
> (Rosenberg and Sutton-Smith, 1960, p. 165)

Using a game checklist made up of 181 games, Rosenberg and Sutton-Smith
compared male and female differences in game play activities. The checklist
yielded eighteen items chosen more frequently by boys than girls and forty
items chosen more frequently by girls than boys.

Rosenberg and Sutton-Smith, in their discussion of the findings, come out in
strong support of an emerging dominant female play role. From their discussion
below and from more recent trends in our liberalized socialization practices, it
would appear that the female role is being expanded, and the male role is being
contracted. What effects will this change in male and female socialization practices have on play service systems of the future? Clearly the merging, blending,
and overlapping of sex roles is evident today in "unisex" clothes, hair styles, and
other traditional bastions of sex distinction. The popularity of male versus
female athletic events (tennis, basketball, swimming, wrestling, etc.) on national
television is another indication that ways are being found to integrate the two
roles when it comes to play behavior. Rosenberg and Sutton-Smith (1960)
pointed out this trend in the blurring of sex roles in play long before it was a
fashionable topic of academic enquiry and commercial exploitation:

> Boys tend to name (select) fewer items which significantly differ-
> entiate them from girls. This finding is consonant with present
> day theories which emphasize the increasing masculinity of the
> feminine self-concept ... many of the games typically seen as
> masculine (baseball, basketball) did not differentiate significantly
> between the sexes at this early age level.
>
> In light of the present findings, it seems probable that an exten-
> sion of the female role perception is occurring in games. The mas-
> culine role appears to have become confined, yielding fewer, wide-
> ly acknowledged ways of seeing the self. It has been observed else-
> where that although modern boys spend as much or more time at
> their play than their predecessors, the variety of their games has
> been considerably reduced.
>
> Brown suggests that there are signs of convergence of the two
> sex roles in our society. The present limited investigation supports
> only the conclusion that the girls now show greater preference for
> boy play roles, not that boys show any greater preference for girl
> play roles. It shows, in additon, that the girls retain their own dis-
> tinctive play roles. The change appears not to be one of role con-
> vergence, but of expansion of female role perception and con-

traction of male role perception.

(Rosenberg and Sutton-Smith, 1960, p. 169)

Most recently, the Roberts and Sutton-Smith (1962) conflict-enculturation theory has been field-tested by Eifermann (1971), an Israeli female psychologist who, in working with rural and urban children, postulated the following hypothesis:

Their [Roberts and Sutton-Smith, 1962] hypothesis leads to the prediction that rural children, who have more opportunities than do urban children for real participation in the adult world (e.g., helping at work), should develop fewer or less intensive conflicts and, hence, a more restricted interest in competitive game styles.

(Eifermann, 1971, p. 291)

Following field observations in three urban and three rural schools, Eifermann (1971), with the exception of one Arab rural village, failed to support the conflict interpretation of play by Roberts and Sutton-Smith (1962). She reported these findings:

The fact that significantly more Jewish rural children participate in competitive games as compared with their urban peers and, moreover, that the difference established is clearly not just a cultural one . . . excludes the possibility of interpreting the results simply in terms of relative cultural differences. To this should be added the fact that a large proportion of fathers in the Arab [rural] village [this village was low in competitive rule-governed games] are employed as construction workers outside their village and are, as a result, often absent from home. The conflict interpretation would lead to the interpretation that conditions should be conducive to greater game involvement than conditions in the more stable Jewish village, which is almost totally agricultural.

(Eifermann, 1971, p. 292)

Thus, while Eifermann (1971) confesses that "the conflict interpretation of game involvement needs revision" (p. 292), she presents reliable data that strongly support the enculturation component of the Roberts and Sutton-Smith (1962) hypothesis:

Now in urban communities, the transition from childhood to adulthood is, in general, less smooth than in rural communities. The roles and modes of interaction acquired in the particularistic family setting will be even less relevant to those required for appropriate

> social behavior in urban surroundings. Preparation for adult life in achievement-oriented societies can be better obtained during childhood and particularly during adolescence by interaction in age-homogeneous groups in which the processes of status acquisition and of achievement evaluation are more like those going on in adult life than those in the family setting.
>
> (Eifermann, 1971, p. 293)

Based upon this theory, Eifermann proved that urban Israeli children play in age-homogeneous groups more often than rural (kibbutz) children.

> In accordance with this theory . . . one should expect that a higher percentage of children will play in age-homogeneous groups in urban than in rural schools. This expectation has indeed been verified in our finding: 66 percent of all players in rural schools played in age-homogeneous groups versus 79 percent in town schools.
>
> (Eifermann, 1971, p. 293)

It would thus appear that the rural environment facilitates an earlier blending of the microworld and macroworld. This may be confirmed by anyone who has seen young farm children riding tractors or assuming critical roles in the management of farm operations, whereas in the urban environment the young children must rely on the microworld of play for a greater contribution to their enculturation (socialization) process.

Play Paradigm

The conflict-enculturation hypothesis of play clearly attempts to interpret play in terms of the determinants, structure, and consequences discussed in the play paradigm. The interpretation of the conflict-enculturation hypothesis vis-à-vis the play paradigm is presented in Figure 15.

ATTRIBUTION THEORY OF PLAY

Learning theorists have pointed out that as a result of socialization by primary (family, relatives, friends, etc.) and secondary (school, church, government, etc.) agents in society, individuals become predisposed to attribute responsibility for the consequences of their behavior differentially. Terms such as "competence," "effectance," "freedom," "inner- and outer-directed autonomy," "causality," "mastery," and "self-confidence" have all been used to denote the "degree to which man is able and believes himself capable of controlling the important events in his life space" (Lefcourt, 1966, p. 186).

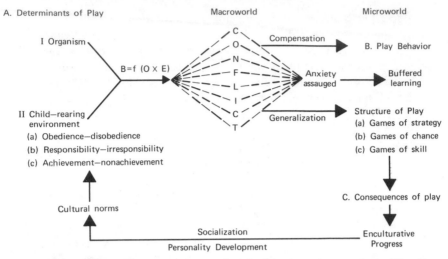

Figure 15   The Conflict-Enculturation Hypothesis in Terms of the Play Paradigm

Over the last two decades, a number of attribution theories have appeared. One of these theories, which has received strong empirical support from clinical, vocational, educational, rehabilitative, and play research, is the internal-external locus of control theory originally developed by Rotter (1966) and de Charms (1968).

Theoretical Definition:
Play is determined by the way in which individuals attribute outcomes and consequences of their behavior. An internal locus of control motivational disposition would direct the individual toward forms of play where the outcome was, to a great degree, under the player's control. On the other hand, an external locus of control motivational disposition would direct the individual toward forms of play where the outcome was, to a great degree, out of the player's control.

Lynn, Phelan, and Kiker (1969) in a study entitled "Beliefs in Internal-External Control of Reinforcement and Participation in Group and Individual Sports," utilized Rotter's (1966) theory to test their hypothesis, which was

> that those Ss in this study (young men, 12 to 15 years of age) and classified as consistently committed to group-team sports endeavor (basketball), would be more actively engaged in striving hence more internally oriented. We further hypothesized that the non-participating Ss would be significantly less internally controlled, and Ss in individual sports would be closer in their orientation to

that of the non-participants.

(Lynn, Phelan and Kiker, 1969, p. 552)

The authors, in a sketchy methodological discussion that is difficult to replicate, confirmed their hypothesis that for

> adolescents, active participants in team sports were significantly more "inner controlled" than the other groups. As predicted; scores of Ss in individual sports approached those of non-participants in showing high alienation or outer-controlled scores.
>
> On the Rotter I-E scale, these junior high Ss earned higher "inner controlled" scores than the college students in the normative group. Team members have higher "inner controlled" scores than all other Ss, also their variability is less than that for Ss in individual sports. Our Ss in individual sports are not significantly different from the non-participant group in degree of alienation shown by their scores on the Rotter I-E Scale.
>
> (Lynn, Phelan and Kiker, 1969, p. 553)

Schneider (1968), in a study whose purpose was to "establish a relationship between . . . locus of control . . . and preferences for participating in skill versus chance activities . . . " (p. 334), points out the *structural* differences between skill and chance activities and the motivational attributes of internal versus externally motivated dispositions.

> It was felt that measurement of the locus of control construct could logically be simplified by means of examining preferences for participation in skill versus chance activities. Skill activities permit the individual to test the effectiveness of his behavior, since success or failure on these tasks is usually seen as being contingent on the adequacy of the individual's performance. Chance activities, on the other hand, do not permit this evaluation since success or failure on these tasks is usually seen as being unrelated to any behaviors in the individual's response repertoire. Therefore, it would be expected that the individual who generally expects to be internally controlled would prefer participating in skill activities since he cannot confirm his expectancies of internal control in chance activities. The externally controlled individual, however, should prefer chance activities which minimize the risk of failure or of success as well as the amount of involvement required, because he believes that "there is no behavior in his repertoire that will allow him to be effective in securing the goal. . . "
>
> (Schneider, 1968, pp. 334–335)

The hypothesis by Schneider (1968) that a predisposition for skill activities should be associated with an internal locus of control and that chance activities should be associated with an external locus of control was strongly supported for male subjects and not supported for female subjects. Schneider explains this sex discrepancy according to a social learning model; that is, women in our society have been socialized into taking part in more passive, less skill-oriented activities. Schneider summarizes this discrepancy in sex role by stating:

> However, the findings for females do support this hypothesis. Since both the skill and the chance activities used in this study are ones which females do not ordinarily participate in or have direct experience with, preference for any of these activities probably reflects something other than the skill-chance dimension. Therefore, females' preference for a particular activity may not have been related to their locus of control, possibly to their preference for a more or less masculine, passive or novel type of activity.
>
> (Schneider, 1968, p. 336)

In an unpublished manuscript entitled Play: A Learning Medium in School, Levy and Schultz (1971) provide the following definition of the locus of control as it applies to play behavior:

> Internal
> Locus of Control — refers to a transaction controlled by the child.
> Co-operative
> Locus of Control — refers to a transaction controlled jointly by the child and one or more other subjects.
> External
> Locus of Control — refers to a transaction controlled by an external agent.
>
> (Levy and Schultz, 1971, p. 6-7)

Building upon the work of Levy and Schultz (1971), Larsen (1973) developed a children's play scale for measuring internal and external locus of control in an unstructured play situation. Using Peanuts-style cartoons and a brief verbal explanation to describe the play situation and outcomes, Larsen compiled twenty-eight play situations (seven male play situations, seven female play situations and fourteen male and female play situations). To date, with the exception of the Larsen (1973) attempt, no research instruments have been reported that measure the degree to which the child or adult is predisposed to attribute outcome in play to either internal or external forces.

SUMMARY

It would appear that the socialization process predisposes individuals to expect certain outcomes (R) following certain environmental situations and experiences (S). Thus, in every novel situation confronting the individual the motivational dispositions direct behavior toward gratification of primary and secondary order needs. Play behavior, while possessing many unique characteristics, is still subject to the laws of social learning and is a product of socialization experiences ingrained into the individual. It therefore follows that socialization determines not only whether the individual gambles, plays bridge, skis, or attends the opera but also how the individual behaves while at the racetrack, card club, ski slope, or opera hall.

STUDY SUGGESTIONS

1. Using the "socialization process at the macrosystem level" in Figure 13, trace the development of a play activity in our society. For example the popular play activity, camping, could have the following development:
   (a) Cultural norms and goals — independence, pioneer spirit, etc.
   (b) Socialization agents — parents, grandparents, uncles, aunts, cousins, etc.
   (c) Secondary reinforcers — recognition and praise for earning camping skill badges; parents avid campers; etc.
   (d) Learned motivations — approach unknown situations with a positive attitude toward success (solo canoeing)
   (e) Human behavior settings — school (athletic leadership), church (cub leader, father a scoutmaster), play (active tipper)

2. Using the definitions of *internal* and *external locus of control*, rate the various play activities listed on the next page. Following this rating, compare your responses with those of the rest of the class.

3. Based upon your own intuitive play experiences, what are the top three internally and externally oriented locus of control play activities? How does your list compare with those of others?

Most Internal Activity_____

Second Most Internal Activity_____

Third Most Internal Activity_____

Most External Activity_____

Second Most External Activity_____

Third Most External Activity_____

Locus of Control Scale

Play Activity:	High Internal	Moderate Internal	Undecided	Moderate External	High External
Kite flying	2	1	0	−1	−2
Weight lifting	2	1	0	−1	−2
Cross—country skiing	2	1	0	−1	−2
Photography hobby	2	1	0	−1	−2
Playing bridge	2	1	0	−1	−2
Running a foot race	2	1	0	−1	−2
Bingo	2	1	0	−1	−2
Flying	2	1	0	−1	−2
Climbing a mountain	2	1	0	−1	−2
Writing poetry	2	1	0	−1	−2
Riding bicycle	2	1	0	−1	−2
Downhill skiing	2	1	0	−1	−2
Watching TV	2	1	0	−1	−2
Playing bridge	2	1	0	−1	−2
Playing Monopoly	2	1	0	−1	−2

11
Play and the Future: A Time for Renaissance

We are slowly awakening to the truth. Teachers, parents, psychiatrists, planners, social workers, and theologians are all beginning to recognize that *play* is the primary activity for confirming our *existence* and affirming our *worth* (Kusyszyn, 1977). If, as a society, we have erred in this century, it is in our failure to realize the importance of play. We have missed this point because we have not understood play behavior as a form of human expression throughout the human life cycle. Play is not, as the theorists would lead us to believe, simply a method of releasing surplus energy or processing information. Nor is it a utilitarian activity preparing us for the more serious and important adult roles in the real world.

Play, as Plato described it, is the answer to the puzzle of our existence. Play is where mankind lives. The goal of each of us, in a simple and trite term, is *happiness*. We are happy when we become one with ourselves, others, the immediate environment, and the universe in general. Play certainly provides the opportunity for this *cosmological unity*.

What are some of the future implications of this definition of play on the person and society?

COLLECTIVE SEARCH FOR IDENTITY: A NEW ROMANTICISM

Although there may be some strong debates raging between sociologists and economists as to whether we have indeed reached the age of leisure, it is not necessary for the age of leisure to reach its zenith to see that people are already playing harder than ever before, longer than ever before, and in new, innovative, and exciting ways. Play is "busting out all over" and unleashing a plethora of life-styles and subterranean energies: parachute jumping, skateboarding, orienteering, survival camping, hang gliding, skin diving, surfing, spiritual meetings, and communal holidays.

What are all these people searching for while risking their lives, money or spouse? Abraham Maslow the American ego psychologist, described it as a "peak experience" brought about by affirmation of our identity and confirmation of

183

our existence. Our technological and computerized approach to most jobs and the loss of the work ethic among the majority of workers has given rise to a search for identity through one's leisure role rather than through the work role. Hence the loss of status, satisfaction, prestige, and self-actualization that were once associated with the work role means that the identity search must be manifested in play behavior.

The number of play identities will increase, and whereas in the past, these identities connoted a parasitic or nonproductive life — philanderer, camper, tennis bum, ski bum, adventurer, traveler — today they have come to have a charismatic halo around them. Recently, it has become very popular for many students to travel either before beginning a long stint of education or during their formal education. This trend has been severely criticized by the more conservative members of our society, who object to the "survival" techniques adopted by these students while on their travels. However, while these conservative groups compare the traveling students to a group of gypsies or hoboes who beg free meals and lodgings, it would be more realistic to interpret this manifestation as another example of a search for identity. There can be little doubt that as the opportunity to find meaningful work diminishes and state support of basic survival becomes a right, there will be an increase in the number of "nonworking" (play) models for identity.

The crucial question facing professionals who monitor play behavior will deal with the *morality of play*. The writing is already on the wall! There is not only a change from a *work identity* to a *play identity* but there is also a concomitant change in *ethos*. This is becoming quite evident from the recent Supreme Court decisions on pornography and drugs — that it will be *right* to derive satisfaction, identity, and fun from play behavior formerly considered *wrong*. Thus, we see that our society is moving toward the moral dictum that the individual has the right to any form of play. Taken to its ultimate philosophical limits, this dictum states that all individuals have the right to find themselves — to achieve self-actualization through smoking pot, watching the movie *Deep Throat,* or parachute jumping. Hedonism in its most crude and vile forms receives societal support when it becomes translated as a *right* to search for identity. Thus the logical argument is that play, which does something for my identity, is *right* because I have a *right* to an identity. But what happens when every person in our society is permitted to assert this right? The result is both progressive and regressive. We have art, culture, sports, philosophy, religion, love, and humanity in all their beautiful manifestations. On the regressive side we have sexual perversions, mental breakdowns, crime, bodily deterioration, and a host of other undesirable human and environmental indicators. Following the trend of our laissez-faire society, there is no point at which society can look at the player and say, "Your lifestyle for achieving self-identity is not in harmony with the collective needs of society."

Hence, our society, which has adopted the philosophy that any means is justified in reaching a state of identity, has gone beyond collective hedonism. It will be encumbent upon the play leaders of the future to educate the citizens of tomorrow in the wholesome and growth-producing expressions of self-identity and actualization if we are to survive through the age of leisure.

TOWARD A WORK-LEISURE AS PLAY SOCIETY

In order to comprehend the contemporary relationship between work and leisure, a brief statement on the holistic nature of human behavior is in order. The human organism is biologically designed to operate through two complementary phases — *effort* and *relaxation.* The biological sciences have provided us with some helpful analogies when they tell us that *effort* is to *relaxation* as catabolism is to anabolism and systole is to diastole. How does effort differ from work and relaxation differ from leisure?

When Plato enunciated that man was born to work, some assume he was echoing the scriptural Commandment, "Six days shalt thou labor and do all thy work." The protestant work ethic still accepts Plato's dictum without serious reservation. Man, needless to say, *was not born to work.* Man was born with an innate capacity for *effort,* which can be dissipated in any activity, be it sailing, cooking, sex, chess, Frisbee, or art.

This innate capacity for effort is the antithesis of the features required to function in the modern work place. Effort is *autonomous, intrinsically motiva ted,* and *stressful,* whereas work is *allonomous, extrinsically motivated,* and *boring* or *overarousing.*

Differentiating effort and work along these parameters helps to explain why some individuals enjoy their jobs and others find them dissatisfying. It is not the unique nature of man's activity (e.g., farming, carpentry, painting, writing, etc.) that makes it work or leisure, but the extent to which the effort involved is inner-directed or outer-directed. Autonomous effort is *competence* and *freedom* in action. Such effort is neither boring nor overarousing; that is, it produces optimal stress. Optimal stress is produced when one has no alternative but to take *responsibility* for one's actions. By taking responsibility for one's actions, one becomes the sole creator of one's effort, one's self, and one's destiny.

Autonomous effort characterizes the intenseness of the pole vaulter, high jumper, or golfer, oblivious of the crowd and unconcerned about the possible consequences of success or failure; or the dedication of the poet, writer, or artist, expressing an inner need for effectance and unconcerned about worldly gain or recognition. All these people are motivated by their intrinsic satisfaction that comes with the freedom of self-expression. Often we hear that competition and stress are to be avoided in healthy interactions. Quite the contrary indeed! Autonomous effort is the genesis of all positive questioning, conflict, and competition. It is only through this healthy risk, challenge, and adventure that we prod our mind and body to undertake new problems and solutions. On the other hand, allonomous or extrinsic-dependent effort is the genesis of unhealthy, over-arousing forms of competition. Autonomous effort leads to healthy competition for the purpose of *improving* ourselves, whereas allonomous effort leads to unhealthy competition for the purpose of *proving* ourselves to external forces.

During the *effort* phase, the individual is logical, rational, literal, deductive, and extremely focused on the activity at hand. This extreme self-commitment requires a great deal of energy. In order to complement this period of dedication, effort, and competence, the organism has the biological and psychological capacity to *relax*. It is during this complementary phase that the body and mind can reflect, synthesize, and engage in inductive, nonfocused behavior. Effort is *output* and relaxation is *input*. The relaxation or leisure phase of life has been of great concern to authorities dating back to early times, when idleness was viewed as a cause of unrest and rebellion. The "give them bread and circuses" philosophy has permeated into the twentieth century, where we have a society overly dependent on external resources for satisfying the relaxation phase of life — hence the tremendous reliance upon television, spectator sports, energy-consuming activities, and many other consumer-oriented forms of relaxation. It is not that these external resources are bad in and of themselves; it is simply that we have become extremely dependent upon them rather than on our inner resources. Play, then, is the complementary relationship between *effort* (output) and *relaxation* (input) at all levels of human biology and psychology.

From the above effort–relaxation paradigm, it is obvious that we want and need effort (work), and we want and need relaxation (leisure). When work (effort) and leisure (relaxation) take that form, the traditional dichotomy of work and leisure, which had each of them subordinate to the other, is removed.

What are the future implications of this *work-leisure as play society?*

1. By embracing this work-leisure as play society, one would move to smaller scales of producing and organizing. The way in which people would relate to one another and to their work experiences would also be changed to the point where people would welcome more integrated cooperative life-styles — life-styles that are based on personal responsibility and accountability and a greater sense of pride and self-worth in what one does to support oneself and society (effort).

2. People are forfeiting extrinsic rewards (money, benefits, bonuses, etc.) in favor of meaningful intrinsic rewards (freedom, responsibility, control, etc.).

3. We have been inclined over the past two decades to assume that man's natural state is a form of homeostasis or tranquility. Recent research by scientists such as Dr. Hans Selye has shown that man seeks some degree of stress, activity, or regularity that provides meaning to his existence. In general, people want to stay active and interactive. The stress of effort

(work), if optimal, helps to provide a form of biological and psychological "tone" analogous to muscle tone brought about by muscle contraction and relaxation. Case studies of retired people have indicated that shortly after retirement, they come to feel useless (effortless) and may be driven to occupy themselves with trivial tasks and "time-killing" activities.

4. Effort must be recognized as worthwhile whether manifested during *work time* or *leisure time*. The new definition of play (effort-relaxation), which accepts the dictum that effort may be financially rewarding or done solely for the value of the activity, will help to give identity to those who volunteer their efforts without financial reimbursement. A wealth of human resources is volunteered each year by individuals who cannot be paid or do not want to be paid. However, in most instances, their efforts are diminished because of society's definition of work in terms of financial remuneration. If economic forecasts are correct and only ten to fifteen percent of our population will be gainfully employed and the other eighty-five to ninety percent will have to fill their leisure time with volunteer efforts, we had better begin to educate our society toward an appreciation and deference for those who volunteer their efforts.

5. The age of leisure will mean that society will have to adopt a playful approach to life where *effort* and *relaxation* are part of a self-fulfilling adaptive life-style. The future will see a tremendous change toward work, since this phase of life will change to effort (autonomous activities), and individuals will graciously consent to undertake unpleasant and even monotonous tasks because they know that they can always assert their full autonomy at any time. This has already been manifested in communal living situations in the United States, Canada, and Israel, where the philosophy is one of "working to live and living to work."

PLAY IS BEING IN CONCERT WITH HUMANITY AND NATURE

Lately, we have witnessed a number of "environmental crises." From these urgent warnings the message should be loud and clear: this generation and the next must learn of the peril that we face from our thoughtless exploitation and ravishment of the earth. We must develop a life-style that will respect the finite nature of our earth and assure us of survival. Nowhere is there more urgently a need for a life-style change than in our "leisure life-styles." People in North America and in some parts of Europe have operated under the mistaken philosophy that "more" would beget "the good life" and "less" would beget "the poor life." This consumer philosophy has led to an overdependence upon an artificial "gadget" mentality supported by a billion dollar mythology that science can cure and fix everything tomorrow.

Both *effort* and *relaxation* must occur in concert with nature, not only so that we might *survive* but also that we might *deserve* to survive. Notwithstanding the fact that failure to respect nature may lead to deadly consequences, there is the need to educate people about the role that nature can play in helping us achieve a state of inner biological rhythm. Nature, in her basic fabric and processes, reveals the miraculous in the commonplace of our lives and the source and sustenance of our very being. Nature in its simplest forms, be it in an inner-city park or a secluded wild river, serves as an antidote to the plastic and artificial "commodity" mentality transcending all our systems of thought and action.

Play is wonder, curiosity, exploration, and appreciation of man and his relationship to his earth. Because nature is literally and endlessly *wonder(ful)* — full of wonders — nature offers innumerable and infinite resources for education, appreciation, and personal growth through the capacity to confirm our existence.

PLAY IS UNITY OF MIND, BODY AND SPIRIT

From our historians and educators we learn that the early Greeks did not separate the body from the mind and spirit in their "scheme of education." However, shortly after Aristotle's Republic came to an end, the great games at Olympia, Nemea, and Delphi took on a professional approach. Winning justified using any approach, and winners were bestowed with great prizes and privileges. The Greek ideal of a balanced person with a holistic body, mind, and spirit became perverted by muscle-bound athletes who could not think and by professional musicians and artists who were physical degenerates addicted to drugs for their physical and moral support.

Unfortunately we have never quite regained Aristotle's ancient ideal of an integrated — body/mind/spirit — person. If anything, our educational system works to the detriment of a unified approach to self-fulfillment. Consider, for example, our "traditional" physical education curriculum in both primary and secondary schools. These educational systems reinforce and perpetuate an elitist and absolute approach to physical, cultural, and artistic expressions. Physical development and expression, as an example, has become synonymous with competitive sports in North America. Furthermore, the competitive sports have become so goal-oriented that only winning is important, and all other aspects become subordinate to winning. The phrase "We're Number One" exemplifies the mentality of our professional approach to sports. It does not matter how one achieves the "Number One" ranking, as long as the records state it is so. However, a more cogent question is, Why do we have to be "Number One"? The absolute goal of becoming "Number One" in some physical attribute clearly rules out the possibility of being "Number One" in some other attribute.

That there is a Renaissance in the education of body/mind/spirit is evidenced by the growing army of joggers, hikers, swimmers, campers, and a host of other "body-conscious" groups. It is exemplified by the ever-increasing popularity of such newly created games as Yogi Tag, New Frisbee, Infinity Volleyball, Boffing, The Mating Game, and Circle Football. These games are of the non-zero sum type, that is, everyone plays and everyone is a "winner."

In the same way that Aristotle described the harmony among bodily movement, cerebral thoughts, and musical playing as a way of achieving "leisure," the Eastern disciplines and philosophies also emphasize a unification of the body, mind, and spirit through movements of the body (yoga), meditation, and deep relaxation. These Eastern cults, which promise a unity with oneself and with the universe, have swept across the Western world because of the vacuum created by our artificial splitting of the body from the mind and spirit.

Young children at play are not able to compartmentalize themselves into physical, cerebral, and affective domains. They play in a holistic way. This similarity holds true for adults at play. We may well discover that in this age, play may provide us with the best option for regaining control over our bodies, minds, and spirits.

PLAY AS A FORUM FOR SOCIETAL INTEGRATION AND NORMALIZATION

Man's behavior is, in good part, determined by his ideologies. By ideology, we mean a combination of beliefs, attitudes, and interpretations or reality that are derived from one's experiences, one's knowledge of what are presumed to be facts, and above all, one's values.

One of the primordial ideologies of our society has centered around deviancy from normality. Individuals who possessed characteristics that set them apart from the mainstream of society were treated differently. Thus, individuals with below-average IQs, physical abnormalities (deafness, blindness, paraplegia, etc.), or emotional aberrations (depression, aggression, schizophrenia, etc.) were automatically isolated from the social and physical environment inhabited by the "normal" population. This isolation led to the development of a series of educational, rehabilitative, and other social services totally isolated from the life space of the nondisabled population.

The past decade has seen an outcry against the segregation of the disabled from the rest of the community, based on humanistic grounds. The new humanism strongly advocates a more integrated approach to our educational, vocational, and avocational systems. Translated into practice, this means designing our environments, modifying our attitudes, and reaching out to the disabled, so that individuals of all levels of ability can become integral members of our societal fabric.

Nowhere has this philosophy of integration become more accepted than in the area of play. Play, through its capacity for fostering *abilities,* has enabled the disabled to achieve self-fulfillment and social recognition, which has heretofore been denied to them in other spheres of life. The integration of the disabled into all our play service systems (theater, park, playground, swimming pool, art gallery, etc.) has been a great human awakening and spiritual uplifting for the average citizen who has taken all of his or her abilities for granted and not recognized the tremendous capabilities we humans possess. Through play as a forum the able and disabled have come closer to recognizing that total integration in all forums of life is a worthwhile human goal for which to strive.

12
An Empirical Study of Children's Competitive Play

Throughout this book the focus has been to stimulate the reader to critically examine the theories of play behavior in light of their heuristic potential. The final chapter of this book presents the results of a large-scale study utilizing the *play paradigm* discussed at length in Chapter 4.

INTRODUCTION

The Study of Play

Historically and traditionally the study of play has been of an intuitive, philosophical, and speculative nature based upon common sense devoid of the so-called "logic of science." Recently, however, social scientists have proposed conceptual models (Levy, 1974; Csikszentmihalyi, 1975b) and empirically explored the motives and outcomes of play (Witt and Bishop, 1970; Neulinger, 1974; Orlick, 1974, 1975a).

The Study of Competitive Play

The desire to strive, excel, master, and succeed in all endeavors of life have been given the ubiquitous label of *achievement motivation.* For the past century the values, norms, and mores of Western society have been based on the premise that man's passion to be more today than he was yesterday and to transcend his old standards appears to be a pervasive motive in human behavior. The elite and mortal idols of our society are described as high achievers in their respective fields, and the values of these models have filtered down to the grass-roots masses. Thus the ubiquity of the motive to achieve is evident, not only in the towering intellectual products of a Shakespeare or an Einstein or in the climactic

athletic performance of a Mark Spitz or a Bobby Hull but also in the first falter-
ing efforts of a toddler to walk unaided or of a pre-school child to print his or
her name. Embraced in this generic concept of achievement motivation, indige-
nous and crucial to our Western entrepreneurship society, are the components of
equity, competition and success, risk taking, and the exploitation of skill.

Since play, games, and sports, at least in part, are microscopic expressive
models of the values and norms that society's dominant institutions use as criteria for the socialization process of their budding citizens, it is little wonder
that play, games, and sports reflect the predominant values of our highly competitive, production, and achievement-oriented society (Kenyon, 1968; Webb,
1969; Petrie, 1971; Orlick, 1974, 1975a, 1975b, 1975c). However, while competitive play may generate, sustain, and reinforce highly reliable "projective or
expressive" models (Roberts and Sutton-Smith, 1962, p. 167) for those children
whose socially conditioned need to win and excel at play far outweighs their fear
of failure or humanistic and moral consideration of others in society (Levy,
1972c; Orlick, 1975a), such is not the case with all children. For those children
who are not   ivated to strive for success, achievement, and conquest at the
risk of self-devaluation and physical injury nor are willing to inflict emotional
and physical pain onto their peers, the competitive play scenario (e.g., hockey,
wrestling, football, soccer, lacrosse, etc.) may indeed be rejected for alternative,
noncompetitive play systems (Orlick, 1975c). To date, there has not been reported an empirical study examining the direct effects of competitive play on
children who are highly motivated to achieve success and those who, when given
the option, would prefer to avoid success–failure, zero-sum types of competitive
play situations.

Purpose of Study

It was the purpose of this study to design a rigorously controlled experiment
that would examine the effects of success and failure on risk-taking behavior in a
competition-oriented play situation as related to children who were either high
or low in their achievement needs.

Conceptual Definitions

Competitive Play

For purposes of the present study, competitive play was defined as a situation in
which success and failure on a skill-perceived task was determined by performing
better than one's opponent, as a result of the degree to which one was prepared
to take risk in one's choice of opponent and playing strategy.

Achievement Motivation

To date, one of the social theories that has shown great promise of evolving postulates and hypotheses that have application in a host of competitive play situ-

ations is John Atkinson's theory of achievement motivation (Atkinson, 1960, 1964; Atkinson and Feather, 1966). Atkinson (1964) attempts to analyze human motivation in terms that account for the fact that behavior does not always lead to the projected outcome and that in competitive play where risk taking is such a vital element, it is necessary to examine the probability of occurrence.

In Atkinson's most recent theory (Atkinson and Feather, 1966) of achievement motivation, an explicit mathematical relationship for predicting an individual's tendency to approach or to avoid achievement-related activity is presented. A person's tendency to *approach* or to *avoid* achievement-oriented activity is thought to be determined by the interaction of parallel constructs:

M_s = a stable personality disposition to strive for success.

M_f = a stable personality disposition to avoid failure.

P_s = the subjective expectancy (probability) that performing the activity will lead to success, ranging on a scale from 0.00 to 1.00.

P_f = the subjective expectancy (probability) that performing the activity will lead to failure, where $P_f = (1 - P_s)$.

I_s = the attractiveness or incentive value of success, where $I_s = (1 - P_s)$.

I_f = incentive value of failure. To capture the notion that more shame is experienced when failing an easy task than when failing a difficult one, it is assumed that $I_f = - P_s$.

The product of the three success variables $(M_s \times P_x \times I_s)$ is conceptualized as a tendency to approach success, while the product of the three failure variables $(M_f \times P_f \times I_f)$ is seen as a tendency to avoid failure. Combining the above success and failure variables results in a resultant achievement motivation score, RAM $= (M_s \times P_s \times I_x) + (M_f \times P_f \times I_f)$. A high RAM score indicates success orientation; a low RAM score indicates avoidance or failure orientation.

Given this general theoretical framework, a variety of predictions can be made. From Figure 16 it may be seen that differences in tendencies to approach achievement tasks are maximized when motive strengths are maximal and $P_s = 0.50$. This is the condition that has the greatest uncertainty regarding the outcome. Thus for the success-motivated subjects $(M_s > M_f)$, intermediate risks produce the greatest motivation, whereas fear-of-failure-motivated subjects $M_f > M_s)$ would experience the greatest avoidance of anxiety at this risk level. On the other hand, when the chances of success are either very high $(P_s = 0.90)$ or very low $(P_s = 0.10)$, the M_s subjects are less likely to be motivated in that activity. In contrast, the M_f subjects are more likely to be motivated when the chances of success are at the two ends of the difficulty continuum.

Risk-taking Behavior

The most outstanding contribution to the field of competitive play behavior by the Atkinson model may be in the domain of risk-taking behavior. Anyone who

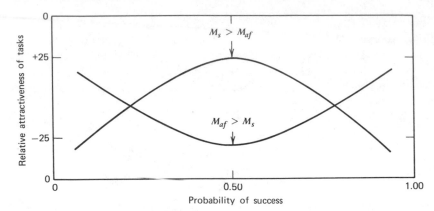

Figure 16 Graphic Representation of the Relative Attractiveness of Tasks that Differ in Subjective Probability of Success, for Individuals Who Differ in Strength of M_s and M_{af}. *Note.* The avoidance curve has been inverted to show that very difficult and very easy tasks arouse less fear of failure and hence are less unattractive than moderately difficult tasks (Atkinson and Feather, 1966, p. 21).

has participated in a competitive play situation is fully aware that decisions made with respect to the strategy often involve the taking of risks. Competition and risk taking, then, are interwoven into the heart of activities in which participants are endeavoring to achieve intrinsic or extrinsic goals of excellence.

Risk-taking behavior, as defined by Atkinson's (1964) theoretical model, may be subdivided into *three* basic categories: (1) those studies that employ the selection of *tasks* varying in degree of probability of success (Hancock and Teevan, 1964); (2) those studies that use the *strategy* selected by the individual as a measure of risk taking (Atkinson and Litwin, 1960; Brody, 1963; and Litwin, 1966); and (3) those studies in which the individual could not select the difficulty of the *task* or the *strategy per se,* but where he or she could select the level of *interpersonal risk* of having one's behavior negatively evaluated (Portnoy and Teevan, 1968; Shaban and Jecker, 1968). For purposes of this study, risk-taking behavior will be operationalized within the latter two categories.

Play Attitudes

Recently, Webb (1969) has supported the hypothesis that children's games and play are expressive models through which the primary and secondary institutions socialize their neophyte citizens in the values characterizing our industrial society. After comparing the ranking of items "important" in play activity of boys and girls at several grade levels through elementary and high school, Webb hypothesized that the major cognitive attitudes in our competitive achieving economic society were those stressing *equity, skill* and *success.* Webb's first step toward confirming the assumption that play and games constitute models of real economic competitive styles was to illustrate that as the child passed through the various school grades, he or she would increasingly emphasize *success* and *skill* at the expense of the element of *fairness*. This change in ranking of attitudes toward competition was termed by Webb the "professionalization" of attitudes toward play.

These play attitudes are clearly a product of the socialization brought about as a result of direct experience within such play service systems as minor league hockey, soccer, football, and baseball, as well as indirect vicarious experiences vis-à-vis the public media (television, radio, newspapers, etc.)

METHOD

Subjects

One hundred and forty-four boys from grades four, five, and six attending three primary schools in a suburban community with a population of 44,000 were randomly selected for the study.

Research Instruments

For purposes of carrying out the present study, three major research instruments were employed.

Children's Achievement Scale (CAS)

Weiner and Kukla (1970) developed a measure of resultant achievement motivation that is a forced-choice inventory consisting of twenty items derived from Atkinson's (1964) theory of resultant achievement motivation and from empirical findings that have been shown to differentiate high from low resultant achievement groups. The items tap, in part, the kind of affect (hope or fear), the direction of behavior (approach or avoidance), and the preference for risk (intermediate versus easy or difficult) expressed in achievement situations. Typical items are:

I prefer jobs
   a. that I might not be able to do.
   b. that I am sure I can do.
I like playing a game when I am
   a. as good as my playmate.
   b. much better than my playmate.
When I play a game I
   a. hate to lose.
   b. love to win.

Professionalization Play Scale

The professionalization Play Scale (Webb, 1969) is a forced-choice instrument that identifies the subject's attitudinal approach toward — fair, play, or beat. Although the items are only at a nominal, that is, categorical, level of measurement, their forced ranking on a "greater importance" basis provides an ordinal level of measurement subject to high-order statistical analysis (Webb, 1969). When the three nominal items are taken together, they provide six permutations, which range from lesser to greater professionalization in terms of the differential ranking of "play," "beat," and "fair." These six permutations are depicted below.

Permutations of Play Items

Play Orientation			Professional Orientation		
1	2	3	4	5	6
Fair	Fair	Play	Play	Beat	Beat
Play	Beat	Fair	Beat	Fair	Play
Beat	Play	Beat	Fair	Play	Fair

Risk-taking Instrument

The risk-taking instrument was an electronically operated "Ray Gun" game connected to a target board made up of three circular lights that turned on and off simultaneously at varying speeds (see Figure 17 for overall system design).

The target board was also equipped with a HIT and BANG light. The BANG light came on every time the subject (S) pulled the trigger, whereas the HIT light came on only when the experimental treatment called for a hit. A BANG light with a HIT light was regarded as a miss.

Situated next to where the S stood to aim his rifle was a knob that prominently displayed five gradations of difficulty, clearly marked VERY EASY, EASY, MEDIUM, HARD, and VERY HARD. By altering the position of the knob from VERY EASY to MEDIUM, the speed with which each of the three lights came on and off simultaneously was also increased, thus simulating greater risks in getting a hit (subjective probability of success is varied by altering the degree of difficulty).

The boys were told that the purpose of the "Ray Gun" game was to aim the rifle in order to hit any one of the three lights coming on and off simultaneously. Accordingly, it was emphasized that hits or misses resulted from the ability to aim the rifle properly and adjust the speed of the target and was therefore a test of skill. In reality, hits and misses were remotely controlled by the experimenter (E).

The technical heart of the "Ray Gun" task was a target range program made up of a thirty-position stepping relay. Each time the S depressed the trigger of

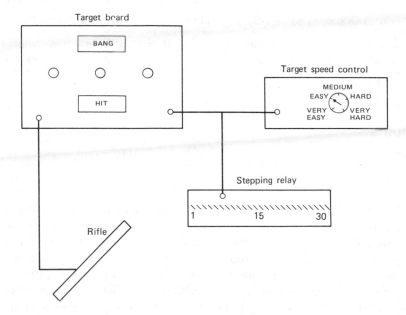

Figure 17 Overall System Block Diagram of Ray Gun Game Apparatus

the rifle, which was an electric switch; the relay advanced one step. Each of the thirty stepper positions was wired to the HIT light through one of the thirty switches. The E set a panel of thirty switches for the desired number and sequence of HITS by turning any number of thirty switches "on" (down). When the stepper selected any particular switch and that switch was down, the HIT light came on. If the switch was *not* "on" (up) the HIT light did not come on; only the BANG light came on, and the S knew he missed.

Preexperimental Procedure

All 144 Ss were administered the CAS and the Professionalization Play Scale prior to the administration of any experimental treatments. Based upon the CAS scores the Ss were divided into two achievement groups using a median split. The high-achievement boys ($N = 72$) were referred to as the HAM group, and the low-achievement boys ($N = 72$) were referred to as the LAM group.

Experimental Procedure

Shooting Competition Groups

The experiment was conducted using four-man shooting competition groups. Three of the members of each group were confederates of the E, while the fourth member of the group was the naive S. The confederates were thoroughly

Table 6   The Scoring System Employed in the Practice and Risk-taking Phase

Difficulty Level	Probability of Success (P_s)	Deviations from $P_s = 0.50$	Points for Each Hit
VERY EASY	1.00	+ 2	2
EASY	0.80	+ 1	3
MEDIUM	0.50	0	4
HARD	0.20	− 1	8
VERY HARD	0.00	− 2	16

coached by E in preexperimental sessions so that they were able to behave as though they were naive subjects. None of the real subjects knew any of the confederates. The groups of confederates were randomly formed from a pool of twelve and were randomly assigned to naive subjects. The above procedure was followed for the high-achievement motive (HAM) group as well as the low-achievement motive (LAM) group. The scoring system that was used in the practice, treatment, and risk-taking phases for the thirty shots is presented in Table 6.

Practice Phase

During the practice phase the E explained that in order to give each of the group members the same opportunity to score and at the same time permit comparisons between members, in preparation for the competition, each of them would take ten shots from each of the VERY EASY, MEDIUM, and VERY HARD difficulty levels. The experimentally controlled results to project the different ability levels to the naive S appear in Table 7.

Preexperiment Risk-taking Preferences

Following the practice phase, the Ss were asked to state their opponent preference and the number of shots that they wanted to take from the three difficulty levels.

Treatment Phase

Through experimental manipulation[1] Ss were assigned to one of the six treatment conditions (Success–Superior; Success–Equal; Success–Inferior; Failure–

[1] The experimental manipulation was carried out by asking the group members, immediately after the practice phase, to write down on a piece of paper whom they would like to compete against. Following their written indications, the E informed the group that two members had requested to compete against the same opponent. In order to alleviate this apparent impasse, the E advised the group that there would be two competitions. The first (which, in fact, was the treatment phase) would involve dyads assigned by the E and obviously selected as a preference by some of the naive Ss and the second competition would be between those individuals denied the opportunity to compete initially. Thus the E assured all the members, including the naive S, that everyone would get the opportunity to compete against the opponent of his choice.

Table 7 The Point-Scoring System to Project Differential Ability Levels of Confederates to Naive Subject

Total Scores for Superior Ability Confederate

Difficulty Level	Hits	Misses	Pts.
VERY EASY	10	0	20
MEDIUM	8	2	32
VERY HARD	7	3	112
TOTAL	25	5	164

Total Scores for Inferior Ability Confederate

Difficulty Level	Hits	Misses	Pts.
VERY EASY	7	3	14
MEDIUM	1	9	4
VERY HARD	0	10	0
TOTAL	8	22	18

Total Scores for Equal Ability Confederate and Naive Subject

Difficulty Level	Hits	Misses	Pts.
VERY EASY	8	2	16
MEDIUM	4	6	16
VERY HARD	1	9	16
TOTAL	13	17	48

Superior; Failure–Equal; Failure–Inferior). During the treatment phase the naive S and his opponent (trained confederate) were informed that they would each be permitted to take ten shots from each of the three difficulty levels (VERY EASY, MEDIUM, VERY HARD). In all cases (144Ss) the success and failure total scores of the confederates and the naive Ss were controlled by the E in order to maintain a constant effect across the three ability level treatments. Thus all confederates or naive Ss experimentally assigned to experience success received a total score equal to 164 points; similarly all confederates or niave Ss supposed to experience failure were assigned a total score equal to 18 points.

Risk-taking Phase

Following one of the six treatment conditions as agreed between E and Ss in the treatment phase, the naive Ss and the three confederates were given the opportunity to compete against their original ability opponent or to select a new ability opponent. In addition to having indicated their ability opponent choice, Ss were also asked to indicate the difficulty level for each of their thirty shots.

Experimental Design

The study outlined herein was a three-factor factorial design (2 x 2 x 3) with the levels of the first factor being the resultant achievement motivation (HAM and LAM). The second factor was the success–failure treatment. The third factor was the three ability opponent levels — superior, equal, and inferior.

Data Analysis

The results of the study were analyzed by carrying out two major statistical procedures. Chi square and analysis of variance (ANOVA) were used to analyze the personality X success–failure X ability opponent interactions for the risk-taking strategy dependent variables — number of shots taken from each difficulty level; and the ability opponent selected to compete against.

The 2 x 2 x 3 experimental design is presented on the next page.

RESULTS

Pretreatment Risk Taking

Immediately following the practice phase in which the 144 Ss obtained a score of 48 and the three confederates accompanying each of the naive Ss obtained either an inferior (18), equal (48), or superior score (164), each S was asked to indicate his choice of ability opponent and distribution of thirty shots across the five difficulty levels (VERY EASY to VERY HARD).

Presented in Table 8 are the chi-square tests comparing the HAM and LAM groups preferences for different risk-taking shooting strategies. Low risk sub-

2 × 2 × 3 Experimental Design

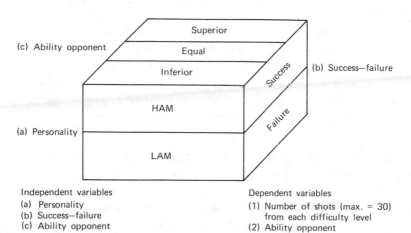

Independent variables
(a) Personality
(b) Success—failure
(c) Ability opponent

Dependent variables
(1) Number of shots (max. = 30)
    from each difficulty level
(2) Ability opponent

Table 8 Risk-taking Shooting Strategies of HAM and LAM Ss in the Ray Gun Game

Achievement Motivation	Risk-taking Shooting Strategy							
	Low	Risk	Interm.	Risk	High	Risk	N	%
	n	%	n	%	n	%		
HAM	9.6	31.9	15.0	50.0	5.4	18.1	30	100.0
LAM	13.3	44.4	7.5	25.0	9.2	30.6	30	100.0

df = 2; χ^2 − 9.79; p < 0.01

sumed VERY EASY and EASY difficulty levels; Intermediate risk subsumed the MEDIUM difficulty level; and high risk subsumed the HARD and VERY HARD difficulty levels.

The results in Table 8 clearly point out that the LAM group preferred the low (n = 13.3; percent = 44.4) and high (n = 9.2; percent = 30.6) risk-taking shooting strategies as opposed to the intermediate risk-taking shooting strategy (n = 7.5; percent = 25.0). The HAM group showed a greater preference for the intermediate (n = 15.0; percent = 50.0) over the low (n = 9.6; percent = 31.9) and high (n = 5.4; percent = 18.1) risk-taking shooting strategies.

Presented in Table 9 are the ability opponent preferences of the HAM and LAM groups.

Table 9 Ability Opponent Strategies of HAM and LAM Ss in the Ray Gun Game

Achievement Motivation	Risk-taking Ability Opponent Strategy							
	Superior Opponent		Equal Opponent		Inferior Opponent		N	%
	N	%	n	%	n	%		
HAM	4.0	5.6	63.0	87.5	5.0	6.9	72	100.0
LAM	10.0	13.9	41.0	56.9	21.0	29.2	72	100.0

df = 2; χ^2 = 17.07; p < 0.001

From Table 9 it may be seen that although a greater proportion of the Ss from both the HAM and LAM groups preferred to compete against equal ability opponents, in the HAM group 87.5 percent of the Ss preferred to compete against an equal ability opponent, while only 5.6 percent selected a superior ability opponent, and 6.9 percent selected an inferior ability opponent. However, in the case of the LAM, while 56.9 percent of Ss selected an equal ability opponent, 13.9 percent selected a superior ability opponent, and 29.2 percent selected an inferior ability opponent.

Summarized in Table 10 are the nine possible risk-taking shooting and ability opponent strategies for the HAM and LAM groups.

Table 10 reveals a clearer risk-taking disposition for the HAM than the LAM group. The HAM group, in keeping with the Atkinson model, clearly preferred the *intermediate-risk shooting* and *equal ability opponent* strategy (n = 34.0; percent = 47.2). The LAM group risk-taking disposition only partly confirms the theoretical risk-taking model by Atkinson. Their failure to strongly select one risk-taking style over another is indicated by their preference for the following risk-taking strategies: *high-risk shooting* and *equal ability opponent* (n = 16.0, percent = 22.2); *low-risk shooting* and *inferior ability opponent* (n = 15.0; percent = 20.8); and *low-risk shooting* and *superior ability opponent* (n = 14.0; percent = 19.4).

Play Professionalization Attitudes

The professionalization attitudes of the HAM and LAM Ss were determined by collapsing the six possible permutations. The "fair" categories are referred to as the *low professionalization attitudes,* while the "beat" categories are referred to as the *high professionalization attitudes.*

The professionalization attitudes of the HAM and LAM groups are presented in Table 11, which reveals that the LAM group accorded "fair" first choice to a greater degree (n = 44.0; percent = 61.1) than the HAM group (n = 22.0; percent = 30.5), while the HAM groups accorded "play" first choice to a greater degree (n = 38.0; percent = 52.8) than the LAM group.

Table 10 Risk-taking Shooting and Ability Opponent Strategies of HAM and LAM Ss in the Ray Gun Game

| Risk Taking Shooting | Achievement Motivation | | | |
| | HAM | | LAM | |
	n	%	n	%
Low-Risk Shooting Superior Ability Opponent	1.0	1.4	3.0	4.2
Low-Risk Shooting Equal Ability Opponent	19.0	26.4	14.0	19.4
Low-Risk Shooting Inferior Ability Opponent	3.0	4.2	15.0	20.8
Intermediate-Risk Shooting Superior Ability Opponent	1.0	1.4	3.0	4.2
Intermediate-Risk Shooting Equal Ability Opponent	34.0	47.2	11.0	15.3
Intermediate-Risk Shooting Inferior Ability Opponent	1.0	1.4	4.0	5.6
High-Risk Shooting Superior Ability Opponent	2.0	2.8	4.0	5.6
High-Risk Shooting Equal Ability Opponent	10.0	13.9	16.0	22.2
High-Risk Shooting Inferior Ability Opponent	1.0	1.4	2.0	2.8
TOTAL	72.0	100.0	72.0	100.0

$df = 8$; $\chi^2 = 17.07$; $p < 0.05$

Table 11 Play Professionalization Attitudes of HAM and LAM Ss

| Play Professionalization Attitude | | Achievement Motivation | | | |
| | | HAM | | LAM | |
		n	%	n	%
Fair (1–2)	Low	22.0	30.5	44.0	61.1
Play (3–4)		38.0	52.8	27.0	37.5
Beat (5–6)	High	12.0	16.7	1.0	1.4
TOTAL		72.0	100.0	72.0	100.0

$df = 5$; $\chi^2 = 19.69$; $p < 0.01$

Although only a minority of the Ss in the two achievement groups ranked "beat" first choice, it is noteworthy that 16.7 percent of the HAM group accorded "beat" first choice, while only 1.4 percent of the LAM group accorded "beat" first choice.

Post-treatment Risk Taking

Following the experimental manipulation, the HAM and LAM groups were asked to indicate their risk-taking preference again. Summarized in Table 12 are the *resultant achievement motivation $\times$ success-failure $\times$ ability opponent ANOVA for risk-taking.*

The results in Table 12 indicate that with the exception of the *ability opponent* dependent variable, there was a strong three-way ANOVA interaction for each of the difficulty levels. The most statistically significant three-way ANOVA interaction was revealed for the MEDIUM difficulty level ($p < 0.01$). A closer examination of Table 12 indicates that the *success-failure* main effect accounted for more of the ability opponent variance than any of the other main or interactive effects. In the case of the present study, the majority of the HAM and LAM Ss selected a *superior* or *equal* ability opponent following the *success* treatment and selected an *inferior* or *equal* ability opponent following the *failure* treatment.

Presented in Table 13 are the actual risk-taking scores for the six treatment conditions.

DISCUSSION

Theoretical Discussion

As predicted by the Atkinson model and related research on socialization, HAM individuals are more concerned with getting an objective evaluation of their abilities, even at the risk of failure which could lead to self- and social devaluation. LAM individuals showed a preference for avoiding the objective range of strategy and opted for the potentially less socially derogatory risk-taking ranges. It was only in their choice of an opponent that the "social desirability" factor intervened. Given the emphasis in our society on males being brave, bold, and daring, it is not surprising that the LAM group made an opponent choice that is congruent with the supposed competitive male role. Hence, when we examine the risk-taking strategy of the LAM individual it fits both the "typical theoretical" predictions of the Atkinson model and the "social desirability" ego-enhancing needs of this individual.

Play Attitudes

In accordance with the theory of achievement motivation (Atkinson, 1964) discussed earlier in the chapter, the HAM group accorded significantly greater

Table 12 Resultant Achievement Motivation × Success–Failure × Ability Opponent ANOVA Summary for Risk-Taking

Source of Variation	df	Very Easy Speed			Medium Speed			Very Hard Speed			Ability Opponent		
		M_s	F	P	M_s	F	P	M_s	F	P	M_s	F	P
Personality (A)	1	154.17	6.17	0.01	568.03	21.20	0.00	210.25	9.91	0.00	0.03	0.07	0.80
Success-failure (B)	1	24.17	0.97	0.33	26.69	0.99	0.32	373.78	16.01	0.00	17.36	41.17	0.00
Ability opponent (C)	2	7.63	0.31	0.74	21.44	0.80	0.45	37.67	1.61	0.20	3.11	7.38	0.00
Personality × success-failure (A × B)	1	11.57	0.47	0.50	1.36	0.05	0.82	2.78	0.12	0.73	0.02	0.70	0.80
Personality × ability opponent (A × C)	2	11.55	0.45	0.63	13.71	0.51	0.60	10.56	0.45	0.64	0.36	0.86	0.43
Success-failure × ability opponent (B × C)	2	0.88	0.04	0.97	7.22	0.27	0.76	6.47	0.28	0.76	1.44	3.43	0.04
Personality × success-failure × ability opponent (A × B × C)	2	101.72	4.07	0.02	127.22	4.75	0.01	69.72	2.99	0.05	0.53	1.25	0.29
Subject (within treat.)	132	25.00			26.80			23.33			0.42		

Table 13 Summary of Risk-taking Results for HAM and LAM *S*s across Treatments

Treatment Conditions	Ability Opponent Strategy[a]		Risk-taking Strategy[b]					
			Very Easy		Medium		Very Hard	
	HAM	LAM	HAM	LAM	HAM	LAM	HAM	LAM
Success superior opponent	1.9	1.9	4.8	5.9	11.6	4.6	5.0	9.8
Success equal opponent	1.3	1.6	3.3	8.8	8.8	4.8	7.3	7.8
Success inferior opponent	1.6	1.4	7.1	4.9	6.2	5.8	8.2	9.2
Failure superior opponent	2.3	2.7	4.8	7.7	9.5	6.8	3.3	3.4
Failure equal opponent	2.7	2.5	6.8	7.4	8.5	6.9	3.8	6.1
Failure inferior opponent	2.0	1.8	4.3	8.8	11.7	3.5	2.8	8.5
Mean	1.96	1.98	5.2	7.3	9.4	5.4	5.1	7.5

[a]1 = Superior
2 = Equal
3 = Inferior
[b]Maximum of 30 shots.

importance to *achievement criteria* (Webb, 1969) than the LAM group. This would seem to be congruent with the "image" that the theory on achievement motivation projects of an *achievement-oriented personality* and of the other individual who is dominated by a dread of failure, a *failure-threatened personality.*

Thus, we see that for the HAM group the paramount factor in play activity becomes "skill" (*Play*). Webb (1969) has used the term "professionalization" to refer to the substitution of "skill" for "fairness' as the preponderant variable in play attitudes. Furthermore, it is also quite evident that the HAM group placed significantly greater importance on "victory" (*beat*) in play than the LAM group.

The diminished emphasis on "equity" and the increase given to "success" and "skill" by the HAM group in this study strongly supports the hypothesis by Webb (1969) that we socialize our young citizens into incorporating the manifesto that "equity may actually inhibit success" (p. 163).

With regard to Webb's (1969) hypothesis concerning the professionalization of play attitudes, it would appear that for the LAM individuals who are concerned about raising their self-expectation, "skill" (*play*) and "victory" (beat) would have to be given precedence over "fairness" in the cognitive formulation of their risk-taking behavior. In the case of the LAM individuals the cognitive formulation of a risk-taking strategy becomes confounded by the *fear of failure*, for although they may not be oriented toward raising their self-expectation level, they are very sensitive about social rejection and, as such, may engage in risk-taking behavior that may appear to be phenotypically oriented toward "skill" and "success," but in genotypical terms, their behavior is intended to avoid anxiety and social embarrassment.

Role of Competitive Play in Promoting a Quality of Life

Most recently a number of play researchers have questioned the value of competitive play in promoting a quality of life conducive to positive growth and development (Levy, 1972a, 1972b, 1976; Orlick, 1974, 1975a, 1975b). Orlick (1975a) questions the "character" value of those competitive play activities that reinforce and ultimately produce negative intrapersonal and interpersonal traits.

> What kinds of models are provided for children in sport and what kinds of behaviors are reinforced? Are children rewarded for respecting the rights and feelings of others, for honesty, and for sharing or are they rewarded for disregarding the rights and feelings of others, for dishonesty and for destructive aggression? Are players encouraged to be self-reliant by such things as self-organization and self-officiating or is it more a nurturing of dependency wherein officials and coaches "call all the shots?" Are athletes given the freedom to take a chance, to improvise, to be creative or is there a

> pre-occupation with outcome, with winning, with authoritarian-
> ism.
>
> (Orlick, 1975a, p. 4)

Thus, while competitive play may be the most attractive form of play for the high achievers, the end product of competitive play — be it excellence, challenge, success, or exploitation of skills, — cannot be justified by the means that are presently imposed on our neophyte citizens by pathological systems, values, and individuals. Orlick (1975a) assails the socially and psychologically deleterious means used to achieve the goals of competitive play.

> In certain sports destructive aggression, dehumanization and ex-
> ploitation of others ("the enemy") is thought to help achieve the
> goal. Therefore these kinds of behaviors are reinforced and made
> to seem necessary and desirable, which results in an increase and
> strengthening in these behaviors. Instead of being training grounds
> for the control of aggression and violence, certain sports appear to
> be training ground for their increase. They serve to stimulate and
> strengthen dehumanizing, exploitive, and aggressive responses. If
> this is "character" then hitting sports appear to be character
> builders.
>
> (Orlick, 1975a, p. 4)

For many decades, educators, psychologists, sociologists, and a host of other behavioral scientists have advocated the use of competitive play in the development and reinforcement of desirable personal and social outcomes. However, the evidence seems to clearly indicate that competitive play, like many other social environments, is not by definition bad or good but rather that it has the capacity to be either, depending on the models and the reinforcement contingencies monitoring the play episode.

It would thus seem justified to state that while the inherent characteristics of competitive play behavior — challenge, risk, objective feedback, self-evaluation, etc. — may be most attractive to the high achievers, each competitive play episode must be assessed to assure that the *means* used to achieve a competitive play experience are conducive for promoting a positive individual and societal quality of life.

Noncompetitive Play Environments

What has been strongly pointed out in the present study is that some individuals who are not risk takers do not wish to compete against an opponent, do not feel that they have control over the outcome, and are more concerned with the *process* (intrinsic motivation) than the *outcome* (extrinsic motivation); competitive play may be contraindicated for these individuals. The growth in popularity among school-age children of drama, music, pottery, weaving, painting, bicycling, kite flying, adventure and creative playgrounds, and a growing field of other noncompetitive play opportunities, indicates the serious shortcomings of competitive play (Orlick, 1974, 1975a, 1975b; Levy, 1976).

It is clearly not the purpose of this study to indict competitive play environments. Quite the contrary! The purpose has been to produce empirical information that will foster discussion based upon unbiased research findings. It is the responsibility of play researchers to examine the phenomena of play from all its perspectives. The perspective chosen for this study was *competition*.

List of Tables

List of Figures

Bibliography

Alderman, R. B. *Psychological behavior in sport.* Toronto: W. B. Saunders, 1974.

Allport, F. W. *Theories of perception and the concept of structure.* New York: John Wiley and Sons, 1955.

Atkinson, J. W. *An introduction to motivation.* Princeton, N. J.: Van Nostrand, 1964.

Atkinson, J. W., and Feather, N. T. *A theory of achievement motivation.* New York: John Wiley and Sons, 1966.

Atkinson, J. W., and Litwin, G. H. Achievement motive and test anxiety conceived as motive to approach success and motive to avoid failure. *Journal of Abnormal and Social Psychology,* 1960, 60, 52-63.

Auden, W. H. Culture and leisure. In G. Bell and J. Tyrwitt (Eds.), *Human identity in the urban environment.* Baltimore: Penguin Books, 1972.

Avedon, E. M., and Sutton-Smith, B. *The study of games.* New York: John Wiley and Sons, 1971.

Ball, D. W. The scaling of gaming skill, strategy, and chance. *Pacific Sociological Review,* July 1972, 277-294.

Barber, T. X. Physiological effects of hypnosis. *Psychological Bulletin,* 1961, 58, 390-419.

Barber, T. X. Physiological effects of hypnosis and suggestion. In L. V. Dicara, T. X. Barber, J. Kamiya, N. E. Miller, D. Shapiro, and J. Stovya (Eds.), *Biofeedback and self-control.* Chicago: Aldine, 1975.

Barcus, C. G., and Bergeson, R. G. Survival training and mental health. *Therapeutic Recreation Journal,* 1972, 6(1), 3-7.

Barker, R. G. *Ecological psychology: Concepts and methods for studying the environment of human behavior.* Stanford, Calif.: Stanford University Press, 1968.

Barker, R. G., and Wright, H. F. *Midwest and its children: The psychological ecology of an American town.* New York: Row, Peterson, 1955.

Beach, F. A. Current concepts of play in animals. *American Naturalist,* 1945, 79, 523-541.

Beisser, A. R. Psychodynamic observations of a sport. *Psychoanalysis and Psychological Review*, 1961, *48*(1), 69–76.

Bengtsson, A. *The child's right to play*. Sheffield: Tartan Press, 1974.

Berger, B. M. The sociology of leisure: Some suggestions. *Industrial Relations*, February 1962, *1*, 31–45.

Berlyne, D. E. Determinants of subjective novelty. *Perception and Psychophysics*, 1960, *3*(6), 415–423.

Berlyne, D. E. Curiosity and exploration. *Science*, 1966, *153*, 25–33.

Berlyne, D. E. Laughter, humor, and play. In G. Lindzey and E. Aronson (Eds.), *Handbook of social psychology*. New York: Addison-Wesley, 1968.

Berne, E. *Games people play*. New York: Grove Press, 1964.

Berns, M. Moving towards a conserver society: "Work or play." *Urban Forum*, Winter 1976, *2*(4), 59-62.

Bernstein, A. Wilderness as a therapeutic setting. *Therapeutic Recreation Journal*, 1972, *6*(4), 160–161, 185.

Bishop, D. W., and Witt, P. A. Sources of behavioral variance during leisure time. *Journal of Personality and Social Psychology*, 1970, *16*(2), 352-360.

Bolan, R. S. Generalist with a specialty — still valid? Educating the urban planner: An expert on experts. *Planning*, 1971, 373–388.

Brightbill, C. *The challenge of leisure*. Englewood Cliffs, N. J.: Prentice-Hall, 1960.

Britt, S. H., and Janus, S. Q. Toward a social psychology of human play. *The Journal of Social Psychology*, 1941, *13*, 351-384.

Brody, N. Need achievement, test anxiety, and subjective probability of success in risk taking behavior. *Journal of Abnormal and Social Psychology*, 1963, *66*, 413–418.

Brok, A. J. Free time and internal-external locus of control: Is socialization for freedom dignified? *Bulletin for Sociology of Leisure, Education and Culture*, 1974, *6*(3), 121–128.

Bronfenbrenner, V. *Two worlds of childhood: U.S. and U.S.S.R.* New York: Simon and Schuster, 1972.

Bruner, J. S. Play is serious business. *Psychology Today*, January 1975, 81–83.

Burlingham, D. Some notes on the development of the blind. *Psychoanalytic Study of the Child*, 1961, *14*, 121–143.

Burlingham, D. Developmental considerations in the occupations of the blind. *Psychoanalytic Study of the Child*, 1967, *22*, 187-198.

Byrne, D. Attitudes and attraction, In L. Berkowitz (Ed.), *Advances in experimental social psychology*, Vol. 4. New York: Academic Press, 1969.

Caillois, R. *Les Jeux et les hommes*. Paris: Gallimard, 1958.

Caillois, R. *Man, play and games*. New York: Free Press, 1961.

Calhoun, J. B. Population density and social pathology. *Scientific American,* 1962, *206,* 139–148.

Caplan, F., and Caplan, T. *The power of play.* New York: Anchor Press, 1974.

Clawson, M. Open space as a new urban resource. In H. S. Perloff (Ed.), *The quality of the urban environment.* Baltimore: John Hopkins Press, 1962.

Crandall, R., and Lewko, J. Leisure research, present and future: Who, what, where. *Journal of Leisure Research,* 1976, *8*(3), 150–159.

Cratty, B. S. *Perceptual and motor development in infants and children.* New York: The Macmillan Co., 1970.

Cratty, B. J. *Learning about human behavior: Through active games.* Englewood Cliffs, N. J.: Prentice-Hall, 1975.

Csikszentmihalyi, M. *Flow: Studies of enjoyment* (PHS Grant Report N. Rol HM 22883-02). Chicago: The University of Chicago, 1974.

Csikszentmihalyi, M. Play and intrinsic rewards. *Journal of Humanistic Psychology,* Summer 1975a, *15*(3), 41–63.

Csikszentimihalyi, M. *Beyond boredom and anxiety.* San Francisco: Jossey-Bass, 1975b.

Day, H. I. A new look at work, play, and job satisfaction. *The School Guidance Worker,* 1971, *27*(2), 4–11.

Day, H. I., Berlyne, D. E., and Hunt, D. E. (Eds.), *Intrinsic motivation: A new direction in education.* Toronto: Holt, Rinehart, and Winston, 1971.

Decharms, R. *Personal causation.* New York: Academic Press, 1968.

Deci, E. L. Effects of externally mediated rewards on intrinsic motivation. *Journal of Personality and Social Psychology,* 1971, *18,* 105–115.

Deci, E. L. *Intrinsic motivation* (Technical Report No. 62). New York: University of Rochester, Management Center, March 1973.

De Grazia, S. *Of time, work and leisure.* New York: The Twentieth Century Fund, 1962.

Dubos, R. *So human an animal.* New York: Charles Scribner's Sons, 1968.

Duffy, E. *Activation and behavior.* New York: John Wiley and Sons, 1962.

Dumazedier, J. *Toward a society of leisure.* New York: The Free Press, 1967.

Dumazedier, J. *Sociology of leisure.* New York: Elsevier, 1974.

Eifermann, R. R. *School children's games.* Washington, D. C.: Office of Education, Department of Health, Education, and Welfare, 1968.

Eifermann, R. R. Social play in childhood. In R. E. Herron and B. Sutton-Smith (Eds.), *Child's play.* New York: John Wiley and Sons, 1971.

Ellis, M. J. *Why people play.* Englewood Cliffs, N.J.: Prentice-Hall, 1973.

Ellis, M. J. *Play as arousal seeking; or the quest for information.* Paper presented to the American Medical Association's conference on Mental Health Aspects of Sports, Exercise and Recreation, Atlantic City, June 1975.

Erikson, E. H. *Childhood and society.* New York: Norton, 1950.

Erikson, E. H. *Identity: Youth and crisis.* New York: Norton, 1968.

Erikson, E. H. Thoughts on the city for human development. *Ekistics,* April 1973, *35*(29), 216–220.

Faunce, W. A. Automation and leisure. In H. Jacobson and J. Roucek (Eds.), *Automation and society.* New York: Philosophical Library, 1955.

Fisher, D., Lewis, J., and Priddle, G. *Land and leisure.* Chicago: Maaroufa Press, 1974.

Fiske, D. W., and Maddi, S. R. A conceptual framework. In D. W. Fiske and S. R. Maddi (Eds.), *Functions of varied experience.* Homewood, Ill.: Dorsey Press, 1961.

Flavell, J. H. *The developmental psychology of Jean Piaget.* Princeton, N. J.: Van Nostrand-Reinhold, 1963.

Fleishman, E. *The structure and measurement of physical fitness.* Englewood Cliffs, N. J.: Prentice-Hall, 1964.

Freud, S. *The ego and the id.* London: Allen and Unwin, 1927.

Freud, S. *A general introduction to psychology.* Garden City, N. Y.: Doubleday, 1943.

Freud, S. *Beyond the pleasure principle.* London: The Hogarth Press, 1948.

Freyberg, J. Hold high the cardboard sword. *Psychology Today,* February 1975, 63–64.

Gallahue, C. L., Werner, P. H., and Leudke, G. C. *A conceptual approach to moving and learning.* New York: John Wiley and Sons, 1975.

Gellhorn, E. *Principles of autonomic-somatic interactions.* Minnesota: University of Minnesota Press, 1967.

Gilmore, J. B. Play: A special behavior. In R. N. Haber (Ed.), *Current research in motivation.* New York: Holt, Rinehart and Winston, 1966, 343–355.

Glasser, W. *The identity society.* New York: Harper and Row, 1972.

Goffman, E. *Encounters: Two studies in the sociology of interaction.* New York: Bobbs-Merrill Co., 1961.

Goffman, E. *Behavior in public places.* Garden City, N. Y.: Doubleday, 1963.

Goffman, E. *Interaction ritual.* Garden City, N. Y.: Doubleday, 1967.

Goffman, E. *Relations in public.* New York: Basic Book, 1971.

Goldstein, H. K. *Research standards and methods for social workers.* New Orleans: The Hauser Press, 1963.

Greendorfer, S. The role of play in pre-history. *The Association for the Anthropological Study of Play Newsletter,* Winter 1975, *1*(3).

Greene, D., and Lepper, M. R. How to turn play into work. *Psychology Today,* September 1974, 49–54.

Griffith, W. Environmental effects on interpersonal affective behavior: Ambient affective temperature and attraction. *Journal of Personality and Social Psychology,* 1970, *1,* 33–48.

Groos, K. *The play of man.* New York: Appleton, 1901.

Gump, P. V. Schoggen, P., and Redl, F. The behavior of the same child in different milieus. In R. G. Barker (Eds.), *The stream of behavior.* New York: Appleton-Century Crofts and Meredith Publishing Company, 1963.

Gump, P. V. and Sutton-Smith, B. Activity-setting and social interaction: A field study. *American Journal of Orthopsychiatry,* 1955a, *25*(4), 755–760.

Gump, P. V., and Sutton-Smith, B. The "it" role in children's games. *The Group,* 1955b, *17*(3), 3–8.

Hall, E. T. *The hidden dimension.* Garden City, N. Y.: Doubleday, 1966.

Hall, G. S. *Youth.* New York: Appleton, 1906.

Hancock, J. G., and Teevan, R. C. Fear of failure and risk-taking behavior. *Journal of Personality,* 1964, *32,* 200–209.

Hanson, R. A. Outdoor challenge and mental health. *Naturalist,* 1973, *24,* 26–30.

Harrison, P. Soccer's tribal wars, *New Society,* 1974, *29,* 602–604.

Harry, J. Work and leisure: Situational attitudes. *Pacific Sociological Review,* July 1971, 301–309.

Hatfield, F. C. Some factors precipitating player violence: A preliminary report. *Sport Sociology Bulletin,* 1973, *2,* 3–5.

Haun, P. *Recreation: A medical viewpoint.* New York: Columbia University Press, 1965.

Hebb, D. O. *The organization of behavior.* New York. John Wiley and Sons, 1949.

Hebb, D. O. Drives and the conceptual nervous system. *Psychological Review,* 1955, *62,* 243–253.

Hebb, D. O. *A textbook of psychology.* Philadelphia: W. B. Saunders Co., 1958.

Hendee, J. C. Rural-urban differences reflected in outdoor recreation participation. *Journal of Leisure Research,* Autumn 1969, *1,* 333–342.

Herron, R. E., and Sutton-Smith, B. *Child's play.* New York: John Wiley and Sons, 1971.

Hilgard, E. S., and Atkinson, R. C. *Introduction to psychology.* New York: Harcourt, Brace and World, 1967.

Hollander, E. P., and Hunt, R. G. (Eds.). *Current perspectives in social psychology.* New York: Oxford University Press, 1971.

Huizinga, J. *Homo ludens.* Boston: Beacon Press, 1955.

Hull, C. L. *Principles of behavior.* New York: Appleton-Century-Crofts, 1943.

Hurlock, E. B. Experimental investigations of childhood play. *Psychological Bulletin,* 1934, *31,* 47–66.

Husman, B. R. Aggression in boxers and wrestlers as measured by projective techniques. *Research Quarterly,* 1965, *26*(4), 421–425.

Ibrahim, H. The future of leisure studies. In D. A. Pelegrino (Ed.). *What recreation research says to the recreation practitioner.* Washington, D. C.: American Alliance for Health, Physical Education and Recreation, 1975.

Inbar, M., and Stoll, C. S. *Autotelic behavior in socialization.* Unpublished manuscript, John Hopkins University, 1968.

Isaacs, S. *Social development in young children.* London: Routledge and Kegan Paul, 1933.

Izumi, K. *Energy and society: Some thoughts for the science council.* Unpublished manuscript, School of Urban and Regional Planning, University of Waterloo, 1972.

Jarvie, I. C. *Towards a sociology of the cinema.* London: Routledge, 1970.

Johnson, M. W. The effect on behavior of variations in the amount of play equipment. *Child Development,* 1935, *6,* 56–58.

Kahn, H., and Weiner, A. J. *The year 2000: A framework for speculation on the next thirty-three years.* New York: Macmillan Co., 1967.

Kando, T. M., and Summers, W. C. The impact of work on leisure: Toward a paradigm and research strategy. *Pacific Sociological Review,* July 1971, *14,* 310–327.

Kaplan, M., and Bosserman, P. (Eds.). *Technology, human values and leisure.* Nashville: Abingdon Press, 1971.

Kaplan, R. Some psychological benefits of gardening. *Environment and Behavior,* 1973, *5,* 145–162.

Kaplan, R. Some psychological benefits of an outdoor challenge program. *Environment and Behavior,* 1974, *6*(1), 101–116.

Keniston, K. *The uncommitted.* New York: Dell Publishing Co., 1970.

Kenyon, G. S. A conceptual model for characterizing physical activity. *Research Quarterly,* 1968, *39,* 96–105.

Kephart, N. C. *The slow learner in the classroom.* Columbus, Ohio: Charles E. Merrill Books, 1960.

Kerlinger, F. N. *Foundation of behavioral research: Educational and psychological inquiry* (2nd ed.). Toronto: Holt, Rinehart and Winston, 1973.

Kingsmore, J. M. The effect of professional wrestling and professional basketball contests upon the aggressive tendencies of spectators. In G. S. Kenyon (Ed.). *Contemporary psychology of sport.* Chicago: Athletic Institute, 1970.

Kluckhohn, C. Culture and behavior. In G. Lindzey (Ed.), *Handbook of social psychology.* New York: Addison-Wesley, 1954, pp. 921–976.

Kusyszyn, I. *Should gambling be legalized?* Paper presented at the First Annual Conference on Gambling, Las Vegas, Nevada, June 1974.

Kusyszyn, I. How gambling saved me from a misspent sabbatical. *Journal of Humanistic Psychology,* Summer 1977, *17*(3).

Kusyszyn, I. *Gambling, leisure, and mental health.* Invited address, Department of Recreation, University of Waterloo, Waterloo, Ontario, Canada, January 14, 1977.

Larsen, A. *An internal-external locus of control play scale.* Unpublished Senior Honors Project, Department of Recreation, University of Waterloo, 1973.

Layman, E. M. The role of play and sport in healthy emotional development: A reappraisal. In G. S. Kenyon (Ed.), *Contemporary psychology of sport.* Proceedings of the Second International Congress of Sport Psychology, Washington, 1968, pp. 249–258.

Lazarus, M. *About the attractions of play.* Berlin: F. Dummler, 1883.

Lefcourt, H. M. Internal versus external control of reinforcement. *Psychological Bulletin,* 1966, *65,* 206–220.

Leonard, G. B. *Education and ecstasy.* New York: Delta Publishing Co., 1968.

Levy, J. An intrinsic-extrinsic motivational framework for therapeutic recreation. *Therapeutic Recreation Journal,* First Quarter, 1971a, 32–38, 43.

Levy, J. Recreation at the crossroads. *Journal of Health, Physical Education and Recreation,* September 1971b, 51–52.

Levy, J. Risk taking as a determinant of competitive play behavior: An extension of Atkinson's theory of achievement motivation. *Journal of the Canadian Association for Health, Physical Education and Recreation,* March-April 1972a, 38(4), 31–37.

Levy, J. Practical implication for the study of a competitive play model: Determinants and consequences of competitive play. *Journal of the Canadian Association for Health, Physical Education and Recreation,* May-June 1972b, *38*(5), 6–8.

Levy, J. *Play attitudes and risk taking as a function of achievement motivation.* Paper presented at the Fourth Canadian Psycho-motor Learning and Sports Psychology Symposium, University of Waterloo, Waterloo, Ontario, October 1972c.

Levy, J. Risk taking and ability opponent strategy as a function of achievement motivation. *Journal of the Canadian Association for Health, Physical Education and Recreation,* January-February 1973, *39*(3), 15–20.

Levy, J. An applied intersystem congruence model of play, recreation, and leisure. *Human Factors,* October 1974, *16*(5), 545–557.

Levy, J. An empirical study of children's competitive play. *The Ontario Psychologist,* 1976, *8*(2), 35–41.

Levy, J. Leisure and the quality of life. *Recreation Research Review,* 1977 (in press).

Levy, J., and Schultz, E. W. *Play: A learning medium in school.* Unpublished manuscript, University of Illinois, 1971.

Lewin, K. *Field theory in social science.* New York: Harper and Row, 1951.

Linder, S. B. *The harried leisure class.* New York: Columbia University Press, 1970.

Litwin, G. H. Achievement motivation, expectancy of success and risk taking behavior. In J. W. Atkinson and N. Y. Feather (Eds.), *A theory of achievement motivation.* New York: John Wiley and Sons, 1966.

Loy, J. The nature of sport: A definitional effort. *Quest Monographs,* May 1968, *10,* 1-15.

Luthe, W. (Ed.). *Autogenic therapy* (5 vol.). New York: Grune & Stratton, 1969.

Luthe, W. Autogenic therapy: Excerpts on applications to cardiovascular disorders and hypercholesterolemia. In L. V. Dicara, T. X. Barber, J. Kamiya, N. E. Miller, D. Shapiro, and J. Stovya (Eds.), *Biofeedback and self-control.* Chicago: Aldine, 1975.

Lynn, R. W. Phelan, J. G., and Kiker, V. L. Beliefs in internal-external control of reinforcement and participation in group and individual sports. *Perceptual and Motor Skills,* 1969, *29,* 551-553.

MacDougall, W. *Social psychology.* Boston: John W. Luce, 1918.

Martin, A. R. The fear of relaxation and leisure. *American Journal of Psychoanalysis,* 1951, *11,* 42-50.

Martin, A. R. Leisure and our inner resources. *Parks and Recreation,* March 1975, 1a-6a.

Martin, P. A. *Leisure and mental health: A psychiatric viewpoint.* New York: American Psychiatric Association, 1967.

Maslow, A. H. Deficiency motivation and growth motivation. In M. R. Jones (Ed.), *Nebraska symposium on motivation.* Lincoln: Nebraska Press, 1955.

Maslow, A. H. *Towards a psychology of being.* Princeton, N. J.: Van Nostrand, 1962.

Maslow, A. H. *Motivation and personality.* New York: Harper and Row, 1964.

Maslow, A. H. *The farther reaches of human nature.* New York: Viking Press, 1971.

Meyersohn, R., and Hollander, P. Leisure. In C. D. Kernig (Ed.), *Marxism, Communism and Western Society.* New York: Herder and Herder, 1973.

Milgram, S. The experience of living in cities. *Science,* 1970, *167,* 1461-1408.

Mitchell, E. D., and Mason, B. S. *The theory of play.* New York: Barnes and Company, 1948.

Moos, R. *Evaluating treatment environments: A social ecological approach.* New York: John Wiley and Sons, 1973.

Moos, R. H., and Insel, P. M. *Issues in social ecology.* Palo Alto, Calif.: National Press Books, 1974.

Morris, D. The response of animals to a restricted environment. *Symposium of the Zoological Society of London,* 1964, *13,* 99–118.

Morris, D. *The human zoo.* New York: McGraw-Hill, 1969.

Murphy, G. *Human potentialities.* New York: Basic Books, 1958.

Murphy, J. F. The counter culture of leisure. *Parks and Recreation,* February 1972, 34–42.

Murray, H. A. *Explorations in personality.* New York: Oxford University Press, 1938.

Neulinger, J. *The psychology of leisure.* Springfield, Ill.: Charles C. Thomas, 1974.

Neumann, E. A. *The elements of play.* Unpublished doctoral dissertation, University of Illinois, 1971.

Newcomb, T. M. Social psychological theory: Integrating individual and social approaches. In J. Rohrer and M. Sherif (Eds.), *Social psychology at the crossroads.* New York: Harper, 1951.

Newman, O. *Gambling: Hazard and reward.* London: Athlone, 1972.

Noble, G. Effects of different forms of filmed aggression on children's constructive and destructive play. *Journal of Personality and Social Psychology,* 1973, *26*(1), 54–59.

Norbeck, E. Human play and its cultural expression. *Humanitas.* 1969. *5*(1), 43–55.

Ogilvie, B. C., and Tutko, T. A. Sport if you want to build character try something else. *Psychology Today,* October 1971, 61–63.

Orlick, T. D. The athletic drop-out: A high price for inefficiency. *The Canadian Association for Health, Physical Education and Recreation,* Nov./Dec. 1974.

Orlick, T. D. *Games of acceptance and psycho-social adjustment.* Paper presented at the Conference on the Mental Health Aspects of Sports, Exercise and Recreation, Atlantic City, N. J., June 1975a.

Orlick, T. D. The sports environment: A capacity to enhance-a capacity to destroy. In B. S. Rushall (Ed.), *The status of psychomotor learning and sport psychology research.* Dartmouth, Nova Scotia: Sport Science Associates, 1975b.

Orlick, T. D., and Botterill, C. *Every kid can win.* Chicago: Nelson Hall, 1975.

Osuna, F. F. D. *The third spiritual alphabet.* London: Benziger, 1931.

Parker, S. *The future of work and leisure.* New York: Praeger, 1971.

Parten, M. B. Social participation among pre-school children. *Journal of Abnormal and Social Psychology,* 1932, *27,* 243–269.

Parten, M. B. Social play among pre-school children. *Journal of Abnormal and Social Psychology,* 1933, *28,* 136–147.

Partridge. The lessons of nature. *Environmental Education,* 1976 (in press).

Patrick, G. T. W. *The psychology of relaxation.* Boston: Houghton Mifflin, 1916.

Pavlov, I. *Conditioned reflexes.* London: Oxford University Press, 1927.

Peller, L. E. Models of children's play. *Mental Hygiene,* 1952, *36,* 66–83.

Petrie, B. M. Achievement orientations in the motivations of canadian university students toward physical activity. *The Canadian Association for Health, Physical Education, and Recreation,* Jan.-Feb. 1971, *37*(3), 7–13.

Piaget, J. *The origins of intelligence in children.* New York: International Universities Press, 1952.

Piaget, J. *Play, dreams and imitation in childhood.* New York: W. W. Norton, 1962.

Pieper, J. *Leisure: The basis of culture.* New York: Pantheon Books, 1952.

Portnoy, S., and Teevan, R. C. *Interpersonal approach-avoidance and fear of failure* (3591-01). Group Psychology Branch, Office of Naval Research, 1968.

Proshansky, H. M., Ittelson, W. H., and Rivlin, L. G. (Eds.). *Environmental psychology.* New York: Holt, Rinehart and Winston, 1970.

Pulaski, A. P. The rich rewards of make believe. *Psychology Today.* January 1974, 68–74.

Rabinovitch, M. S. Violence perception as a function of entertainment value and TV violence. *Psychonomic Science,* 1972, *29,* 360–362.

Roberts, J. M., and Sutton-Smith, B. Child training and game involvement. *Ethnology,* 1962, *1,* 166–185.

Rogers, C. R. *On becoming a person.* Boston: Houghton Mifflin, 1961.

Rosenberg, B. G., and Sutton-Smith, B. A. A revised conception of masculine-feminine differences in play activities. *Journal of Genetic Psychology,* 1960, *96,* 165–170.

Rotter, J. B. *Social learning and clinical psychology.* Englewood Cliffs, N. J.: Prentice-Hall, 1954.

Rotter, J. B. Generalized expectancies for internal versus external control of reinforcement. *Psychological Monographs,* 1966, *80,* (1, whole no. 609).

Rubin, K. H., and Maioni, T. L. Play preferences and its relationship to ego-centrism, popularity and classification skills in preschoolers. *Merrill-Palmer Quarterly of Behavior and Development,* 1975, *21*(3), 171–179.

Schiller, F. V. *Essays aesthetical and philosophical.* London: George Bell, 1875.

Schneider, J. M. Skill versus chance activity preference and locus of control. *Journal of Consulting and Clinical Psychology.* 1968, *32*(3), 333–337.

Schultz, D. D. *Sensory restriction: Effects on behavior.* New York: Academic Press, 1965.

Sells, S. B. An interactionist looks at the environment. *American Psychologist,* 1963, *18,* 696–702.

Senters, J. M. A function of uncertainty and stakes in recreation. *Pacific Sociological Review*, July 1971, 259–269.

Shaban, J., and Jecker, J. Risk preferences in choosing an evaluator: An extension of Atkinson's achievement motivation model. *Journal of Experimental Social Psychology*, 1968, *4*, 34–45.

Sheehan, G. A. *Dr. Sheehan on running*. Mountain View, Calif.: World Publications, 1975.

Sheldon, W. H., and Stevens, S. S. *The varieties of temperament: A psychology of differences* New York: Harper, 1942.

Sieghart, P., The social obligations of the scientist. *The Hastings Centre Studies*, 1973, *1*(2), 7–16.

Singer, R. N. *Coaching, athletics and psychology*. New York: McGraw-Hill, 1972.

Smilansky, S. *The effects of sociodramatic play on disadvantaged preschool children*. New York: John Wiley and Sons, 1968.

Sommer, R. Small group ecology, *Psychological Bulletin*, 1967, *67*, 145–152.

Spencer, H. *Principles of psychology*. New York: D. Appleton, 1873.

Staley, E. J., and Miller, N. P. *Leisure and the quality of life*. Washington, D. C.: American Association for Health, Physical Education and Recreation, 1972.

Sutton-Smith, B. Play preference and play behavior: A validity study. *Psychological Reports*, 1965, *16*, 65–66.

Sutton-Smith, B. Piaget on play: A critique. *Psychological Review*, 1966, *73*(1), 104–110.

Sutton-Smith, B. The role of play in cognitive development. *Young Children*, 1967, *22*, 361–370.

Sutton-Smith, B. Novel responses to toys. *Merrill-Palmer Quarterly*, 1968, *14*, 151–158.

Sutton-Smith, B., and Roberts, J. M. Rubrics of competitive behavior. *The Journal of Genetic Psychology*. 1964, *105*, 13–37.

Sutton-Smith, B., Roberts, J. M., and Kozelka, R. M. Game involvement in adults. *The Journal of Social Psychology*, 1963, *60*, 15–30.

Sutton-Smith, B., Rosenberg, B. G., and Morgan, E. F. Development of sex differences in play choices during pre-adolescence. *Child Development*, 1963, *34*, 119–126.

Taylor, I. R. Soccer consciousness and soccer hooliganism. In S. Cohen (Ed.), *Images of Deviance*. London: Penguin, 1971.

Toffler, A. *Future shock*. New York: Random House, 1971.

Veblen, T. *The theory of the leisure class*. New York: New American Library, 1953.

Waelder, R. The psychoanalytic theory of play. *Psychoanalytic Quarterly*, 1933, *2*, 208–224.

Warning on aging: Two generations may be retired by 2000. *Kitchener-Waterloo Record*, February 7, 1976, p. 20.

Webb, H. Professionalization of attitudes toward play among adolescents. In G. S. Kenyon (Ed.), *Aspects of contemporary sport sociology*. Chicago: Athletic Institute, 1969.

Weiner, B., and Kukla, A. An attributional analysis of achievement motivation. *Journal of Personality and Social Psychology*, 1970, *15*(1), 1–20.

Whatever the reasons booze use is on the rise. *Kitchener-Waterloo Record*, February 20, 1976, p. 36.

White, R. W. Motivation reconsidered: The concept of competence. *Psychological Review*, 1959, *66*, 297–333.

Wills, D. M. Problems of play and mastery in the blind child. *British Journal of Medical Psychology*, 1968, *41*, 213–221.

Witt, P. A., and Bishop, D. W. Situational antecedents to leisure behavior. *Journal of Leisure Research*, Winter 1970, 2, 64–77.

Author Index

Subject Index